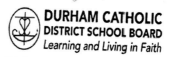

DURHAM CATHOLIC
DISTRICT SCHOOL BOARD
Learning and Living in Faith

Welcome to DCDSB may your journey in Catholic Education be fulfilled with joy and hope. In order to educate it is necessary to step out of ourselves and be among young people, to accompany them in the stages of their growth and to set ourselves beside them. ~Pope Francis

D1501279

The GOSPELS

    for Young Catholics

This BIBLE belongs to:

_____

The **GOSPELS**

 for Young Catholics

Imprimatur: +Most Reverend Robert J. McManus, S.T.D., Bishop of Worcester, June 4, 2021.

PUBLISHER: David Dziena

EDITORS: David Mead and Mark Zimmermann

COVER DESIGN: Jamie Wyatt

DESIGNER: David Mead

ILLUSTRATIONS: Marcelino Truong

Printed in South Korea

Published in Canada by Novalis Publishing Office
1 Eglinton Avenue East, Suite 800
Toronto, Ontario, Canada
M4P 3A1

Head Office
4475 Frontenac Street
Montréal, Québec, Canada
H2H 2S2
www.novalis.ca

Cataloguing in Publication Data is available from Library and Archives Canada.

Published in the United States by
Pflaum Publishing Group, a division of Bayard, Inc.
3055 Kettering Blvd., Suite 100
Dayton, OH 45439
www.pflaum.com

CEO: Hugues de Foucauld

ISBN Novalis: 978-2-89688-968-6

ISBN Pflaum: 978-1-947358-61-4

TABLE of CONTENTS

Detachable GOSPEL BOOKMARKS can be found at the back of this book.

INTRODUCTION

> **Many people have done their best to write a report of the things that have taken place among us.**
>
> **They wrote what we have been told by those who saw these things from the beginning and who proclaimed the message.**
> *Luke 1:1-2*

The story of the life, Death and Resurrection of Jesus comes from the Bible's four **Gospel** books—**Matthew, Mark, Luke** and **John.** In the years after Jesus ascended into Heaven, the story of the Gospels was told in spoken words to early Christian church groups. These words were written down for more people to know the Good News of the salvation from sin, death and the devil that Jesus won for the whole world. Eyewitnesses to the events of Jesus' life told of their experiences to the Gospel writers toward the end of the first century, when it became clear that the message needed to be recorded for future generations.

The Gospels were first written in Greek, a common language of the Roman Empire, presumably so that they could be read by the greatest number of people. **The Gospel of Mark** was written first, most likely around 70 A.D., about 40 years after Jesus ascended. **Matthew and Luke** were written next, between 80 and 90 A.D. Then, **the Gospel of John** appeared last, around 95 A.D.

The Gospels of Matthew, Mark and Luke are known as the **Synoptic** (sin-OP-tick) **Gospels** because they are so similar to one another. *Synoptic* means "the same view." Since Mark came first, it is assumed that the authors of Matthew and Luke knew about the Gospel of Mark and used much of it in their own Gospels, adding further details along with material from another common source not yet known.

The Gospel of John stands alone from the Synoptic Gospels in the way it is organized and explains the events of Jesus' life. The Synoptics present a more chronological picture of Jesus' activities, words and movements spreading the message of forgiveness and new life in him. John expresses a more holy and richly reflective nature of Jesus. All four Gospels end with Christ's trial, crucifixion and Resurrection.

We are fortunate to have these four "windows" to see four views of the central events of Christianity. This book provides you with an even larger view of what the Gospels mean for you as a young Catholic. Along with the Gospels themselves, the additional resources on these pages will help you to see Jesus even more clearly and to know him even more deeply. The word **Gospel** means "Good News." **The Good News** revealed in this book is that you belong to Jesus and you always will.

My **GUIDE** to the **GOSPELS**

The first four books of the **New Testament of the Bible** are the **Gospels**. The word *Gospel* comes from the Latin word for **"Good News."** Each Gospel tells the story of the life, ministry, Death and Resurrection of Jesus in a different way. The four Gospels are **Matthew, Mark, Luke** and **John.** Each of the Gospels follows the same general order, telling of:

1. **The divine nature of Jesus**
2. **The miracles and teachings of Jesus**
3. **Jesus' betrayal, suffering and Death**
4. **Jesus' Resurrection and direction to his disciples to spread the Good News**

There are four different Gospels because **four different people** chose to write the story of Jesus from their own perspective, to a particular audience, with a certain purpose in mind. They are the inspired **Word of God** and are accepted by the Church as part of the Bible. Looking at each Gospel individually, we find themes that are unique to each of them.

Each Gospel was intended to be read in one sitting. Consider setting aside time to read each Gospel from start to finish at once. This helps to understand the the meaning of the Gospel. Many times, when we read quotes from the Gospels by themselves, we do not get a good sense of what was happening before and after this quote. That is why it is helpful to read sections of the Gospel instead of single verses.

Ask yourself the following questions as you read to help you better understand the Gospels:

- **Who is Jesus?**
- **Who is Jesus speaking to?**
- **What is Jesus telling us about God?**

- **How does Jesus react to various situations?**
- **What is Jesus telling us to do?**

The Gospels are a great way to get to know Jesus and to understand what he came to earth to do. He came for you, and everything that he said and did was to bring life and love to us all, so that we might live with God forever in Heaven, forgiven and freed through his Death and Resurrection. There is no other way for us to be saved except through him. **What a great story to tell!**

The GOSPEL of MATTHEW dwells a great deal on **Jesus as King**, and focuses heavily on the teachings of Jesus. It was written by **Matthew the Apostle** and tax collector, who was Jewish. Since the audience for the Gospel of Matthew was Jewish, Matthew connects the words of Jewish Law and the Prophets to the things Jesus said and did. In this way, Matthew serves as the bridge between the Old Testament and New Testament, a helpful way to remember that Matthew is first in the New Testament, even though the Gospel of Mark was likely written first.

> **She will have a son, and you will name him Jesus—because he will save his people from their sins.** *Matthew 1:21*

Matthew the Evangelist is symbolized by **a winged man or an angel**. This Gospel opens with listing of Jesus' ancestors starting with Abraham. Jesus' humanity is emphasized throughout the book. **When you see the angel symbol** in this book, the Gospel verse or story can be found in the Gospel of Matthew!

The GOSPEL of MARK appears next in the Bible, and in many ways serves as a condensed version of Matthew. It is the shortest of the four Gospels, and may have been written in this way so that it could be memorized and told orally by disciples as they traveled from town to town. That idea makes sense since the writer of the Gospel of Mark, **John Mark**, was part of missionary trips with Paul, Barnabas and Peter. This Gospel is characterized by action, and things happen "immediately" over and over again. This Gospel, then, reads more like a story than the other Gospels.

> **For even the Son of Man did not come to be served; he came to serve and to give his life to redeem many people.** *Mark 10:45*

Mark the Evangelist is symbolized by a **winged lion**—a sign of Jesus' leadership and royalty. This Gospel begins with John the Baptist, whose preaching is described as a voice crying in the wilderness like the roar of a lion. **When you see the lion symbol** in this book, the Gospel verse or story can be found in the Gospel of Mark!

The GOSPEL of LUKE is the third and longest Gospel in the Bible. It is like reading a news story about Jesus and is very orderly in its set-up. The author **Luke is a physician**, so there is an emphasis on healing and the physical nature of Jesus. Luke also wrote the Book of Acts, so he is familiar with and involved in the spreading of the story of Jesus. Many believe that Luke interviewed eyewitnesses who were part of Jesus' life, including Mary, the mother of Jesus. A non-Jew himself, Luke wrote his Gospel in a way that could be read and understood by Jews and non-Jews alike. Luke emphasizes that **Jesus is the Savior** of all people.

The Son of Man came to seek and to save the lost. *Luke 19:10*

Luke the Evangelist is symbolized by a **winged ox or bull**—a figure showing Jesus' sacrifice, service and strength. This Gospel opens with a narrative involving Zechariah's priestly duties and temple services, a reminder that Christians should be prepared to sacrifice themselves in following Christ. **When you see the ox symbol** in this book, the Gospel verse or story can be found in the Gospel of Luke!

The GOSPEL of JOHN was written by **John the Apostle**. It stands apart from the first three Gospels because its structure and tone are largely different than the others, and it includes content not included in the others. By showing the miracles of Jesus, John is designed not just to tell a story, but to persuade the reader to believe in Jesus and have everlasting life. John wants to make clear that **Jesus is God** and has the divine power within him to destroy sin, death and the devil. The series of "signs" and speeches by Jesus in John's Gospel declare Christ's divinity.

These have been written in order that you may believe that Jesus is the Messiah, the Son of God, and that through your faith in him you may have life. *John 20:31*

John the Evangelist is symbolized by an **eagle**—a figure of the sky. It represents Jesus' Ascension, and Christ's divine nature. This Gospel begins with Jesus existing in heaven as "the Word of God" before he came to earth. **When you see the eagle symbol** in this book, the Gospel verse or story can be found in the Gospel of John!

How to **LOOK UP** a **BIBLE VERSE**

Do you have a favorite Bible story?

Do you know where and how to find it?

Bible citations (sigh-TAY-shuns) show you how to find a verse or a longer passage in the Bible. There are three steps to looking up a Bible verse:

Chapter 21
The Widow's Offering

[1] Jesus looked around and saw rich people dropping their gifts in the Temple treasury, [2] and he also saw a very poor widow dropping in two little copper coins. [3] He said, "I tell you that this poor widow put in more than all the others. [4] For the others offered their gifts from what they had to spare of their riches; but she, poor as she is, gave all she had to live on."

1. FIND THE BOOK.
Example: Luke
Hint: Look in the New Testament, between the books of Mark and John.

2. FIND THE CHAPTER.
Example: Luke 21
Say: Luke, chapter twenty-one.
Hint: The chapter is the first number after the name of the book.

3. FIND THE VERSE NUMBER(S)*
Example: Luke 21:4
Say: Luke, twenty-one, four.
Hint: The verse is the second number, found after the chapter number. They are separated by a colon (:).

*If two verse numbers are separated with a hyphen (-), read all of the verses in between. For example, **Luke 21:1-4**. Read all the verses beginning with verse 1, through the end of verse 4.

*If the verse numbers are separated with a comma (,), read only the verses whose numbers are given. For example, **Luke 21:1, 4**. Read only verse 1 and verse 4.

Try looking up some passages from the Bible on your own!

BOOKS of the NEW TESTAMENT

The GOSPELS and ACTS
Matthew
Mark
Luke
John
Acts

The LETTERS and REVELATION

Romans
1 Corinthians
2 Corinthians
Galatians
Ephesians
Philippians
Colossians
1 Thessalonians
2 Thessalonians
1 Timothy
2 Timothy

Titus
Philemon
Hebrews
James
1 Peter
2 Peter
1 John
2 John
3 John
Jude
Revelation

The GOSPEL according to MATTHEW

The Gospel of Matthew is believed to be **written by Matthew,** also called Levi, who was one of the 12 disciples of Jesus. **Matthew was a tax collector** and one of the very first disciples Jesus called. Matthew's Gospel was written sometime between 80 and 90 A.D., after the temple in Jerusalem was destroyed, and draws heavily from the Gospel of Mark, which was written first, around 70 A.D.

Matthew is unique in that it **quotes Old Testament Scripture to connect Jesus to the prophecies of old.** Verses from the Old Testament occur in Matthew 96 times, more than in any other Gospel. This high number of references to the Old Testament reveals that Matthew is of Jewish descent and that he is most likely writing to those of Jewish descent. His readers would know and recognize these verses from the old books of Scripture referring to the coming of the Messiah, the Chosen One sent by God to save us from sin, death, and the devil. **Jesus was the One long awaited,** Matthew was declaring.

What's the story?

Matthew follows chronologically the life of Jesus on earth, beginning with the birth and early years of Jesus. This section includes **the family tree of Jesus** (called a genealogy), then tells of Jesus' birth—through the eyes of Joseph—and the visit by the wise men. This section ends with Jesus' journey to Egypt with Mary and Joseph to escape King Herod.

The story of Jesus' ministry in the region of Galilee follows, which includes Jesus' **Sermon on the Mount,** his miracles, his selection of the 12 disciples and his parables of the Kingdom. Jesus expands his ministry beyond Galilee in Matthew's Gospel, to Judea and Perea, where he teaches and heals, preaches parables and speaks with those who come to him with questions and requests.

The events of **Holy Week** are described in detail, including Jesus' entry into Jerusalem, his cleansing of the temple, the anointing of his feet, and his arrest, trial and Death. The last section highlights the Resurrection of Jesus with an earthquake, angels, Jesus' encounter with the women and his **Great Commission** to his disciples to go and preach the Gospel.

The GOSPEL according to MATTHEW

Chapter 1
The Ancestors of Jesus Christ

¹ This is the list of the ancestors of Jesus Christ, a descendant of David, who was a descendant of Abraham.

²⁻⁶ᵃ From Abraham to King David, the following ancestors are listed: Abraham, Isaac, Jacob, Judah and his brothers; then Perez and Zerah (their mother was Tamar), Hezron, Ram, Amminadab, Nahshon, Salmon, Boaz (his mother was Rahab), Obed (his mother was Ruth), Jesse, and King David.

⁶ᵇ⁻¹¹ From David to the time when the people of Israel were taken into exile in Babylon, the following ancestors are listed: David, Solomon (his mother was the woman who had been Uriah's wife), Rehoboam, Abijah, Asa, Jehoshaphat, Jehoram, Uzziah, Jotham, Ahaz, Hezekiah, Manasseh, Amon, Josiah, and Jehoiachin and his brothers.

¹²⁻¹⁶ From the time after the exile in Babylon to the birth of Jesus, the following ancestors are listed: Jehoiachin, Shealtiel, Zerubbabel, Abiud, Eliakim, Azor, Zadok, Achim, Eliud, Eleazar, Matthan, Jacob, and Joseph, who married Mary, the mother of Jesus, who was called the Messiah.

¹⁷ So then, there were fourteen generations from Abraham to David, and fourteen from David to the exile in Babylon, and fourteen from then to the birth of the Messiah.

The Birth of Jesus Christ

¹⁸ This was how the birth of Jesus Christ took place. His mother Mary was engaged to Joseph, but before they were married, she found out that she was going to have a baby by the Holy Spirit. ¹⁹ Joseph was a man who always did what was right, but he did not want to disgrace Mary publicly; so he made plans to break the engagement privately. ²⁰ While he was thinking about this, an angel of the Lord appeared to him in a dream and said, "Joseph, descendant of David, do not be afraid to take Mary to be your wife. For it is by the Holy Spirit that she has conceived. ²¹ She will have a son, and you will name him Jesus—because he will save his people from their sins."

²² Now all this happened in order to make come true what the Lord had said through the prophet, ²³ "A virgin will become pregnant and have a son, and he will be called Immanuel" (which means, "God is with us").

²⁴ So when Joseph woke up, he married Mary, as the angel of the Lord had told him to. ²⁵ But he had no sexual relations with her before she gave birth to her son. And Joseph named him Jesus.

Chapter 2
Visitors from the East

Learn more on page 159.

¹ Jesus was born in the town of Bethlehem in Judea, during the time when Herod was king. Soon afterward, some men who studied the stars came from the East to Jerusalem ² and asked, "Where is the baby born to be the king of the Jews? We saw his star when it came up in the east, and we have come to worship him."

³ When King Herod heard about this, he was very upset, and so was everyone else in Jerusalem. ⁴ He called together all the chief priests and the teachers of the Law and asked them, "Where will the Messiah be born?"

⁵ "In the town of Bethlehem in Judea," they answered. "For this is what the prophet wrote:

⁶ 'Bethlehem in the land of Judah,
    you are by no means the least of
    the leading cities of Judah;

Learn more on page 156.

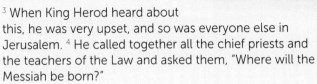

for from you will come a leader
who will guide my people Israel.'"

7 So Herod called the visitors from the East to a secret meeting and found out from them the exact time the star had appeared. 8 Then he sent them to Bethlehem with these instructions: "Go and make a careful search for the child; and when you find him, let me know, so that I too may go and worship him."

9-10 And so they left, and on their way they saw the same star they had seen in the East. When they saw it, how happy they were, what joy was theirs! It went ahead of them until it stopped over the place where the child was. 11 They went into the house, and when they saw the child with his mother Mary, they knelt down and worshiped him. They brought out their gifts of gold, frankincense, and myrrh, and presented them to him.

12 Then they returned to their country by another road, since God had warned them in a dream not to go back to Herod.

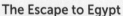

The Escape to Egypt

13 After they had left, an angel of the Lord appeared in a dream to Joseph and said, "Herod will be looking for the child in order to kill him. So get up, take the child and his mother and escape to Egypt, and stay there until I tell you to leave."

14 Joseph got up, took the child and his mother, and left during the night for Egypt, 15 where he stayed until Herod died. This was done to make come true what the Lord had said through the prophet, "I called my Son out of Egypt."

The Killing of the Children

16 When Herod realized that the visitors from the East had tricked him, he was furious. He gave orders to kill all the boys in Bethlehem and its neighborhood who were two years old and younger—this was done in accordance with what he had learned from the visitors about the time when the star had appeared.

17 In this way what the prophet Jeremiah had said came true:

18 "A sound is heard in Ramah,
   the sound of bitter weeping.
Rachel is crying for her children;
   she refuses to be comforted,
   for they are dead."

The Return from Egypt

19 After Herod died, an angel of the Lord appeared in a dream to Joseph in Egypt 20 and said, "Get up, take the child and his mother, and go back to the land of Israel, because those who tried to kill the child are dead." 21 So Joseph got up, took the child and his mother, and went back to Israel.

22 But when Joseph heard that Archelaus had succeeded his father Herod as king of Judea, he was afraid to go there. He was given more instructions in a dream, so he went to the province of Galilee 23 and made his home in a town named Nazareth. And so what the prophets had said came true: "He will be called a Nazarene."

Chapter 3
The Preaching of John the Baptist

1 At that time John the Baptist came to the desert of Judea and started preaching. 2 "Turn away from your sins," he said, "because the Kingdom of heaven is near!"

3 John was the man the prophet Isaiah was talking about when he said,

"Someone is shouting in the desert,
   'Prepare a road for the Lord;
   make a straight path for him to travel!'"

4 John's clothes were made of camel's hair; he wore a leather belt around his waist, and his food was locusts and wild honey. 5 People came to him from Jerusalem,

from the whole province of Judea, and from all over the country near the Jordan River. [6] They confessed their sins, and he baptized them in the Jordan.

[7] When John saw many Pharisees and Sadducees coming to him to be baptized, he said to them, "You snakes—who told you that you could escape from the punishment God is about to send? [8] Do those things that will show that you have turned from your sins. [9] And don't think you can escape punishment by saying that Abraham is your ancestor. I tell you that God can take these rocks and make descendants for Abraham! [10] The ax is ready to cut down the trees at the roots; every tree that does not bear good fruit will be cut down and thrown in the fire. [11] I baptize you with water to show that you have repented, but the one who will come after me will baptize you with the Holy Spirit and fire. He is much greater than I am; and I am not good enough even to carry his sandals. [12] He has his winnowing shovel with him to thresh out all the grain. He will gather his wheat into his barn, but he will burn the chaff in a fire that never goes out."

The Baptism of Jesus

[13] At that time Jesus arrived from Galilee and came to John at the Jordan to be baptized by him. [14] But John tried to make him change his mind. "I ought to be baptized by you," John said, "and yet you have come to me!"

[15] But Jesus answered him, "Let it be so for now. For in this way we shall do all that God requires." So John agreed.

Learn more on page 162.

[16] As soon as Jesus was baptized, he came up out of the water. Then heaven was opened to him, and he saw the Spirit of God coming down like a dove and lighting on him. [17] Then a voice said from heaven, "This is my own dear Son, with whom I am pleased."

Chapter 4
The Temptation of Jesus

[1] Then the Spirit led Jesus into the desert to be tempted by the Devil. [2] After spending forty days and nights without food, Jesus was hungry. [3] Then the Devil came to him and said, "If you are God's Son, order these stones to turn into bread."

[4] But Jesus answered, "The scripture says, 'Human beings cannot live on bread alone, but need every word that God speaks.'"

[5] Then the Devil took Jesus to Jerusalem, the Holy City, set him on the highest point of the Temple, [6] and said to him, "If you are God's Son, throw yourself down, for the scripture says,

'God will give orders to his angels about you;
  they will hold you up with their hands, so that not even your feet will be hurt on the stones.'"

[7] Jesus answered, "But the scripture also says, 'Do not put the Lord your God to the test.'"

[8] Then the Devil took Jesus to a very high mountain and showed him all the kingdoms of the world in all their greatness. [9] "All this I will give you," the Devil said, "if you kneel down and worship me."

Learn more on page 163.

[10] Then Jesus answered, "Go away, Satan! The scripture says, 'Worship the Lord your God and serve only him!'"

[11] Then the Devil left Jesus; and angels came and helped him.

Jesus Begins His Work in Galilee

[12] When Jesus heard that John had been put in prison, he went away to Galilee. [13] He did not stay in Nazareth, but went to live in Capernaum, a town by Lake Galilee, in the territory of Zebulun and Naphtali. [14] This was done to

make come true what the prophet Isaiah had said,

¹⁵ "Land of Zebulun and land of Naphtali,
    on the road to the sea,
on the other side of the Jordan,
    Galilee, land of the Gentiles!
¹⁶ The people who live in darkness
    will see a great light.
On those who live in the dark land of death
    the light will shine."

¹⁷ From that time Jesus began to preach his message: "Turn away from your sins, because the Kingdom of heaven is near!"

Jesus Calls Four Fishermen

¹⁸ As Jesus walked along the shore of Lake Galilee, he saw two brothers who were fishermen, Simon (called Peter) and his brother Andrew, catching fish in the lake with a net. ¹⁹ Jesus said to them, "Come with me, and I will teach you to catch people." ²⁰ At once they left their nets and went with him.

²¹ He went on and saw two other brothers, James and John, the sons of Zebedee. They were in their boat with their father Zebedee, getting their nets ready. Jesus called them, ²² and at once they left the boat and their father, and went with him.

Jesus Teaches, Preaches, and Heals

²³ Jesus went all over Galilee, teaching in the synagogues, preaching the Good News about the Kingdom, and healing people who had all kinds of disease and sickness. ²⁴ The news about him spread through the whole country of Syria, so that people brought to him all those who were sick, suffering from all kinds of diseases and disorders: people with demons, and epileptics, and paralyzed people—and Jesus healed them all. ²⁵ Large crowds followed him from Galilee and the Ten Towns, from Jerusalem, Judea, and the land on the other side of the Jordan.

Chapter 5

The Sermon on the Mount

¹ Jesus saw the crowds and went up a hill, where he sat down. His disciples gathered around him, ² and he began to teach them:

True Happiness

³ "Happy are those who know they are spiritually poor;
    the Kingdom of heaven belongs to them!
⁴ "Happy are those who mourn;
    God will comfort them!
⁵ "Happy are those who are humble;
    they will receive what God has promised!
⁶ "Happy are those whose greatest desire is to do
        what God requires;
    God will satisfy them fully!
⁷ "Happy are those who are merciful to others;
    God will be merciful to them!
⁸ "Happy are the pure in heart;
    they will see God!
⁹ "Happy are those who work for peace;
    God will call them his children!
¹⁰ "Happy are those who are persecuted because they
        do what God requires;
    the Kingdom of heaven belongs to them!

¹¹ "Happy are you when people insult you and persecute you and tell all kinds of evil lies against you because you are my followers. ¹² Be happy and glad, for a great reward is kept for you in heaven. This is how the prophets who lived before you were persecuted.

Salt and Light

¹³ "You are like salt for the whole human race. But if salt loses its saltiness, there is no way to make it salty again. It has become worthless, so it is thrown out and people trample on it.

¹⁴ "You are like light for the whole world. A city built on a hill cannot be hid. ¹⁵ No one lights a lamp and puts it under a bowl; instead it is put on the lampstand, where it gives light for everyone in the house. ¹⁶ In the same way

Learn more on page 166.

your light must shine before people, so that they will see the good things you do and praise your Father in heaven.

Teaching about the Law

17 "Do not think that I have come to do away with the Law of Moses and the teachings of the prophets. I have not come to do away with them, but to make their teachings come true. 18 Remember that as long as heaven and earth last, not the least point nor the smallest detail of the Law will be done away with—not until the end of all things. 19 So then, whoever disobeys even the least important of the commandments and teaches others to do the same, will be least in the Kingdom of heaven. On the other hand, whoever obeys the Law and teaches others to do the same, will be great in the Kingdom of heaven. 20 I tell you, then, that you will be able to enter the Kingdom of heaven only if you are more faithful than the teachers of the Law and the Pharisees in doing what God requires.

Teaching about Anger

21 "You have heard that people were told in the past, 'Do not commit murder; anyone who does will be brought to trial.' 22 But now I tell you: if you are angry with your brother you will be brought to trial, if you call your brother 'You good-for-nothing!' you will be brought before the Council, and if you call your brother a worthless fool you will be in danger of going to the fire of hell. 23 So if you are about to offer your gift to God at the altar and there you remember that your brother has something against you, 24 leave your gift there in front of the altar, go at once and make peace with your brother, and then come back and offer your gift to God.

25 "If someone brings a lawsuit against you and takes you to court, settle the dispute while there is time, before you get to court. Once you are there, you will be turned over to the judge, who will hand you over to the police, and you will be put in jail.

26 There you will stay, I tell you, until you pay the last penny of your fine.

Teaching about Adultery

27 "You have heard that it was said, 'Do not commit adultery.' 28 But now I tell you: anyone who looks at a woman and wants to possess her is guilty of committing adultery with her in his heart. 29 So if your right eye causes you to sin, take it out and throw it away! It is much better for you to lose a part of your body than to have your whole body thrown into hell. 30 If your right hand causes you to sin, cut it off and throw it away! It is much better for you to lose one of your limbs than to have your whole body go off to hell.

Teaching about Divorce

31 "It was also said, 'Anyone who divorces his wife must give her a written notice of divorce.' 32 But now I tell you: if a man divorces his wife for any cause other than her unfaithfulness, then he is guilty of making her commit adultery if she marries again; and the man who marries her commits adultery also.

Teaching about Vows

33 "You have also heard that people were told in the past, 'Do not break your promise, but do what you have vowed to the Lord to do.' 34 But now I tell you: do not use any vow when you make a promise. Do not swear by heaven, for it is God's throne; 35 nor by earth, for it is the resting place for his feet; nor by Jerusalem, for it is the city of the great King. 36 Do not even swear by your head, because you cannot make a single hair white or black. 37 Just say 'Yes' or 'No'—anything else you say comes from the Evil One.

Teaching about Revenge

38 "You have heard that it was said, 'An eye for an eye, and a tooth for a tooth.' 39 But now I tell you: do not take revenge on someone who wrongs you. If anyone slaps you on the right cheek, let him slap your left cheek too. 40 And if someone takes you to court to sue you for your shirt, let him have your coat as well. 41 And if one of the occupation troops forces you to carry his pack one mile,

carry it two miles. [42] When someone asks you for something, give it to him; when someone wants to borrow something, lend it to him.

Love for Enemies

[43] "You have heard that it was said, 'Love your friends, hate your enemies.' [44] But now I tell you: love your enemies and pray for those who persecute you, [45] so that you may become the children of your Father in heaven. For he makes his sun to shine on bad and good people alike, and gives rain to those who do good and to those who do evil. [46] Why should God reward you if you love only the people who love you? Even the tax collectors do that! [47] And if you speak only to your friends, have you done anything out of the ordinary? Even the pagans do that! [48] You must be perfect—just as your Father in heaven is perfect.

Chapter 6

Teaching about Charity

[1] "Make certain you do not perform your religious duties in public so that people will see what you do. If you do these things publicly, you will not have any reward from your Father in heaven.

[2] "So when you give something to a needy person, do not make a big show of it, as the hypocrites do in the houses of worship and on the streets. They do it so that people will praise them. I assure you, they have already been paid in full. [3] But when you help a needy person, do it in such a way that even your closest friend will not know about it. [4] Then it will be a private matter. And your Father, who sees what you do in private, will reward you.

Teaching about Prayer

[5] "When you pray, do not be like the hypocrites! They love to stand up and pray in the houses of worship and on the street corners, so that everyone will see them. I assure you, they have already been paid in full. [6] But when you pray, go to your room, close the door, and pray to your Father, who is unseen. And your Father, who sees what you do in private, will reward you.

[7] "When you pray, do not use a lot of meaningless words, as the pagans do, who think that their gods will hear them because their prayers are long. [8] Do not be like them. Your Father already knows what you need before you ask him. [9] This, then, is how you should pray:

'Our Father in heaven:
　　May your holy name be honored;
[10] may your Kingdom come;
　　may your will be done on earth as it is in heaven.
[11] Give us today the food we need.
[12] Forgive us the wrongs we have done,
　　as we forgive the wrongs that others have done to us.
[13] Do not bring us to hard testing,
　　but keep us safe from the Evil One.'

[14] "If you forgive others the wrongs they have done to you, your Father in heaven will also forgive you. [15] But if you do not forgive others, then your Father will not forgive the wrongs you have done.

Teaching about Fasting

[16] "And when you fast, do not put on a sad face as the hypocrites do. They neglect their appearance so that everyone will see that they are fasting. I assure you, they have already been paid in full. [17] When you go without food, wash your face and comb your hair, [18] so that others cannot know that you are fasting—only your Father, who is unseen, will know. And your Father, who sees what you do in private, will reward you.

Riches in Heaven

[19] "Do not store up riches for yourselves here on earth, where moths and rust destroy, and robbers break in and steal. [20] Instead, store up riches for yourselves in heaven, where moths and rust cannot destroy, and robbers cannot break in and steal. [21] For your heart will always be where your riches are.

The Light of the Body

22 "The eyes are like a lamp for the body. If your eyes are sound, your whole body will be full of light; 23 but if your eyes are no good, your body will be in darkness. So if the light in you is darkness, how terribly dark it will be!

God and Possessions

24 "You cannot be a slave of two masters; you will hate one and love the other; you will be loyal to one and despise the other. You cannot serve both God and money.

25 "This is why I tell you: do not be worried about the food and drink you need in order to stay alive, or about clothes for your body. After all, isn't life worth more than food? And isn't the body worth more than clothes? 26 Look at the birds: they do not plant seeds, gather a harvest and put it in barns; yet your Father in heaven takes care of them! Aren't you worth much more than birds? 27 Can any of you live a bit longer by worrying about it?

28 "And why worry about clothes? Look how the wild flowers grow: they do not work or make clothes for themselves. 29 But I tell you that not even King Solomon with all his wealth had clothes as beautiful as one of these flowers. 30 It is God who clothes the wild grass—grass that is here today and gone tomorrow, burned up in the oven. Won't he be all the more sure to clothe you? What little faith you have!

31 "So do not start worrying: 'Where will my food come from? or my drink? or my clothes?' 32 (These are the things the pagans are always concerned about.) Your Father in heaven knows that you need all these things. 33 Instead, be concerned above everything else with the

Kingdom of God and with what he requires of you, and he will provide you with all these other things. 34 So do not worry about tomorrow; it will have enough worries of its own. There is no need to add to the troubles each day brings.

Chapter 7

Judging Others

1 "Do not judge others, so that God will not judge you, 2 for God will judge you in the same way you judge others, and he will apply to you the same rules you apply to others. 3 Why, then, do you look at the speck in your brother's eye and pay no attention to the log in your own eye? 4 How dare you say to your brother, 'Please, let me take that speck out of your eye,' when you have a log in your own eye? 5 You hypocrite! First take the log out of your own eye, and then you will be able to see clearly to take the speck out of your brother's eye.

6 "Do not give what is holy to dogs—they will only turn and attack you. Do not throw your pearls in front of pigs—they will only trample them underfoot.

Ask, Seek, Knock

7 "Ask, and you will receive; seek, and you will find; knock, and the door will be opened to you. 8 For everyone who asks will receive, and anyone who seeks will find, and the door will be opened to those who knock. 9 Would any of you who are fathers give your son a stone when he asks for bread? 10 Or would you give him a snake when he asks for a fish? 11 As bad as you are, you know how to give good things to your children. How much more, then, will your Father in heaven give good things to those who ask him!

12 "Do for others what you want them to do for you: this is the meaning of the Law of Moses and of the teachings of the prophets.

The Narrow Gate

13 "Go in through the narrow gate, because the gate to hell is wide and the road that leads to it is easy, and there are many who travel it. 14 But the gate to life is narrow and the way that leads to it is hard, and there are few people who find it.

A Tree and Its Fruit

15 "Be on your guard against false prophets; they come

to you looking like sheep on the outside, but on the inside they are really like wild wolves. ¹⁶ You will know them by what they do. Thorn bushes do not bear grapes, and briers do not bear figs. ¹⁷ A healthy tree bears good fruit, but a poor tree bears bad fruit. ¹⁸ A healthy tree cannot bear bad fruit, and a poor tree cannot bear good fruit. ¹⁹ And any tree that does not bear good fruit is cut down and thrown in the fire. ²⁰ So then, you will know the false prophets by what they do.

I Never Knew You

²¹ "Not everyone who calls me 'Lord, Lord' will enter the Kingdom of heaven, but only those who do what my Father in heaven wants them to do. ²² When the Judgment Day comes, many will say to me, 'Lord, Lord! In your name we spoke God's message, by your name we drove out many demons and performed many miracles!' ²³ Then I will say to them, 'I never knew you. Get away from me, you wicked people!'

The Two House Builders

²⁴ "So then, anyone who hears these words of mine and obeys them is like a wise man who built his house on rock. ²⁵ The rain poured down, the rivers flooded over, and the wind blew hard against that house. But it did not fall, because it was built on rock.

Learn more on page 167.

²⁶ "But anyone who hears these words of mine and does not obey them is like a foolish man who built his house on sand. ²⁷ The rain poured down, the rivers flooded over, the wind blew hard against that house, and it fell. And what a terrible fall that was!"

The Authority of Jesus

²⁸ When Jesus finished saying these things, the crowd was amazed at the way he taught. ²⁹ He wasn't like the teachers of the Law; instead, he taught with authority.

Chapter 8

Jesus Heals a Man

¹ When Jesus came down from the hill, large crowds followed him. ² Then a man suffering from a dreaded skin disease came to him, knelt down before him, and said, "Sir, if you want to, you can make me clean."

³ Jesus reached out and touched him. "I do want to," he answered. "Be clean!" At once the man was healed of his disease. ⁴ Then Jesus said to him, "Listen! Don't tell anyone, but go straight to the priest and let him examine you; then in order to prove to everyone that you are cured, offer the sacrifice that Moses ordered."

Jesus Heals a Roman Officer's Servant

⁵ When Jesus entered Capernaum, a Roman officer met him and begged for help: ⁶ "Sir, my servant is sick in bed at home, unable to move and suffering terribly."

⁷ "I will go and make him well," Jesus said.

⁸ "Oh no, sir," answered the officer. "I do not deserve to have you come into my house. Just give the order, and my servant will get well. ⁹ I, too, am a man under the authority of superior officers, and I have soldiers under me. I order this one, 'Go!' and he goes; and I order that one, 'Come!' and he comes; and I order my slave, 'Do this!' and he does it."

¹⁰ When Jesus heard this, he was surprised and said to the people following him, "I tell you, I have never found anyone in Israel with faith like this. ¹¹ I assure you that many will come from the east and the west and sit down with Abraham, Isaac, and Jacob at the feast in the Kingdom of heaven. ¹² But those who should be in the Kingdom will be thrown out into the darkness, where they will cry and gnash their teeth." ¹³ Then Jesus said to the officer, "Go home, and what you believe will be done for you."

And the officer's servant was healed that very moment.

Jesus Heals Many People

¹⁴ Jesus went to Peter's home, and there he saw Peter's

mother-in-law sick in bed with a fever. [15] He touched her hand; the fever left her, and she got up and began to wait on him.

[16] When evening came, people brought to Jesus many who had demons in them. Jesus drove out the evil spirits with a word and healed all who were sick. [17] He did this to make come true what the prophet Isaiah had said, "He himself took our sickness and carried away our diseases."

The Would-Be Followers of Jesus

[18] When Jesus noticed the crowd around him, he ordered his disciples to go to the other side of the lake. [19] A teacher of the Law came to him. "Teacher," he said, "I am ready to go with you wherever you go."

[20] Jesus answered him, "Foxes have holes, and birds have nests, but the Son of Man has no place to lie down and rest."

[21] Another man, who was a disciple, said, "Sir, first let me go back and bury my father."

[22] "Follow me," Jesus answered, "and let the dead bury their own dead."

Jesus Calms a Storm

[23] Jesus got into a boat, and his disciples went with him. [24] Suddenly a fierce storm hit the lake, and the boat was in danger of sinking. But Jesus was asleep. [25] The disciples went to him and woke him up. "Save us, Lord!" they said. "We are about to die!"

[26] "Why are you so frightened?" Jesus answered. "What little faith you have!" Then he got up and ordered the winds and the waves to stop, and there was a great calm.

[27] Everyone was amazed. "What kind of man is this?" they said. "Even the winds and the waves obey him!"

Jesus Heals Two Men with Demons

[28] When Jesus came to the territory of Gadara on the other side of the lake, he was met by two men who came out of the burial caves there. These men had demons in them

and were so fierce that no one dared travel on that road. [29] At once they screamed, "What do you want with us, you Son of God? Have you come to punish us before the right time?"

[30] Not far away there was a large herd of pigs feeding. [31] So the demons begged Jesus, "If you are going to drive us out, send us into that herd of pigs."

[32] "Go," Jesus told them; so they left and went off into the pigs. The whole herd rushed down the side of the cliff into the lake and was drowned.

[33] The men who had been taking care of the pigs ran away and went into the town, where they told the whole story and what had happened to the men with the demons. [34] So everyone from the town went out to meet Jesus; and when they saw him, they begged him to leave their territory.

Chapter 9

Jesus Heals a Paralyzed Man

[1] Jesus got into the boat and went back across the lake to his own town, [2] where some people brought to him a paralyzed man, lying on a bed. When Jesus saw how much faith they had, he said to the paralyzed man, "Courage, my son! Your sins are forgiven."

[3] Then some teachers of the Law said to themselves, "This man is speaking blasphemy!"

[4] Jesus perceived what they were thinking, and so he said, "Why are you thinking such evil things? [5] Is it easier to say, 'Your sins are forgiven,' or to say, 'Get up and walk'? [6] I will prove to you, then, that the Son of Man has authority on earth to forgive sins." So he said to the paralyzed man, "Get up, pick up your bed, and go home!"

[7] The man got up and went home. [8] When the people saw it, they were afraid, and praised God for giving such authority to people.

Jesus Calls Matthew

[9] Jesus left that place, and as he walked along, he saw a

tax collector, named Matthew, sitting in his office. He said to him, "Follow me."

Matthew got up and followed him.

[10] While Jesus was having a meal in Matthew's house, many tax collectors and other outcasts came and joined Jesus and his disciples at the table. [11] Some Pharisees saw this and asked his disciples, "Why does your teacher eat with such people?"

[12] Jesus heard them and answered, "People who are well do not need a doctor, but only those who are sick. [13] Go and find out what is meant by the scripture that says: 'It is kindness that I want, not animal sacrifices.' I have not come to call respectable people, but outcasts."

The Question about Fasting

[14] Then the followers of John the Baptist came to Jesus, asking, "Why is it that we and the Pharisees fast often, but your disciples don't fast at all?"

[15] Jesus answered, "Do you expect the guests at a wedding party to be sad as long as the bridegroom is with them? Of course not! But the day will come when the bridegroom will be taken away from them, and then they will fast.

[16] "No one patches up an old coat with a piece of new cloth, for the new patch will shrink and make an even bigger hole in the coat. [17] Nor does anyone pour new wine into used wineskins, for the skins will burst, the wine will pour out, and the skins will be ruined. Instead, new wine is poured into fresh wineskins, and both will keep in good condition."

The Official's Daughter and the Woman Who Touched Jesus' Cloak

[18] While Jesus was saying this, a Jewish official came to him, knelt down before him, and said, "My daughter has just died; but come and place your hands on her, and she will live."

[19] So Jesus got up and followed him, and his disciples went along with him.

[20] A woman who had suffered from severe bleeding for twelve years came up behind Jesus and touched the edge of his cloak. [21] She said to herself, "If only I touch his cloak, I will get well."

[22] Jesus turned around and saw her, and said, "Courage, my daughter! Your faith has made you well." At that very moment the woman became well.

[23] Then Jesus went into the official's house. When he saw the musicians for the funeral and the people all stirred up, [24] he said, "Get out, everybody! The little girl is not dead—she is only sleeping!" Then they all started making fun of him. [25] But as soon as the people had been put out, Jesus went into the girl's room and took hold of her hand, and she got up. [26] The news about this spread all over that part of the country.

Jesus Heals Two Blind Men

[27] Jesus left that place, and as he walked along, two blind men started following him. "Have mercy on us, Son of David!" they shouted.

[28] When Jesus had gone indoors, the two blind men came to him, and he asked them, "Do you believe that I can heal you?"

"Yes, sir!" they answered.

[29] Then Jesus touched their eyes and said, "Let it happen, then, just as you believe!"— [30] and their sight was restored. Jesus spoke sternly to them, "Don't tell this to anyone!"

[31] But they left and spread the news about Jesus all over that part of the country.

Jesus Heals a Man Who Could Not Speak

[32] As the men were leaving, some people brought to Jesus a man who could not talk because he had a demon. [33] But as soon as the demon was driven out, the man

started talking, and everyone was amazed. "We have never seen anything like this in Israel!" they exclaimed.

34 But the Pharisees said, "It is the chief of the demons who gives Jesus the power to drive out demons."

Jesus Has Pity for the People
35 Jesus went around visiting all the towns and villages. He taught in the synagogues, preached the Good News about the Kingdom, and healed people with every kind of disease and sickness. 36 As he saw the crowds, his heart was filled with pity for them, because they were worried and helpless, like sheep without a shepherd. 37 So he said to his disciples, "The harvest is large, but there are few workers to gather it in. 38 Pray to the owner of the harvest that he will send out workers to gather in his harvest."

Chapter 10
The Twelve Apostles
1 Jesus called his twelve disciples together and gave them authority to drive out evil spirits and to heal every disease and every sickness. 2 These are the names of the twelve apostles: first, Simon (called Peter) and his brother Andrew; James and his brother John, the sons of Zebedee; 3 Philip and Bartholomew; Thomas and Matthew, the tax collector; James son of Alphaeus, and Thaddaeus; 4 Simon the Patriot, and Judas Iscariot, who betrayed Jesus.

The Mission of the Twelve
5 These twelve men were sent out by Jesus with the following instructions: "Do not go to any Gentile territory or any Samaritan towns. 6 Instead, you are to go to the lost sheep of the people of Israel. 7 Go and preach, 'The Kingdom of heaven is near!' 8 Heal the sick, bring the dead back to life, heal those who suffer from dreaded skin diseases, and drive out demons. You have received without paying, so give without being paid. 9 Do not carry any gold, silver, or copper money in your pockets; 10 do not carry a beggar's bag for the trip or an extra shirt or shoes or a walking stick. Workers should be given what they need.

11 "When you come to a town or village, go in and look for someone who is willing to welcome you, and stay with him until you leave that place. 12 When you go into a house, say, 'Peace be with you.' 13 If the people in that house welcome you, let your greeting of peace remain; but if they do not welcome you, then take back your greeting. 14 And if some home or town will not welcome you or listen to you, then leave that place and shake the dust off your feet. 15 I assure you that on the Judgment Day God will show more mercy to the people of Sodom and Gomorrah than to the people of that town!

Coming Persecutions
16 "Listen! I am sending you out just like sheep to a pack of wolves. You must be as cautious as snakes and as gentle as doves. 17 Watch out, for there will be those who will arrest you and take you to court, and they will whip you in the synagogues. 18 For my sake you will be brought to trial before rulers and kings, to tell the Good News to them and to the Gentiles. 19 When they bring you to trial, do not worry about what you are going to say or how you will say it; when the time comes, you will be given what you will say. 20 For the words you will speak will not be yours; they will come from the Spirit of your Father speaking through you.

21 "People will hand over their own brothers to be put to death, and fathers will do the same to their children; children will turn against their parents and have them put to death. 22 Everyone will hate you because of me. But whoever holds out to the end will be saved. 23 When they persecute you in one town, run away to another one. I assure you that you will not finish your work in all the towns of Israel before the Son of Man comes.

24 "No pupil is greater than his teacher; no slave is greater than his master. 25 So a pupil should be satisfied to become like his teacher, and a slave like his master. If the head of the family is called Beelzebul, the members of the family will be called even worse names!

Whom to Fear

26 "So do not be afraid of people. Whatever is now covered up will be uncovered, and every secret will be made known. 27 What I am telling you in the dark you must repeat in broad daylight, and what you have heard in private you must announce from the housetops. 28 Do not be afraid of those who kill the body but cannot kill the soul; rather be afraid of God, who can destroy both body and soul in hell. 29 For only a penny you can buy two sparrows, yet not one sparrow falls to the ground without your Father's consent. 30 As for you, even the hairs of your head have all been counted. 31 So do not be afraid; you are worth much more than many sparrows!

Confessing and Rejecting Christ

32 "Those who declare publicly that they belong to me, I will do the same for them before my Father in heaven. 33 But those who reject me publicly, I will reject before my Father in heaven.

Not Peace, but a Sword

34 "Do not think that I have come to bring peace to the world. No, I did not come to bring peace, but a sword. 35 I came to set sons against their fathers, daughters against their mothers, daughters-in-law against their mothers-in-law; 36 your worst enemies will be the members of your own family.

37 "Those who love their father or mother more than me are not fit to be my disciples; those who love their son or daughter more than me are not fit to be my disciples. 38 Those who do not take up their cross and follow in my steps are not fit to be my disciples. 39 Those who try to gain their own life will lose it; but those who lose their life for my sake will gain it.

Rewards

40 "Whoever welcomes you welcomes me; and whoever welcomes me welcomes the one who sent me. 41 Whoever welcomes God's messenger because he is God's messenger, will share in his reward. And whoever welcomes a good man because he is good, will share in his reward. 42 You can be sure that whoever gives even a drink of cold water to one of the least of these my followers because he is my follower, will certainly receive a reward."

Chapter 11

The Messengers from John the Baptist

1 When Jesus finished giving these instructions to his twelve disciples, he left that place and went off to teach and preach in the towns near there.

2 When John the Baptist heard in prison about the things that Christ was doing, he sent some of his disciples to him. 3 "Tell us," they asked Jesus, "are you the one John said was going to come, or should we expect someone else?"

4 Jesus answered, "Go back and tell John what you are hearing and seeing: 5 the blind can see, the lame can walk, those who suffer from dreaded skin diseases are made clean, the deaf hear, the dead are brought back to life, and the Good News is preached to the poor. 6 How happy are those who have no doubts about me!"

7 While John's disciples were leaving, Jesus spoke about him to the crowds: "When you went out to John in the desert, what did you expect to see? A blade of grass bending in the wind? 8 What did you go out to see? A man dressed up in fancy clothes? People who dress like that live in palaces! 9 Tell me, what did you go out to see? A prophet? Yes indeed, but you saw much more than a prophet. 10 For John is the one of whom the scripture

says: 'God said, I will send my messenger ahead of you to open the way for you.' [11] I assure you that John the Baptist is greater than anyone who has ever lived. But the one who s least in the Kingdom of heaven is greater than John. [12] From the time John preached his message until this very day the Kingdom of heaven has suffered violent attacks, and violent men try to seize it. [13] Until the time of John all the prophets and the Law of Moses spoke about the Kingdom; [14] and if you are willing to believe their message, John is Elijah, whose coming was predicted. [15] Listen, then, if you have ears!

[16] "Now, to what can I compare the people of this day? They are like children sitting in the marketplace. One group shouts to the other, [17] 'We played wedding music for you, but you wouldn't dance! We sang funeral songs, but you wouldn't cry!' [18] When John came, he fasted and drank no wine, and everyone said, 'He has a demon in him!' [19] When the Son of Man came, he ate and drank, and everyone said, 'Look at this man! He is a glutton and wine drinker, a friend of tax collectors and other outcasts!' God's wisdom, however, is shown to be true by its results."

The Unbelieving Towns

[20] The people in the towns where Jesus had performed most of his miracles did not turn from their sins, so he reproached those towns. [21] "How terrible it will be for you, Chorazin! How terrible for you too, Bethsaida! If the miracles which were performed in you had been performed in Tyre and Sidon, the people there would have long ago put on sackcloth and sprinkled ashes on themselves, to show that they had turned from their sins! [22] I assure you that on the Judgment Day God will show more mercy to the people of Tyre and Sidon than to you! [23] And as for you, Capernaum! Did you want to lift yourself up to heaven? You will be thrown down to hell! If the miracles which were performed in you had been performed in Sodom, it would still be in existence today! [24] You can be sure that on the Judgment Day God will show more mercy to Sodom than to you!"

Come to Me and Rest

[25] At that time Jesus said, "Father, Lord of heaven and earth! I thank you because you have shown to the unlearned what you have hidden from the wise and learned. [26] Yes, Father, this was how you were pleased to have it happen.

[27] "My Father has given me all things. No one knows the Son except the Father, and no one knows the Father except the Son and those to whom the Son chooses to reveal him.

[28] "Come to me, all of you who are tired from carrying heavy loads, and I will give you rest. [29] Take my yoke and put it on you, and learn from me, because I am gentle and humble in spirit; and you will find rest. [30] For the yoke I will give you is easy, and the load I will put on you is light."

Chapter 12

The Question about the Sabbath

[1] Not long afterward Jesus was walking through some wheat fields on a Sabbath. His disciples were hungry, so they began to pick heads of wheat and eat the grain. [2] When the Pharisees saw this, they said to Jesus, "Look, it is against our Law for your disciples to do this on the Sabbath!"

[3] Jesus answered, "Have you never read what David did that time when he and his men were hungry? [4] He went into the house of God, and he and his men ate the bread offered to God, even though it was against the Law for them to eat it—only the priests were allowed to eat that bread. [5] Or have you not read in the Law of Moses that every Sabbath the priests in the Temple actually break the Sabbath law, yet they are not guilty? [6] I tell you that there is something here greater than the Temple. [7] The scripture says, 'It is kindness that I want, not animal sacrifices.' If you really knew what this means, you would not condemn people who are not guilty; [8] for the Son of Man is Lord of the Sabbath."

The Man with a Paralyzed Hand

[9] Jesus left that place and went to a synagogue, [10] where

there was a man who had a paralyzed hand. Some people were there who wanted to accuse Jesus of doing wrong, so they asked him, "Is it against our Law to heal on the Sabbath?"

11 Jesus answered, "What if one of you has a sheep and it falls into a deep hole on the Sabbath? Will you not take hold of it and lift it out? 12 And a human being is worth much more than a sheep! So then, our Law does allow us to help someone on the Sabbath." 13 Then he said to the man with the paralyzed hand, "Stretch out your hand."

He stretched it out, and it became well again, just like the other one. 14 Then the Pharisees left and made plans to kill Jesus.

God's Chosen Servant

15 When Jesus heard about the plot against him, he went away from that place; and large crowds followed him. He healed all the sick 16 and gave them orders not to tell others about him. 17 He did this so as to make come true what God had said through the prophet Isaiah:

18 "Here is my servant, whom I have chosen,
the one I love, and with whom I am pleased.
I will send my Spirit upon him,
and he will announce my judgment to the nations.
19 He will not argue or shout,
or make loud speeches in the streets.
20 He will not break off a bent reed,
nor put out a flickering lamp.
He will persist until he causes justice to triumph,
21 and on him all peoples will put their hope."

Jesus and Beelzebul

22 Then some people brought to Jesus a man who was blind and could not talk because he had a demon. Jesus healed the man, so that he was able to talk and see. 23 The crowds were all amazed at what Jesus had done. "Could he be the Son of David?" they asked.

24 When the Pharisees heard this, they replied, "He drives out demons only because their ruler Beelzebul gives him power to do so."

25 Jesus knew what they were thinking, and so he said to them, "Any country that divides itself into groups which fight each other will not last very long. And any town or family that divides itself into groups which fight each other will fall apart. 26 So if one group is fighting another in Satan's kingdom, this means that it is already divided into groups and will soon fall apart! 27 You say that I drive out demons because Beelzebul gives me the power to do so. Well, then, who gives your followers the power to drive them out? What your own followers do proves that you are wrong! 28 No, it is not Beelzebul, but God's Spirit, who gives me the power to drive out demons, which proves that the Kingdom of God has already come upon you.

29 "No one can break into a strong man's house and take away his belongings unless he first ties up the strong man; then he can plunder his house.

30 "Anyone who is not for me is really against me; anyone who does not help me gather is really scattering. 31 For this reason I tell you: people can be forgiven any sin and any evil thing they say; but whoever says evil things against the Holy Spirit will not be forgiven. 32 Anyone who says something against the Son of Man can be forgiven; but whoever says something against the Holy Spirit will not be forgiven—now or ever.

A Tree and Its Fruit

33 "To have good fruit you must have a healthy tree; if you have a poor tree, you will have bad fruit. A tree is known by the kind of fruit it bears. 34 You snakes—how can you say good things when you are evil? For the mouth speaks what the heart is full of. 35 A good person brings good things out of a treasure of good things; a bad person brings bad things out of a treasure of bad things.

36 "You can be sure that on the Judgment Day you will have to give account of every useless word you have ever spoken. 37 Your words will be used to judge you—to declare you either innocent or guilty."

The Demand for a Miracle
38 Then some teachers of the Law and some Pharisees spoke up. "Teacher," they said, "we want to see you perform a miracle."

39 "How evil and godless are the people of this day!" Jesus exclaimed. "You ask me for a miracle? No! The only miracle you will be given is the miracle of the prophet Jonah. 40 In the same way that Jonah spent three days and nights in the big fish, so will the Son of Man spend three days and nights in the depths of the earth. 41 On the Judgment Day the people of Nineveh will stand up and accuse you, because they turned from their sins when they heard Jonah preach; and I tell you that there is something here greater than Jonah! 42 On the Judgment Day the Queen of Sheba will stand up and accuse you, because she traveled all the way from her country to listen to King Solomon's wise teaching; and I assure you that there is something here greater than Solomon!

The Return of the Evil Spirit
43 "When an evil spirit goes out of a person, it travels over dry country looking for a place to rest. If it can't find one, 44 it says to itself, 'I will go back to my house.' So it goes back and finds the house empty, clean, and all fixed up. 45 Then it goes out and brings along seven other spirits even worse than itself, and they come and live there. So when it is all over, that person is in worse shape than at the beginning. This is what will happen to the evil people of this day."

Jesus' Mother and Brothers
46 Jesus was still talking to the people when his mother and brothers arrived. They stood outside, asking to speak with him. 47 So one of the people there said to him, "Look, your mother and brothers are standing outside, and they want to speak with you."

48 Jesus answered, "Who is my mother? Who are my brothers?" 49 Then he pointed to his disciples and said, "Look! Here are my mother and my brothers! 50 Whoever does what my Father in heaven wants is my brother, my sister, and my mother."

Chapter 13
The Parable of the Sower
1 That same day Jesus left the house and went to the lakeside, where he sat down to teach. 2 The crowd that gathered around him was so large that he got into a boat and sat in it, while the crowd stood on the shore. 3 He used parables to tell them many things.

"Once there was a man who went out to sow grain. 4 As he scattered the seed in the field, some of it fell along the path, and the birds came and ate it up. 5 Some of it fell on rocky ground, where there was little soil. The seeds soon sprouted, because the soil wasn't deep. 6 But when the sun came up, it burned the young plants; and because the roots had not grown deep enough, the plants soon dried up. 7 Some of the seed fell among thorn bushes, which grew up and choked the plants. 8 But some seeds fell in good soil, and the plants bore grain: some had one hundred grains, others sixty, and others thirty."

9 And Jesus concluded, "Listen, then, if you have ears!"

The Purpose of the Parables
10 Then the disciples came to Jesus and asked him, "Why do you use parables when you talk to the people?"

11 Jesus answered, "The knowledge about the secrets of the Kingdom of heaven has been given to you, but not to them. 12 For the person who has something will be given more, so that he will have more than enough; but the person who has nothing will have taken away from him even the little he has. 13 The reason I use parables in talking to them is that they look, but do not see, and they listen, but do not hear or understand. 14 So the prophecy of Isaiah applies to them:

'This people will listen and listen, but not understand;
    they will look and look, but not see,

15 because their minds are dull,
    and they have stopped up their ears
    and have closed their eyes.
Otherwise, their eyes would see,
    their ears would hear,
    their minds would understand,
and they would turn to me, says God,
    and I would heal them.'

16 "As for you, how fortunate you are! Your eyes see and your ears hear. 17 I assure you that many prophets and many of God's people wanted very much to see what you see, but they could not, and to hear what you hear, but they did not.

Learn more on page 170.

Jesus Explains the Parable of the Sower

18 "Listen, then, and learn what the parable of the sower means. 19 Those who hear the message about the Kingdom but do not understand it are like the seeds that fell along the path. The Evil One comes and snatches away what was sown in them. 20 The seeds that fell on rocky ground stand for those who receive the message gladly as soon as they hear it. 21 But it does not sink deep into them, and they don't last long. So when trouble or persecution comes because of the message, they give up at once. 22 The seeds that fell among thorn bushes stand for those who hear the message; but the worries about this life and the love for riches choke the message, and they don't bear fruit. 23 And the seeds sown in the good soil stand for those who hear the message and understand it: they bear fruit, some as much as one hundred, others sixty, and others thirty."

The Parable of the Weeds

24 Jesus told them another parable: "The Kingdom of heaven is like this. A man sowed good seed in his field.

25 One night, when everyone was asleep, an enemy came and sowed weeds among the wheat and went away. 26 When the plants grew and the heads of grain began to form, then the weeds showed up. 27 The man's servants came to him and said, 'Sir, it was good seed you sowed in your field; where did the weeds come from?' 28 'It was some enemy who did this,' he answered. 'Do you want us to go and pull up the weeds?' they asked him. 29 'No,' he answered, 'because as you gather the weeds you might pull up some of the wheat along with them. 30 Let the wheat and the weeds both grow together until harvest. Then I will tell the harvest workers to pull up the weeds first, tie them in bundles and burn them, and then to gather in the wheat and put it in my barn.'"

The Parable of the Mustard Seed

31 Jesus told them another parable: "The Kingdom of heaven is like this. A man takes a mustard seed and sows it in his field. 32 It is the smallest of all seeds, but when it grows up, it is the biggest of all plants. It becomes a tree, so that birds come and make their nests in its branches."

The Parable of the Yeast

33 Jesus told them still another parable: "The Kingdom of heaven is like this. A woman takes some yeast and mixes it with a bushel of flour until the whole batch of dough rises."

Jesus' Use of Parables

34 Jesus used parables to tell all these things to the crowds; he would not say a thing to them without using a parable. 35 He did this to make come true what the prophet had said,

"I will use parables when I speak to them;
    I will tell them things unknown since the creation of
    the world."

Jesus Explains the Parable of the Weeds

36 When Jesus had left the crowd and gone indoors, his disciples came to him and said, "Tell us what the parable about the weeds in the field means."

[37] Jesus answered, "The man who sowed the good seed is the Son of Man; [38] the field is the world; the good seed is the people who belong to the Kingdom; the weeds are the people who belong to the Evil One; [39] and the enemy who sowed the weeds is the Devil. The harvest is the end of the age, and the harvest workers are angels. [40] Just as the weeds are gathered up and burned in the fire, so the same thing will happen at the end of the age: [41] the Son of Man will send out his angels to gather up out of his Kingdom all those who cause people to sin and all others who do evil things, [42] and they will throw them into the fiery furnace, where they will cry and gnash their teeth. [43] Then God's people will shine like the sun in their Father's Kingdom. Listen, then, if you have ears!

The Parable of the Hidden Treasure
[44] "The Kingdom of heaven is like this. A man happens to find a treasure hidden in a field. He covers it up again, and is so happy that he goes and sells everything he has, and then goes back and buys that field.

The Parable of the Pearl
[45] "Also, the Kingdom of heaven is like this. A man is looking for fine pearls, [46] and when he finds one that is unusually fine, he goes and sells everything he has, and buys that pearl.

The Parable of the Net
[47] "Also, the Kingdom of heaven is like this. Some fishermen throw their net out in the lake and catch all kinds of fish. [48] When the net is full, they pull it to shore and sit down to divide the fish: the good ones go into the buckets, the worthless ones are thrown away. [49] It will be like this at the end of the age: the angels will go out and gather up the evil people from among the good [50] and will throw them into the fiery furnace, where they will cry and gnash their teeth.

New Truths and Old
[51] "Do you understand these things?" Jesus asked them.

"Yes," they answered.

[52] So he replied, "This means, then, that every teacher of the Law who becomes a disciple in the Kingdom of heaven is like a homeowner who takes new and old things out of his storage room."

Jesus Is Rejected at Nazareth
[53] When Jesus finished telling these parables, he left that place [54] and went back to his hometown. He taught in the synagogue, and those who heard him were amazed. "Where did he get such wisdom?" they asked. "And what about his miracles? [55] Isn't he the carpenter's son? Isn't Mary his mother, and aren't James, Joseph, Simon, and Judas his brothers? [56] Aren't all his sisters living here? Where did he get all this?" [57] And so they rejected him.

Jesus said to them, "A prophet is respected everywhere except in his hometown and by his own family." [58] Because they did not have faith, he did not perform many miracles there.

Chapter 14
The Death of John the Baptist
[1] At that time Herod, the ruler of Galilee, heard about Jesus. [2] "He is really John the Baptist, who has come back to life," he told his officials. "That is why he has this power to perform miracles."

[3] For Herod had earlier ordered John's arrest, and he had him tied up and put in prison. He had done this because of Herodias, his brother Philip's wife. [4] For some time John the Baptist had told Herod, "It isn't right for you to be married to Herodias!" [5] Herod wanted to kill him, but he was afraid of the Jewish people, because they considered John to be a prophet.

MATTHEW 14

[6] On Herod's birthday the daughter of Herodias danced in front of the whole group. Herod was so pleased [7] that he promised her, "I swear that I will give you anything you ask for!"

[8] At her mother's suggestion she asked him, "Give me here and now the head of John the Baptist on a plate!"

[9] The king was sad, but because of the promise he had made in front of all his guests he gave orders that her wish be granted. [10] So he had John beheaded in prison. [11] The head was brought in on a plate and given to the girl, who took it to her mother. [12] John's disciples came, carried away his body, and buried it; then they went and told Jesus.

Jesus Feeds Five Thousand

[13] When Jesus heard the news about John, he left there in a boat and went to a lonely place by himself. The people heard about it, and so they left their towns and followed him by land. [14] Jesus got out of the boat, and when he saw the large crowd, his heart was filled with pity for them, and he healed their sick.

[15] That evening his disciples came to him and said, "It is already very late, and this is a lonely place. Send the people away and let them go to the villages to buy food for themselves."

[16] "They don't have to leave," answered Jesus. "You yourselves give them something to eat!"

[17] "All we have here are five loaves and two fish," they replied.

[18] "Then bring them here to me," Jesus said. [19] He ordered the people to sit down on the grass; then he took the five loaves and the two fish, looked up to heaven, and gave thanks to God. He broke the loaves and gave them to the disciples, and the disciples gave them to the people. [20] Everyone ate and had enough. Then the disciples took up twelve baskets full of what was left over. [21] The number of men who ate was about five thousand, not counting the women and children.

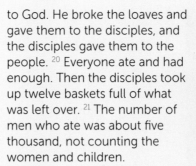

Jesus Walks on the Water

[22] Then Jesus made the disciples get into the boat and go on ahead to the other side of the lake, while he sent the people away. [23] After sending the people away, he went up a hill by himself to pray. When evening came, Jesus was there alone; [24] and by this time the boat was far out in the lake, tossed about by the waves, because the wind was blowing against it.

[25] Between three and six o'clock in the morning Jesus came to the disciples, walking on the water. [26] When they saw him walking on the water, they were terrified. "It's a ghost!" they said, and screamed with fear.

[27] Jesus spoke to them at once. "Courage!" he said. "It is I. Don't be afraid!"

[28] Then Peter spoke up. "Lord, if it is really you, order me to come out on the water to you."

[29] "Come!" answered Jesus. So Peter got out of the boat and started walking on the water to Jesus. [30] But when he noticed the strong wind, he was afraid and started to sink down in the water. "Save me, Lord!" he cried.

[31] At once Jesus reached out and grabbed hold of him and said, "What little faith you have! Why did you doubt?"

[32] They both got into the boat, and the wind died down. [33] Then the disciples in the boat worshiped Jesus. "Truly you are the Son of God!" they exclaimed.

Jesus Heals the Sick in Gennesaret

[34] They crossed the lake and came to land at Gennesaret,

35 where the people recognized Jesus. So they sent for the sick people in all the surrounding country and brought them to Jesus. 36 They begged him to let the sick at least touch the edge of his cloak; and all who touched it were made well.

Chapter 15

The Teaching of the Ancestors

1 Then some Pharisees and teachers of the Law came from Jerusalem to Jesus and asked him, 2 "Why is it that your disciples disobey the teaching handed down by our ancestors? They don't wash their hands in the proper way before they eat!"

3 Jesus answered, "And why do you disobey God's command and follow your own teaching? 4 For God said, 'Respect your father and your mother,' and 'If you curse your father or your mother, you are to be put to death.' 5 But you teach that if people have something they could use to help their father or mother, but say, 'This belongs to God,' 6 they do not need to honor their father. In this way you disregard God's command, in order to follow your own teaching. 7 You hypocrites! How right Isaiah was when he prophesied about you!

8 'These people, says God, honor me with their words,
    but their heart is really far away from me.
9 It is no use for them to worship me,
    because they teach human rules as though they
    were my laws!'"

The Things That Make a Person Unclean

10 Then Jesus called the crowd to him and said to them, "Listen and understand! 11 It is not what goes into your mouth that makes you ritually unclean; rather, what comes out of it makes you unclean."

12 Then the disciples came to him and said, "Do you know that the Pharisees had their feelings hurt by what you said?"

13 "Every plant which my Father in heaven did not plant will be pulled up," answered Jesus. 14 "Don't worry about them!

They are blind leaders of the blind; and when one blind man leads another, both fall into a ditch."

15 Peter spoke up, "Explain this saying to us."

16 Jesus said to them, "You are still no more intelligent than the others. 17 Don't you understand? Anything that goes into your mouth goes into your stomach and then on out of your body. 18 But the things that come out of the mouth come from the heart, and these are the things that make you ritually unclean. 19 For from your heart come the evil ideas which lead you to kill, commit adultery, and do other immoral things; to rob, lie, and slander others. 20 These are the things that make you unclean. But to eat without washing your hands as they say you should—this doesn't make you unclean."

A Woman's Faith

Learn more on page 174.

21 Jesus left that place and went off to the territory near the cities of Tyre and Sidon. 22 A Canaanite woman who lived in that region came to him. "Son of David!" she cried out. "Have mercy on me, sir! My daughter has a demon and is in a terrible condition."

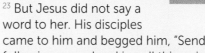

23 But Jesus did not say a word to her. His disciples came to him and begged him, "Send her away! She is following us and making all this noise!"

24 Then Jesus replied, "I have been sent only to the lost sheep of the people of Israel."

25 At this the woman came and fell at his feet. "Help me, sir!" she said.

26 Jesus answered, "It isn't right to take the children's food and throw it to the dogs."

27 "That's true, sir," she answered, "but even the dogs eat

the leftovers that fall from their masters' table."

28 So Jesus answered her, "You are a woman of great faith! What you want will be done for you." And at that very moment her daughter was healed.

Jesus Heals Many People

29 Jesus left there and went along by Lake Galilee. He climbed a hill and sat down. 30 Large crowds came to him, bringing with them the lame, the blind, the crippled, the dumb, and many other sick people, whom they placed at Jesus' feet; and he healed them. 31 The people were amazed as they saw the dumb speaking, the crippled made whole, the lame walking, and the blind seeing; and they praised the God of Israel.

Jesus Feeds Four Thousand

32 Jesus called his disciples to him and said, "I feel sorry for these people, because they have been with me for three days and now have nothing to eat. I don't want to send them away without feeding them, for they might faint on their way home."

33 The disciples asked him, "Where will we find enough food in this desert to feed this crowd?"

34 "How much bread do you have?" Jesus asked.

"Seven loaves," they answered, "and a few small fish."

35 So Jesus ordered the crowd to sit down on the ground. 36 Then he took the seven loaves and the fish, gave thanks to God, broke them, and gave them to the disciples; and the disciples gave them to the people. 37 They all ate and had enough. Then the disciples took up seven baskets full of pieces left over. 38 The number of men who ate was four thousand, not counting the women and children.

39 Then Jesus sent the people away, got into a boat, and went to the territory of Magadan.

Chapter 16

The Demand for a Miracle

1 Some Pharisees and Sadducees who came to Jesus wanted to trap him, so they asked him to perform a miracle for them, to show that God approved of him. 2 But Jesus answered, "When the sun is setting, you say, 'We are going to have fine weather, because the sky is red.' 3 And early in the morning you say, 'It is going to rain, because the sky is red and dark.' You can predict the weather by looking at the sky, but you cannot interpret the signs concerning these times! 4 How evil and godless are the people of this day! You ask me for a miracle? No! The only miracle you will be given is the miracle of Jonah."

So he left them and went away.

The Yeast of the Pharisees and Sadducees

5 When the disciples crossed over to the other side of the lake, they forgot to take any bread. 6 Jesus said to them, "Take care; be on your guard against the yeast of the Pharisees and Sadducees."

7 They started discussing among themselves, "He says this because we didn't bring any bread."

8 Jesus knew what they were saying, so he asked them, "Why are you discussing among yourselves about not having any bread? What little faith you have! 9 Don't you understand yet? Don't you remember when I broke the five loaves for the five thousand men? How many baskets did you fill? 10 And what about the seven loaves for the four thousand men? How many baskets did you fill? 11 How is it that you don't understand that I was not talking to you about bread? Guard yourselves from the yeast of the Pharisees and Sadducees!"

12 Then the disciples understood that he was not warning them to guard themselves from the yeast used in bread but from the teaching of the Pharisees and Sadducees.

Peter's Declaration about Jesus

13 Jesus went to the territory near the town of Caesarea Philippi, where he asked his disciples, "Who do people say the Son of Man is?"

14 "Some say John the Baptist," they answered. "Others say Elijah, while others say Jeremiah or some other prophet."

15 "What about you?" he asked them. "Who do you say I am?"

16 Simon Peter answered, "You are the Messiah, the Son of the living God."

17 "Good for you, Simon son of John!" answered Jesus. "For this truth did not come to you from any human being, but it was given to you directly by my Father in heaven. 18 And so I tell you, Peter: you are a rock, and on this rock foundation I will build my church, and not even death will ever be able to overcome it. 19 I will give you the keys of the Kingdom of heaven; what you prohibit on earth will be prohibited in heaven, and what you permit on earth will be permitted in heaven."

20 Then Jesus ordered his disciples not to tell anyone that he was the Messiah.

Jesus Speaks about His Suffering and Death

21 From that time on Jesus began to say plainly to his disciples, "I must go to Jerusalem and suffer much from the elders, the chief priests, and the teachers of the Law. I will be put to death, but three days later I will be raised to life."

22 Peter took him aside and began to rebuke him. "God forbid it, Lord!" he said. "That must never happen to you!"

23 Jesus turned around and said to Peter, "Get away from me, Satan! You are an obstacle in my way, because these thoughts of yours don't come from God, but from human nature."

24 Then Jesus said to his disciples, "If any of you want to come with me, you must forget yourself, carry your cross, and follow me. 25 For if you want to save your own life, you will lose it; but if you lose your life for my sake, you will find it. 26 Will you gain anything if you win the whole world but lose your life? Of course not! There is nothing you can give to regain your life. 27 For the Son of Man is about to come in the glory of his Father with his angels, and then he will reward each one according to his deeds. 28 I assure you that there are some here who will not die until they have seen the Son of Man come as King."

Chapter 17
The Transfiguration

1 Six days later Jesus took with him Peter and the brothers James and John and led them up a high mountain where they were alone. 2 As they looked on, a change came over Jesus: his face was shining like the sun, and his clothes were dazzling white. 3 Then the three disciples saw Moses and Elijah talking with Jesus. 4 So Peter spoke up and said to Jesus, "Lord, how good it is that we are here! If you wish, I will make three tents here, one for you, one for Moses, and one for Elijah."

5 While he was talking, a shining cloud came over them, and a voice from the cloud said, "This is my own dear Son, with whom I am pleased—listen to him!"

6 When the disciples heard the voice, they were so terrified that they threw themselves face downward on the ground. 7 Jesus came to them and touched them. "Get up," he said. "Don't be afraid!" 8 So they looked up and saw no one there but Jesus.

9 As they came down the mountain, Jesus ordered them, "Don't tell anyone about this vision you have seen until the Son of Man has been raised from death."

10 Then the disciples asked Jesus, "Why do the teachers of the Law say that Elijah has to come first?"

11 "Elijah is indeed coming first," answered Jesus, "and he will get everything ready. 12 But I tell you that Elijah has already come and people did not recognize him, but treated him just as they pleased. In the same way they will also mistreat the Son of Man."

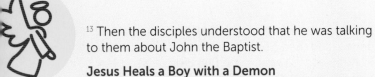

¹³ Then the disciples understood that he was talking to them about John the Baptist.

Jesus Heals a Boy with a Demon

¹⁴ When they returned to the crowd, a man came to Jesus, knelt before him, ¹⁵ and said, "Sir, have mercy on my son! He is an epileptic and has such terrible attacks that he often falls in the fire or into water. ¹⁶ I brought him to your disciples, but they could not heal him."

¹⁷ Jesus answered, "How unbelieving and wrong you people are! How long must I stay with you? How long do I have to put up with you? Bring the boy here to me!" ¹⁸ Jesus gave a command to the demon, and it went out of the boy, and at that very moment he was healed.

¹⁹ Then the disciples came to Jesus in private and asked him, "Why couldn't we drive the demon out?"

²⁰ "It was because you do not have enough faith," answered Jesus. "I assure you that if you have faith as big as a mustard seed, you can say to this hill, 'Go from here to there!' and it will go. You could do anything!"

Jesus Speaks Again about His Death

²² When the disciples all came together in Galilee, Jesus said to them, "The Son of Man is about to be handed over to those ²³ who will kill him; but three days later he will be raised to life."

The disciples became very sad.

Payment of the Temple Tax

²⁴ When Jesus and his disciples came to Capernaum, the collectors of the Temple tax came to Peter and asked, "Does your teacher pay the Temple tax?"

²⁵ "Of course," Peter answered.

When Peter went into the house, Jesus spoke up first, "Simon, what is your opinion? Who pays duties or taxes to the kings of this world? The citizens of the country or the foreigners?"

²⁶ "The foreigners," answered Peter.

"Well, then," replied Jesus, "that means that the citizens don't have to pay. ²⁷ But we don't want to offend these people. So go to the lake and drop in a line. Pull up the first fish you hook, and in its mouth you will find a coin worth enough for my Temple tax and yours. Take it and pay them our taxes."

Chapter 18
Who Is the Greatest?

¹ At that time the disciples came to Jesus, asking, "Who is the greatest in the Kingdom of heaven?"

² So Jesus called a child to come and stand in front of them, ³ and said, "I assure you that unless you change and become like children, you will never enter the Kingdom of heaven. ⁴ The greatest in the Kingdom of heaven is the one who humbles himself and becomes like this child. ⁵ And whoever welcomes in my name one such child as this, welcomes me.

Temptations to Sin

⁶ "If anyone should cause one of these little ones to lose his faith in me, it would be better for that person to have a large millstone tied around his neck and be drowned in the deep sea. ⁷ How terrible for the world that there are things that make people lose their faith! Such things will always happen—but how terrible for the one who causes them!

⁸ "If your hand or your foot makes you lose your faith, cut it off and throw it away! It is better for you to enter life without a hand or a foot than to keep both hands and both feet and be thrown into the eternal fire. ⁹ And if your eye makes you lose your faith, take it out and throw it away! It is better for you to enter life with only one eye than to keep both eyes and be thrown into the fire of hell.

The Parable of the Lost Sheep

¹⁰ "See that you don't despise any of these little ones. Their angels in heaven, I tell you, are always in the presence of my Father in heaven. ¹¹ For the Son of Man came to save the lost.

12 "What do you think a man does who has one hundred sheep and one of them gets lost? He will leave the other ninety-nine grazing on the hillside and go and look for the lost sheep. 13 When he finds it, I tell you, he feels far happier over this one sheep than over the ninety-nine that did not get lost. 14 In just the same way your Father in heaven does not want any of these little ones to be lost.

When Someone Sins

15 "If your brother sins against you, go to him and show him his fault. But do it privately, just between your-selves. If he listens to you, you have won your brother back. 16 But if he will not listen to you, take one or two other persons with you, so that 'every accusation may be upheld by the testimony of two or more witnesses,' as the scripture says. 17 And if he will not listen to them, then tell the whole thing to the church. Finally, if he will not listen to the church, treat him as though he were a pagan or a tax collector.

Prohibiting and Permitting

18 "And so I tell all of you: what you prohibit on earth will be prohibited in heaven, and what you permit on earth will be permitted in heaven.

19 "And I tell you more: whenever two of you on earth agree about anything you pray for, it will be done for you by my Father in heaven. 20 For where two or three come together in my name, I am there with them."

The Parable of the Unforgiving Servant

21 Then Peter came to Jesus and asked, "Lord, if my brother keeps on sinning against me, how many times do I have to forgive him? Seven times?"

22 "No, not seven times," answered Jesus, "but seventy times seven, 23 because the Kingdom of heaven is like this. Once there was a king who decided to check on his servants' accounts. 24 He had just begun to do so when one of them was brought in who owed him millions of dollars. 25 The servant did not have enough to pay his debt, so the king ordered him to be sold as a slave, with his wife and his children and all that he had, in order to pay the debt. 26 The servant fell on his knees before the king. 'Be patient with me,' he begged, 'and I will pay you everything!' 27 The king felt sorry for him, so he forgave him the debt and let him go.

28 "Then the man went out and met one of his fellow servants who owed him a few dollars. He grabbed him and started choking him. 'Pay back what you owe me!' he said. 29 His fellow servant fell down and begged him, 'Be patient with me, and I will pay you back!' 30 But he refused; instead, he had him thrown into jail until he should pay the debt. 31 When the other servants saw what had happened, they were very upset and went to the king and told him everything. 32 So he called the ser-vant in. 'You worthless slave!' he said. 'I forgave you the whole amount you owed me, just because you asked me to. 33 You should have had mercy on your fellow servant, just as I had mercy on you.' 34 The king was very angry, and he sent the servant to jail to be punished until he should pay back the whole amount."

35 And Jesus concluded, "That is how my Father in heaven will treat every one of you unless you forgive your broth-er from your heart."

Chapter 19
Jesus Teaches about Divorce

1 When Jesus finished saying these things, he left Galilee and went to the territory of Judea on the other side of the Jordan River. 2 Large crowds fol-lowed him, and he healed them there.

Learn more on page 178.

3 Some Pharisees came to him and tried to trap him by asking, "Does our Law allow a man to divorce his wife for whatever reason he wishes?"

4 Jesus answered, "Haven't you read the scripture that says that in the beginning the Creator made people male and female? 5 And God said, 'For this reason a man will leave his father and mother and unite with his wife, and the two will become one.' 6 So they are no longer two, but one. No human being must separate, then, what God has joined together."

7 The Pharisees asked him, "Why, then, did Moses give the law for a man to hand his wife a divorce notice and send her away?"

8 Jesus answered, "Moses gave you permission to divorce your wives because you are so hard to teach. But it was not like that at the time of creation. 9 I tell you, then, that any man who divorces his wife for any cause other than her unfaithfulness, commits adultery if he marries some other woman."

10 His disciples said to him, "If this is how it is between a man and his wife, it is better not to marry."

11 Jesus answered, "This teaching does not apply to everyone, but only to those to whom God has given it. 12 For there are different reasons why men cannot marry: some, because they were born that way; others, because men made them that way; and others do not marry for the sake of the Kingdom of heaven. Let him who can accept this teaching do so."

Jesus Blesses Little Children

13 Some people brought children to Jesus for him to place his hands on them and to pray for them, but the disciples scolded the people. 14 Jesus said, "Let the children come to me and do not stop them, because the Kingdom of heaven belongs to such as these."

15 He placed his hands on them and then went away.

The Rich Young Man

16 Once a man came to Jesus. "Teacher," he asked, "what good thing must I do to receive eternal life?"

17 "Why do you ask me concerning what is good?" answered Jesus. "There is only One who is good. Keep the commandments if you want to enter life."

18 "What commandments?" he asked.

Jesus answered, "Do not commit murder; do not commit adultery; do not steal; do not accuse anyone falsely; 19 respect your father and your mother; and love your neighbor as you love yourself."

20 "I have obeyed all these commandments," the young man replied. "What else do I need to do?"

21 Jesus said to him, "If you want to be perfect, go and sell all you have and give the money to the poor, and you will have riches in heaven; then come and follow me."

22 When the young man heard this, he went away sad, because he was very rich.

23 Jesus then said to his disciples, "I assure you: it will be very hard for rich people to enter the Kingdom of heaven. 24 I repeat: it is much harder for a rich person to enter the Kingdom of God than for a camel to go through the eye of a needle."

25 When the disciples heard this, they were completely amazed. "Who, then, can be saved?" they asked.

26 Jesus looked straight at them and answered, "This is impossible for human beings, but for God everything is possible."

27 Then Peter spoke up. "Look," he said, "we have left everything and followed you. What will we have?"

28 Jesus said to them, "You can be sure that when the Son of Man sits on his glorious throne in the New Age, then you twelve followers of mine will also sit on thrones, to rule the twelve tribes of Israel. 29 And everyone who has left houses or brothers or sisters or father or mother or children or fields for my sake, will receive

a hundred times more and will be given eternal life. ³⁰ But many who now are first will be last, and many who now are last will be first.

rn more on page 181.

Chapter 20
The Workers in the Vineyard
¹ "The Kingdom of heaven is like this. Once there was a man who went out early in the morning to hire some men to work in his vineyard. ² He agreed to pay them the regular wage, a silver coin a day, and sent them to work in his vineyard. ³ He went out again to the marketplace at nine o'clock and saw some men standing there doing nothing, ⁴ so he told them, 'You also go and work in the vineyard, and I will pay you a fair wage.' ⁵ So they went. Then at twelve o'clock and again at three o'clock he did the same thing. ⁶ It was nearly five o'clock when he went to the marketplace and saw some other men still standing there. 'Why are you wasting the whole day here doing nothing?' he asked them. ⁷ 'No one hired us,' they answered. 'Well, then, you go and work in the vineyard,' he told them.

⁸ "When evening came, the owner told his foreman, 'Call the workers and pay them their wages, starting with those who were hired last and ending with those who were hired first.' ⁹ The men who had begun to work at five o'clock were paid a silver coin each. ¹⁰ So when the men who were the first to be hired came to be paid, they thought they would get more; but they too were given a silver coin each. ¹¹ They took their money and started grumbling against the employer. ¹² 'These men who were hired last worked only one hour,' they said, 'while we put up with a whole day's work in the hot sun—yet you paid them the same as you paid us!' ¹³ 'Listen, friend,' the owner answered one of them, 'I have not cheated you. After all, you agreed to do a day's work for one silver coin. ¹⁴ Now take your pay and go

home. I want to give this man who was hired last as much as I gave you. ¹⁵ Don't I have the right to do as I wish with my own money? Or are you jealous because I am generous?'"

¹⁶ And Jesus concluded, "So those who are last will be first, and those who are first will be last."

Jesus Speaks a Third Time about His Death
¹⁷ As Jesus was going up to Jerusalem, he took the twelve disciples aside and spoke to them privately, as they walked along. ¹⁸ "Listen," he told them, "we are going up to Jerusalem, where the Son of Man will be handed over to the chief priests and the teachers of the Law. They will condemn him to death ¹⁹ and then hand him over to the Gentiles, who will make fun of him, whip him, and crucify him; but three days later he will be raised to life."

A Mother's Request
²⁰ Then the wife of Zebedee came to Jesus with her two sons, bowed before him, and asked him for a favor.

²¹ "What do you want?" Jesus asked her.

She answered, "Promise me that these two sons of mine will sit at your right and your left when you are King."

²² "You don't know what you are asking for," Jesus answered the sons. "Can you drink the cup of suffering that I am about to drink?"

"We can," they answered.

²³ "You will indeed drink from my cup," Jesus told them, "but I do not have the right to choose who will sit at my right and my left. These places belong to those for whom my Father has prepared them."

²⁴ When the other ten disciples heard about this, they became angry with the two brothers. ²⁵ So Jesus called them all together and said, "You know that the rulers of the heathen have power over them, and the leaders have complete authority. ²⁶ This, however, is not the way it shall be among you. If one of you wants to be great, you must be the servant of the rest; ²⁷ and if one of you wants to be

first, you must be the slave of the others— 28 like the Son of Man, who did not come to be served, but to serve and to give his life to redeem many people."

Jesus Heals Two Blind Men

29 As Jesus and his disciples were leaving Jericho, a large crowd was following. 30 Two blind men who were sitting by the road heard that Jesus was passing by, so they began to shout, "Son of David! Have mercy on us, sir!"

31 The crowd scolded them and told them to be quiet. But they shouted even more loudly, "Son of David! Have mercy on us, sir!"

32 Jesus stopped and called them. "What do you want me to do for you?" he asked them.

33 "Sir," they answered, "we want you to give us our sight!"

34 Jesus had pity on them and touched their eyes; at once they were able to see, and they followed him.

Chapter 21

The Triumphant Entry into Jerusalem

1 As Jesus and his disciples approached Jerusalem, they came to Bethphage at the Mount of Olives. There Jesus sent two of the disciples on ahead 2 with these instructions: "Go to the village there ahead of you, and at once you will find a donkey tied up with her colt beside her. Untie them and bring them to me. 3 And if anyone says anything, tell him, 'The Master needs them'; and then he will let them go at once."

4 This happened in order to make come true what the prophet had said:

5 "Tell the city of Zion,
    Look, your king is coming to you!
He is humble and rides on a donkey
    and on a colt, the foal of a donkey."

6 So the disciples went and did what Jesus had told them to do: 7 they brought the donkey and the colt, threw their cloaks over them, and Jesus got on. 8 A large crowd of people spread their cloaks on the road while others cut branches from the trees and spread them on the road. 9 The crowds walking in front of Jesus and those walking behind began to shout, "Praise to David's Son! God bless him who comes in the name of the Lord! Praise be to God!"

10 When Jesus entered Jerusalem, the whole city was thrown into an uproar. "Who is he?" the people asked.

11 "This is the prophet Jesus, from Nazareth in Galilee," the crowds answered.

Jesus Goes to the Temple

12 Jesus went into the Temple and drove out all those who were buying and selling there. He overturned the tables of the moneychangers and the stools of those who sold pigeons, 13 and said to them, "It is written in the Scriptures that God said, 'My Temple will be called a house of prayer.' But you are making it a hideout for thieves!"

14 The blind and the crippled came to him in the Temple, and he healed them. 15 The chief priests and the teachers of the Law became angry when they saw the wonderful things he was doing and the children shouting in the Temple, "Praise to David's Son!" 16 So they asked Jesus, "Do you hear what they are saying?"

"Indeed I do," answered Jesus. "Haven't you ever read this scripture? 'You have trained children and babies to offer perfect praise.'"

17 Jesus left them and went out of the city to Bethany, where he spent the night.

Jesus Curses the Fig Tree

18 On his way back to the city early next morning, Jesus was hungry. 19 He saw a fig tree by the side of the road and went to it, but found nothing on it except leaves. So he said to the tree, "You

will never again bear fruit!" At once the fig tree dried up.

20 The disciples saw this and were astounded. "How did the fig tree dry up so quickly?" they asked.

21 Jesus answered, "I assure you that if you believe and do not doubt, you will be able to do what I have done to this fig tree. And not only this, but you will even be able to say to this hill, 'Get up and throw yourself in the sea,' and it will. 22 If you believe, you will receive whatever you ask for in prayer."

The Question about Jesus' Authority
23 Jesus came back to the Temple; and as he taught, the chief priests and the elders came to him and asked, "What right do you have to do these things? Who gave you such right?"

24 Jesus answered them, "I will ask you just one question, and if you give me an answer, I will tell you what right I have to do these things. 25 Where did John's right to baptize come from: was it from God or from human beings?"

They started to argue among themselves, "What shall we say? If we answer, 'From God,' he will say to us, 'Why, then, did you not believe John?' 26 But if we say, 'From human beings,' we are afraid of what the people might do, because they are all convinced that John was a prophet." 27 So they answered Jesus, "We don't know."

And he said to them, "Neither will I tell you, then, by what right I do these things.

The Parable of the Two Sons
28 "Now, what do you think? There was once a man who had two sons. He went to the older one and said, 'Son, go and work in the vineyard today.' 29 'I don't want to,' he answered, but later he changed his mind and went. 30 Then the father went to the other son and said the same thing. 'Yes, sir,' he answered, but he did not go. 31 Which one of the two did what his father wanted?"

"The older one," they answered.

So Jesus said to them, "I tell you: the tax collectors and the prostitutes are going into the Kingdom of God ahead of you. 32 For John the Baptist came to you showing you the right path to take, and you would not believe him; but the tax collectors and the prostitutes believed him. Even when you saw this, you did not later change your minds and believe him.

The Parable of the Tenants in the Vineyard
33 "Listen to another parable," Jesus said. "There was once a landowner who planted a vineyard, put a fence around it, dug a hole for the wine press, and built a watchtower. Then he rented the vineyard to tenants and left home on a trip. 34 When the time came to gather the grapes, he sent his slaves to the tenants to receive his share of the harvest. 35 The tenants grabbed his slaves, beat one, killed another, and stoned another. 36 Again the man sent other slaves, more than the first time, and the tenants treated them the same way. 37 Last of all he sent his son to them. 'Surely they will respect my son,' he said. 38 But when the tenants saw the son, they said to themselves, 'This is the owner's son. Come on, let's kill him, and we will get his property!' 39 So they grabbed him, threw him out of the vineyard, and killed him.

40 "Now, when the owner of the vineyard comes, what will he do to those tenants?" Jesus asked.

41 "He will certainly kill those evil men," they answered, "and rent the vineyard out to other tenants, who will give him his share of the harvest at the right time."

42 Jesus said to them, "Haven't you ever read what the Scriptures say?

'The stone which the builders rejected as worthless
    turned out to be the most important of all.
This was done by the Lord;
    what a wonderful sight it is!'

43 "And so I tell you," added Jesus, "the Kingdom of God will be taken away from you and given to a people who will produce the proper fruits."

MATTHEW 22

45 The chief priests and the Pharisees heard Jesus' parables and knew that he was talking about them, 46 so they tried to arrest him. But they were afraid of the crowds, who considered Jesus to be a prophet.

Chapter 22
The Parable of the Wedding Feast

1 Jesus again used parables in talking to the people. 2 "The Kingdom of heaven is like this. Once there was a king who prepared a wedding feast for his son. 3 He sent his servants to tell the invited guests to come to the feast, but they did not want to come. 4 So he sent other servants with this message for the guests: 'My feast is ready now; my steers and prize calves have been butchered, and everything is ready. Come to the wedding feast!' 5 But the invited guests paid no attention and went about their business: one went to his farm, another to his store, 6 while others grabbed the servants, beat them, and killed them. 7 The king was very angry; so he sent his soldiers, who killed those murderers and burned down their city. 8 Then he called his servants and said to them, 'My wedding feast is ready, but the people I invited did not deserve it. 9 Now go to the main streets and invite to the feast as many people as you find.' 10 So the servants went out into the streets and gathered all the people they could find, good and bad alike; and the wedding hall was filled with people.

11 "The king went in to look at the guests and saw a man who was not wearing wedding clothes. 12 'Friend, how did you get in here without wedding clothes?' the king asked him. But the man said nothing. 13 Then the king told the servants, 'Tie him up hand and foot, and throw him outside in the dark. There he will cry and gnash his teeth.'"

14 And Jesus concluded, "Many are invited, but few are chosen."

The Question about Paying Taxes

15 The Pharisees went off and made a plan to trap Jesus with questions. 16 Then they sent to him some of their disciples and some members of Herod's party. "Teacher," they said, "we know that you tell the truth. You teach the truth about God's will for people, without worrying about what others think, because you pay no attention to anyone's status. 17 Tell us, then, what do you think? Is it against our Law to pay taxes to the Roman Emperor, or not?"

18 Jesus, however, was aware of their evil plan, and so he said, "You hypocrites! Why are you trying to trap me? 19 Show me the coin for paying the tax!"

They brought him the coin, 20 and he asked them, "Whose face and name are these?"

21 "The Emperor's," they answered.

So Jesus said to them, "Well, then, pay to the Emperor what belongs to the Emperor, and pay to God what belongs to God."

22 When they heard this, they were amazed; and they left him and went away.

The Question about Rising from Death

23 That same day some Sadducees came to Jesus and claimed that people will not rise from death. 24 "Teacher," they said, "Moses said that if a man who has no children dies, his brother must marry the widow so that they can have children who will be considered the dead man's children. 25 Now, there were seven brothers who used to live here. The oldest got married and died without having children, so he left his widow to his brother. 26 The same thing happened to the second brother, to the third, and finally to all seven. 27 Last of all, the woman died. 28 Now, on the day when the dead rise to life, whose wife will she be? All of them had married her."

29 Jesus answered them, "How wrong you are! It is because you don't know the Scriptures or God's power. 30 For when the dead rise to life, they will be like the an-

Learn more on page 192.

gels in heaven and will not marry. ³¹ Now, as for the dead rising to life: haven't you ever read what God has told you? He said, ³² 'I am the God of Abraham, the God of Isaac, and the God of Jacob.' He is the God of the living, not of the dead."

³³ When the crowds heard this, they were amazed at his teaching.

earn more on page 180.

The Great Commandment
³⁴ When the Pharisees heard that Jesus had silenced the Sadducees, they came together, ³⁵ and one of them, a teacher of the Law, tried to trap him with a question. ³⁶ "Teacher," he asked, "which is the greatest commandment in the Law?"

³⁷ Jesus answered, "'Love the Lord your God with all your heart, with all your soul, and with all your mind.' ³⁸ This is the greatest and the most important commandment. ³⁹ The second most important commandment is like it: 'Love your neighbor as you love yourself.' ⁴⁰ The whole Law of Moses and the teachings of the prophets depend on these two commandments."

The Question about the Messiah
⁴¹ When some Pharisees gathered together, Jesus asked them, ⁴² "What do you think about the Messiah? Whose descendant is he?"

"He is David's descendant," they answered.

⁴³ "Why, then," Jesus asked, "did the Spirit inspire David to call him 'Lord'? David said,

⁴⁴ 'The Lord said to my Lord:
Sit here at my right side
until I put your enemies under your feet.'

⁴⁵ If, then, David called him 'Lord,' how can the Messiah be David's descendant?"

⁴⁶ No one was able to give Jesus any answer, and from that day on no one dared to ask him any more questions.

Chapter 23
Jesus Warns against the Teachers of the Law and the Pharisees
¹ Then Jesus spoke to the crowds and to his disciples. ² "The teachers of the Law and the Pharisees are the authorized interpreters of Moses' Law. ³ So you must obey and follow everything they tell you to do; do not, however, imitate their actions, because they don't practice what they preach. ⁴ They tie onto people's backs loads that are heavy and hard to carry, yet they aren't willing even to lift a finger to help them carry those loads. ⁵ They do everything so that people will see them. Look at the straps with scripture verses on them which they wear on their foreheads and arms, and notice how large they are! Notice also how long are the tassels on their cloaks! ⁶ They love the best places at feasts and the reserved seats in the synagogues; ⁷ they love to be greeted with respect in the marketplaces and to have people call them 'Teacher.' ⁸ You must not be called 'Teacher,' because you are all equal and have only one Teacher. ⁹ And you must not call anyone here on earth 'Father,' because you have only the one Father in heaven. ¹⁰ Nor should you be called 'Leader,' because your one and only leader is the Messiah. ¹¹ The greatest one among you must be your servant. ¹² Whoever makes himself great will be humbled, and whoever humbles himself will be made great.

Jesus Condemns Their Hypocrisy
¹³ "How terrible for you, teachers of the Law and Pharisees! You hypocrites! You lock the door to the Kingdom of heaven in people's faces, but you yourselves don't go in, nor do you allow in those who are trying to enter!

¹⁵ "How terrible for you, teachers of the Law and Pharisees! You hypocrites! You sail the seas and cross whole countries to win one convert; and when you succeed,

you make him twice as deserving of going to hell as you yourselves are!

16 "How terrible for you, blind guides! You teach, 'If someone swears by the Temple, he isn't bound by his vow; but if he swears by the gold in the Temple, he is bound.' 17 Blind fools! Which is more important, the gold or the Temple which makes the gold holy? 18 You also teach, 'If someone swears by the altar, he isn't bound by his vow; but if he swears by the gift on the altar, he is bound.' 19 How blind you are! Which is the more important, the gift or the altar which makes the gift holy? 20 So then, when a person swears by the altar, he is swearing by it and by all the gifts on it; 21 and when he swears by the Temple, he is swearing by it and by God, who lives there; 22 and when someone swears by heaven, he is swearing by God's throne and by him who sits on it.

23 "How terrible for you, teachers of the Law and Pharisees! You hypocrites! You give to God one tenth even of the seasoning herbs, such as mint, dill, and cumin, but you neglect to obey the really important teachings of the Law, such as justice and mercy and honesty. These you should practice, without neglecting the others. 24 Blind guides! You strain a fly out of your drink, but swallow a camel!

25 "How terrible for you, teachers of the Law and Pharisees! You hypocrites! You clean the outside of your cup and plate, while the inside is full of what you have gotten by violence and selfishness. 26 Blind Pharisee! Clean what is inside the cup first, and then the outside will be clean too!

27 "How terrible for you, teachers of the Law and Pharisees! You hypocrites! You are like whitewashed tombs, which look fine on the outside but are full of bones and decaying corpses on the inside. 28 In the same way, on the outside you appear good to everybody, but inside you are full of hypocrisy and sins.

Jesus Predicts Their Punishment

29 "How terrible for you, teachers of the Law and Pharisees! You hypocrites! You make fine tombs for the prophets and

decorate the monuments of those who lived good lives; 30 and you claim that if you had lived during the time of your ancestors, you would not have done what they did and killed the prophets. 31 So you actually admit that you are the descendants of those who murdered the prophets! 32 Go on, then, and finish up what your ancestors started!

33 You snakes and children of snakes! How do you expect to escape from being condemned to hell? 34 And so I tell you that I will send you prophets and wise men and teachers; you will kill some of them, crucify others, and whip others in the synagogues and chase them from town to town. 35 As a result, the punishment for the murder of all innocent people will fall on you, from the murder of innocent Abel to the murder of Zechariah son of Berechiah, whom you murdered between the Temple and the altar. 36 I tell you indeed: the punishment for all these murders will fall on the people of this day!

Jesus' Love for Jerusalem

37 "Jerusalem, Jerusalem! You kill the prophets and stone the messengers God has sent you! How many times I wanted to put my arms around all your people, just as a hen gathers her chicks under her wings, but you would not let me! 38 And so your Temple will be abandoned and empty. 39 From now on, I tell you, you will never see me again until you say, 'God bless him who comes in the name of the Lord.'"

Chapter 24
Jesus Speaks of the Destruction of the Temple

1 Jesus left and was going away from the Temple when his disciples came to him to call his attention to its buildings. 2 "Yes," he said, "you may well look at all these. I tell you this: not a single stone here will be left in its place; every one of them will be thrown down."

Troubles and Persecutions

3 As Jesus sat on the Mount of Olives, the disciples came to him in private. "Tell us when all this will be," they asked, "and what will happen to show that it is the time for your coming and the end of the age."

4 Jesus answered, "Watch out, and do not let anyone fool you. 5 Many men, claiming to speak for me, will come and say, 'I am the Messiah!' and they will fool many people. 6 You are going to hear the noise of battles close by and the news of battles far away; but do not be troubled. Such things must happen, but they do not mean that the end has come. 7 Countries will fight each other; kingdoms will attack one another. There will be famines and earthquakes everywhere. 8 All these things are like the first pains of childbirth.

9 "Then you will be arrested and handed over to be punished and be put to death. Everyone will hate you because of me. 10 Many will give up their faith at that time; they will betray one another and hate one another. 11 Then many false prophets will appear and fool many people. 12 Such will be the spread of evil that many people's love will grow cold. 13 But whoever holds out to the end will be saved. 14 And this Good News about the Kingdom will be preached through all the world for a witness to all people; and then the end will come.

The Awful Horror

15 "You will see 'The Awful Horror' of which the prophet Daniel spoke. It will be standing in the holy place." (Note to the reader: understand what this means!) 16 "Then those who are in Judea must run away to the hills. 17 Someone who is on the roof of a house must not take the time to go down and get any belongings from the house. 18 Someone who is in the field must not go back to get a cloak. 19 How terrible it will be in those days for women who are pregnant and for mothers with little babies! 20 Pray to God that you will not have to run away during the winter or on a Sabbath! 21 For the trouble at that time will be far more terrible than any there has ever been, from the beginning of the world to this very day. Nor will there ever be any-

thing like it again. 22 But God has already reduced the number of days; had he not done so, nobody would survive. For the sake of his chosen people, however, God will reduce the days.

23 "Then, if anyone says to you, 'Look, here is the Messiah!' or 'There he is!'—do not believe it. 24 For false Messiahs and false prophets will appear; they will perform great miracles and wonders in order to deceive even God's chosen people, if possible. 25 Listen! I have told you this ahead of time.

26 "Or, if people should tell you, 'Look, he is out in the desert!'—don't go there; or if they say, 'Look, he is hiding here!'—don't believe it. 27 For the Son of Man will come like the lightning which flashes across the whole sky from the east to the west.

28 "Wherever there is a dead body, the vultures will gather.

The Coming of the Son of Man

29 "Soon after the trouble of those days, the sun will grow dark, the moon will no longer shine, the stars will fall from heaven, and the powers in space will be driven from their courses. 30 Then the sign of the Son of Man will appear in the sky; and all the peoples of earth will weep as they see the Son of Man coming on the clouds of heaven with power and great glory. 31 The great trumpet will sound, and he will send out his angels to the four corners of the earth, and they will gather his chosen people from one end of the world to the other.

The Lesson of the Fig Tree

32 "Let the fig tree teach you a lesson. When its branches become green and tender and it starts putting out leaves, you know that summer is near. 33 In the same way, when you see all these things, you will know that the time is near, ready to begin. 34 Remember that all these things will happen before the people now living have all died. 35 Heaven and earth will pass away, but my words will never pass away.

Learn more on page 193.

No One Knows the Day and Hour

36 "No one knows, however, when that day and hour will come—neither the angels in heaven nor the Son; the Father alone knows. 37 The coming of the Son of Man will be like what happened in the time of Noah. 38 In the days before the flood people ate and drank, men and women married, up to the very day Noah went into the boat; 39 yet they did not realize what was happening until the flood came and swept them all away. That is how it will be when the Son of Man comes. 40 At that time two men will be working in a field: one will be taken away, the other will be left behind. 41 Two women will be at a mill grinding meal: one will be taken away, the other will be left behind. 42 Watch out, then, because you do not know what day your Lord will come. 43 If the owner of a house knew the time when the thief would come, you can be sure that he would stay awake and not let the thief break into his house. 44 So then, you also must always be ready, because the Son of Man will come at an hour when you are not expecting him.

The Faithful or the Unfaithful Servant

45 "Who, then, is a faithful and wise servant? It is the one that his master has placed in charge of the other servants to give them their food at the proper time. 46 How happy that servant is if his master finds him doing this when he comes home! 47 Indeed, I tell you, the master will put that servant in charge of all his property. 48 But if he is a bad servant, he will tell himself that his master will not come back for a long time, 49 and he will begin to beat his fellow servants and to eat and drink with drunkards. 50 Then that servant's master will come back one day when the servant does not expect him and at a time he does not know. 51 The master will cut him in pieces and make him share the fate of the hypocrites. There he will cry and gnash his teeth.

Chapter 25

The Parable of the Ten Young Women

1 "At that time the Kingdom of heaven will be like this. Once there were ten young women who took their oil lamps and went out to meet the bridegroom. 2 Five of them were foolish, and the other five were wise. 3 The foolish ones took their lamps but did not take any extra oil with them, 4 while the wise ones took containers full of oil for their lamps. 5 The bridegroom was late in coming, so they began to nod and fall asleep.

6 "It was already midnight when the cry rang out, 'Here is the bridegroom! Come and meet him!' 7 The ten young women woke up and trimmed their lamps. 8 Then the foolish ones said to the wise ones, 'Let us have some of your oil, because our lamps are going out.' 9 'No, indeed,' the wise ones answered, 'there is not enough for you and for us. Go to the store and buy some for yourselves.' 10 So the foolish ones went off to buy some oil; and while they were gone, the bridegroom arrived. The five who were ready went in with him to the wedding feast, and the door was closed.

11 "Later the others arrived. 'Sir, sir! Let us in!' they cried out. 12 'Certainly not! I don't know you,' the bridegroom answered."

13 And Jesus concluded, "Watch out, then, because you do not know the day or the hour.

The Parable of the Three Servants

14 "At that time the Kingdom of heaven will be like this. Once there was a man who was about to leave home on a trip; he called his servants and put them in charge of his property. 15 He gave to each one according to his ability: to one he gave five thousand gold coins, to another he gave two thousand, and to another he gave one thousand. Then he left on his trip. 16 The servant who had received five thousand coins went at once and invested his money and earned another five thousand. 17 In the same way the servant who had received two thousand coins

earned another two thousand. ¹⁸ But the servant who had received one thousand coins went off, dug a hole in the ground, and hid his master's money.

¹⁹ "After a long time the master of those servants came back and settled accounts with them. ²⁰ The servant who had received five thousand coins came in and handed over the other five thousand. 'You gave me five thousand coins, sir,' he said. 'Look! Here are another five thousand that I have earned.' ²¹ 'Well done, you good and faithful servant!' said his master. 'You have been faithful in managing small amounts, so I will put you in charge of large amounts. Come on in and share my happiness!'
²² Then the servant who had been given two thousand coins came in and said, 'You gave me two thousand coins, sir. Look! Here are another two thousand that I have earned.' ²³ 'Well done, you good and faithful servant!' said his master. 'You have been faithful in managing small amounts, so I will put you in charge of large amounts. Come on in and share my happiness!' ²⁴ Then the servant who had received one thousand coins came in and said, 'Sir, I know you are a hard man; you reap harvests where you did not plant, and you gather crops where you did not scatter seed. ²⁵ I was afraid, so I went off and hid your money in the ground. Look! Here is what belongs to you.' ²⁶ 'You bad and lazy servant!' his master said. 'You knew, did you, that I reap harvests where I did not plant, and gather crops where I did not scatter seed? ²⁷ Well, then, you should have deposited my money in the bank, and I would have received it all back with interest when I returned. ²⁸ Now, take the money away from him and give it to the one who has ten thousand coins. ²⁹ For to every person who has something, even more will be given, and he will have more than enough; but the person who has nothing, even the little that he has will be taken away from him.

Learn more on page 194.

³⁰ As for this useless servant—throw him outside in the darkness; there he will cry and gnash his teeth.'

The Final Judgment

³¹ "When the Son of Man comes as King and all the angels with him, he will sit on his royal throne, ³² and the people of all the nations will be gathered before him. Then he will divide them into two groups, just as a shepherd separates the sheep from the goats. ³³ He will put the righteous people at his right and the others at his left. ³⁴ Then the King will say to the people on his right, 'Come, you that are blessed by my Father! Come and possess the kingdom which has been prepared for you ever since the creation of the world. ³⁵ I was hungry and you fed me, thirsty and you gave me a drink; I was a stranger and you received me in your homes, ³⁶ naked and you clothed me; I was sick and you took care of me, in prison and you visited me.' ³⁷ The righteous will then answer him, 'When, Lord, did we ever see you hungry and feed you, or thirsty and give you a drink? ³⁸ When did we ever see you a stranger and welcome you in our homes, or naked and clothe you? ³⁹ When did we ever see you sick or in prison, and visit you?' ⁴⁰ The King will reply, 'I tell you, whenever you did this for one of the least important of these followers of mine, you did it for me!'

Learn more on page 195.

⁴¹ "Then he will say to those on his left, 'Away from me, you that are under God's curse! Away to the eternal fire which has been prepared for the Devil and his angels! ⁴² I was hungry but you would not feed me, thirsty but you would not give me a drink; ⁴³ I was a stranger but you would not welcome me in your homes, naked but you would not clothe me; I was sick and in prison but you would not take care of me.' ⁴⁴ Then they will answer him, 'When, Lord, did we ever see you hungry or thirsty

or a stranger or naked or sick or in prison, and we would not help you?' ⁴⁵ The King will reply, 'I tell you, whenever you refused to help one of these least important ones, you refused to help me.'

⁴⁶ These, then, will be sent off to eternal punishment, but the righteous will go to eternal life."

Chapter 26
The Plot against Jesus
¹ When Jesus had finished teaching all these things, he said to his disciples, ² "In two days, as you know, it will be the Passover Festival, and the Son of Man will be handed over to be crucified."

³ Then the chief priests and the elders met together in the palace of Caiaphas, the High Priest, ⁴ and made plans to arrest Jesus secretly and put him to death. ⁵ "We must not do it during the festival," they said, "or the people will riot."

Jesus Is Anointed at Bethany
⁶ Jesus was in Bethany at the house of Simon, a man who had suffered from a dreaded skin disease. ⁷ While Jesus was eating, a woman came to him with an alabaster jar filled with an expensive perfume, which she poured on his head. ⁸ The disciples saw this and became angry. "Why all this waste?" they asked. ⁹ "This perfume could have been sold for a large amount and the money given to the poor!"

¹⁰ Jesus knew what they were saying, and so he said to them, "Why are you bothering this woman? It is a fine and beautiful thing that she has done for me. ¹¹ You will always have poor people with you, but you will not always have me. ¹² What she did was to pour this perfume on my body to get me ready for burial. ¹³ Now, I assure you that wherever this gospel is preached all over the world, what she has done will be told in memory of her."

Judas Agrees to Betray Jesus
¹⁴ Then one of the twelve disciples—the one named Judas Iscariot—went to the chief priests ¹⁵ and asked, "What will you give me if I betray Jesus to you?" They counted out thirty silver coins and gave them to him. ¹⁶ From then on Judas was looking for a good chance to hand Jesus over to them.

Jesus Eats the Passover Meal with His Disciples
¹⁷ On the first day of the Festival of Unleavened Bread the disciples came to Jesus and asked him, "Where do you want us to get the Passover meal ready for you?"

¹⁸ "Go to a certain man in the city," he said to them, "and tell him: 'The Teacher says, My hour has come; my disciples and I will celebrate the Passover at your house.'"

¹⁹ The disciples did as Jesus had told them and prepared the Passover meal.

²⁰ When it was evening, Jesus and the twelve disciples sat down to eat. ²¹ During the meal Jesus said, "I tell you, one of you will betray me."

²² The disciples were very upset and began to ask him, one after the other, "Surely, Lord, you don't mean me?"

²³ Jesus answered, "One who dips his bread in the dish with me will betray me. ²⁴ The Son of Man will die as the Scriptures say he will, but how terrible for that man who will betray the Son of Man! It would have been better for that man if he had never been born!"

²⁵ Judas, the traitor, spoke up. "Surely, Teacher, you don't mean me?" he asked.

Jesus answered, "So you say."

Learn more on page 196

The Lord's Supper
²⁶ While they were eating, Jesus took a piece of bread, gave a prayer of thanks, broke it, and gave it to his disciples. "Take and eat it," he said; "this is my body."

²⁷ Then he took a cup, gave thanks to God, and gave it to them. "Drink it, all of you," he said; ²⁸ "this is my blood, which seals God's covenant, my blood poured out for many for

the forgiveness of sins. 29 I tell you, I will never again drink this wine until the day I drink the new wine with you in my Father's Kingdom."

30 Then they sang a hymn and went out to the Mount of Olives.

Jesus Predicts Peter's Denial
31 Then Jesus said to them, "This very night all of you will run away and leave me, for the scripture says, 'God will kill the shepherd, and the sheep of the flock will be scattered.' 32 But after I am raised to life, I will go to Galilee ahead of you."

33 Peter spoke up and said to Jesus, "I will never leave you, even though all the rest do!"

34 Jesus said to Peter, "I tell you that before the rooster crows tonight, you will say three times that you do not know me."

35 Peter answered, "I will never say that, even if I have to die with you!"

And all the other disciples said the same thing.

Jesus Prays in Gethsemane
36 Then Jesus went with his disciples to a place called Gethsemane, and he said to them, "Sit here while I go over there and pray." 37 He took with him Peter and the two sons of Zebedee. Grief and anguish came over him, 38 and he said to them, "The sorrow in my heart is so great that it almost crushes me. Stay here and keep watch with me."

39 He went a little farther on, threw himself face downward on the ground, and prayed, "My Father, if it is possible, take this cup of suffering from me! Yet not what I want, but what you want."

40 Then he returned to the three disciples and found them asleep; and he said to Peter, "How is it that you three were not able to keep watch with me for even one hour? 41 Keep watch and pray that you will not fall into temptation. The spirit is willing, but the flesh is weak."

42 Once more Jesus went away and prayed, "My Father, if this cup of suffering cannot be taken away unless I drink it, your will be done." 43 He returned once more and found the disciples asleep; they could not keep their eyes open.

44 Again Jesus left them, went away, and prayed the third time, saying the same words. 45 Then he returned to the disciples and said, "Are you still sleeping and resting? Look! The hour has come for the Son of Man to be handed over to the power of sinners. 46 Get up, let us go. Look, here is the man who is betraying me!"

The Arrest of Jesus
47 Jesus was still speaking when Judas, one of the twelve disciples, arrived. With him was a large crowd armed with swords and clubs and sent by the chief priests and the elders. 48 The traitor had given the crowd a signal: "The man I kiss is the one you want. Arrest him!"

49 Judas went straight to Jesus and said, "Peace be with you, Teacher," and kissed him.

50 Jesus answered, "Be quick about it, friend!"

Then they came up, arrested Jesus, and held him tight. 51 One of those who were with Jesus drew his sword and struck at the High Priest's slave, cutting off his ear. 52 "Put your sword back in its place," Jesus said to him. "All who take the sword will die by the sword. 53 Don't you know that I could call on my Father for help, and at once he would send me more than twelve armies of angels? 54 But in that case, how could the Scriptures come true which say that this is what must happen?"

55 Then Jesus spoke to the crowd, "Did you have to come with swords and clubs to capture me, as though I were an outlaw? Every day I sat down and taught in the Temple, and you did not arrest me. 56 But all this has happened in order to make come true what the prophets wrote in the Scriptures."

Then all the disciples left him and ran away.

Jesus Before the Council

57 Those who had arrested Jesus took him to the house of Caiaphas, the High Priest, where the teachers of the Law and the elders had gathered together. 58 Peter followed from a distance, as far as the courtyard of the High Priest's house. He went into the courtyard and sat down with the guards to see how it would all come out. 59 The chief priests and the whole Council tried to find some false evidence against Jesus to put him to death; 60 but they could not find any, even though many people came forward and told lies about him. Finally two men stepped up 61 and said, "This man said, 'I am able to tear down God's Temple and three days later build it back up.'"

62 The High Priest stood up and said to Jesus, "Have you no answer to give to this accusation against you?" 63 But Jesus kept quiet. Again the High Priest spoke to him, "In the name of the living God I now put you under oath: tell us if you are the Messiah, the Son of God."

64 Jesus answered him, "So you say. But I tell all of you: from this time on you will see the Son of Man sitting at the right side of the Almighty and coming on the clouds of heaven!"

65 At this the High Priest tore his clothes and said, "Blasphemy! We don't need any more witnesses! You have just heard his blasphemy! 66 What do you think?"

They answered, "He is guilty and must die."

67 Then they spat in his face and beat him; and those who slapped him 68 said, "Prophesy for us, Messiah! Guess who hit you!"

Peter Denies Jesus

69 Peter was sitting outside in the courtyard when one of the High Priest's servant women came to him and said, "You, too, were with Jesus of Galilee."

70 But he denied it in front of them all. "I don't know what you are talking about," he answered, 71 and went on out to the entrance of the courtyard. Another servant woman saw him and said to the men there, "He was with Jesus of Nazareth."

72 Again Peter denied it and answered, "I swear that I don't know that man!"

73 After a little while the men standing there came to Peter. "Of course you are one of them," they said. "After all, the way you speak gives you away!"

74 Then Peter said, "I swear that I am telling the truth! May God punish me if I am not! I do not know that man!"

Just then a rooster crowed, 75 and Peter remembered what Jesus had told him: "Before the rooster crows, you will say three times that you do not know me." He went out and wept bitterly.

Chapter 27

Jesus Is Taken to Pilate

1 Early in the morning all the chief priests and the elders made their plans against Jesus to put him to death. 2 They put him in chains, led him off, and handed him over to Pilate, the Roman governor.

The Death of Judas

3 When Judas, the traitor, learned that Jesus had been condemned, he repented and took back the thirty silver coins to the chief priests and the elders. 4 "I have sinned by betraying an innocent man to death!" he said.

"What do we care about that?" they answered. "That is your business!"

5 Judas threw the coins down in the Temple and left; then he went off and hanged himself.

6 The chief priests picked up the coins and said, "This is blood money, and it is against our Law to put it in the Temple treasury." 7 After reaching an agreement about it, they used the money to buy Potter's Field, as a cemetery for foreigners. 8 That is why that field is called

"Field of Blood" to this very day.

⁹ Then what the prophet Jeremiah had said came true: "They took the thirty silver coins, the amount the people of Israel had agreed to pay for him, ¹⁰ and used the money to buy the potter's field, as the Lord had commanded me."

Pilate Questions Jesus
¹¹ Jesus stood before the Roman governor, who questioned him. "Are you the king of the Jews?" he asked.

"So you say," answered Jesus. ¹² But he said nothing in response to the accusations of the chief priests and elders.

¹³ So Pilate said to him, "Don't you hear all these things they accuse you of?"

¹⁴ But Jesus refused to answer a single word, with the result that the Governor was greatly surprised.

Jesus Is Sentenced to Death
¹⁵ At every Passover Festival the Roman governor was in the habit of setting free any one prisoner the crowd asked for. ¹⁵ At that time there was a well-known prisoner named Jesus Barabbas. ¹⁷ So when the crowd gathered, Pilate asked them, "Which one do you want me to set free for you? Jesus Barabbas or Jesus called the Messiah?" ¹⁸ He knew very well that the Jewish authorities had handed Jesus over to him because they were jealous.

¹⁹ While Pilate was sitting in the judgment hall, his wife sent him a message: "Have nothing to do with that innocent man, because in a dream last night I suffered much on account of him."

²⁰ The chief priests and the elders persuaded the crowd to ask Pilate to set Barabbas free and have Jesus put to death. ²¹ But Pilate asked the crowd, "Which one of these two do you want me to set free for you?"

"Barabbas!" they answered.

²² "What, then, shall I do with Jesus called the Messiah?" Pilate asked them.

"Crucify him!" they all answered.

²³ But Pilate asked, "What crime has he committed?"

Then they started shouting at the top of their voices: "Crucify him!"

²⁴ When Pilate saw that it was no use to go on, but that a riot might break out, he took some water, washed his hands in front of the crowd, and said, "I am not responsible for the death of this man! This is your doing!"

²⁵ The whole crowd answered, "Let the responsibility for his death fall on us and on our children!"

²⁶ Then Pilate set Barabbas free for them; and after he had Jesus whipped, he handed him over to be crucified.

The Soldiers Make Fun of Jesus
²⁷ Then Pilate's soldiers took Jesus into the governor's palace, and the whole company gathered around him. ²⁸ They stripped off his clothes and put a scarlet robe on him. ²⁹ Then they made a crown out of thorny branches and placed it on his head, and put a stick in his right hand; then they knelt before him and made fun of him. "Long live the King of the Jews!" they said. ³⁰ They spat on him, and took the stick and hit him over the head. ³¹ When they had finished making fun of him, they took the robe off and put his own clothes back on him. Then they led him out to crucify him.

Jesus Is Crucified
³² As they were going out, they met a man from Cyrene named Simon, and the soldiers forced him to carry Jesus' cross. ³³ They came to a place called Golgotha, which means, "The Place of the Skull." ³⁴ There they offered Jesus wine mixed with a bitter substance; but after tasting it, he would not drink it.

35 They crucified him and then divided his clothes among them by throwing dice. 36 After that they sat there and watched him. 37 Above his head they put the written notice of the accusation against him: "This is Jesus, the King of the Jews." 38 Then they crucified two bandits with Jesus, one on his right and the other on his left.

39 People passing by shook their heads and hurled insults at Jesus: 40 "You were going to tear down the Temple and build it back up in three days! Save yourself if you are God's Son! Come on down from the cross!"

41 In the same way the chief priests and the teachers of the Law and the elders made fun of him: 42 "He saved others, but he cannot save himself! Isn't he the king of Israel? If he will come down off the cross now, we will believe in him! 43 He trusts in God and claims to be God's Son. Well, then, let us see if God wants to save him now!"

44 Even the bandits who had been crucified with him insulted him in the same way.

The Death of Jesus

45 At noon the whole country was covered with darkness, which lasted for three hours. 46 At about three o'clock Jesus cried out with a loud shout, *"Eli, Eli, lema sabachthani?"* which means, "My God, my God, why did you abandon me?"

47 Some of the people standing there heard him and said, "He is calling for Elijah!" 48 One of them ran up at once, took a sponge, soaked it in cheap wine, put it on the end of a stick, and tried to make him drink it.

49 But the others said, "Wait, let us see if Elijah is coming to save him!"

50 Jesus again gave a loud cry and breathed his last.

51 Then the curtain hanging in the Temple was torn in two from top to bottom. The earth shook, the rocks split apart, 52 the graves broke open, and many of God's people who had died were raised to life. 53 They left the graves, and after Jesus rose from death, they went into the Holy City, where many people saw them.

54 When the army officer and the soldiers with him who were watching Jesus saw the earthquake and everything else that happened, they were terrified and said, "He really was the Son of God!"

55 There were many women there, looking on from a distance, who had followed Jesus from Galilee and helped him. 56 Among them were Mary Magdalene, Mary the mother of James and Joseph, and the wife of Zebedee.

The Burial of Jesus

57 When it was evening, a rich man from Arimathea arrived; his name was Joseph, and he also was a disciple of Jesus. 58 He went into the presence of Pilate and asked for the body of Jesus. Pilate gave orders for the body to be given to Joseph. 59 So Joseph took it, wrapped it in a new linen sheet, 60 and placed it in his own tomb, which he had just recently dug out of solid rock. Then he rolled a large stone across the entrance to the tomb and went away. 61 Mary Magdalene and the other Mary were sitting there, facing the tomb.

The Guard at the Tomb

62 The next day, which was a Sabbath, the chief priests and the Pharisees met with Pilate 63 and said, "Sir, we remember that while that liar was still alive he said, 'I will be raised to life three days later.' 64 Give orders, then, for his tomb to be carefully guarded until the third day, so that his disciples will not be able to go and steal the body, and then tell the people that he was raised from death. This last lie would be even worse than the first one."

65 "Take a guard," Pilate told them; "go and make the tomb as secure as you can."

66 So they left and made the tomb secure by putting a seal on the stone and leaving the guard on watch.

Chapter 28
The Resurrection

1 After the Sabbath, as Sunday morning was dawning, Mary Magdalene and the other Mary went to look at the tomb. 2 Suddenly there was a violent earthquake; an angel of the Lord came down from heaven, rolled the stone away, and sat on it. 3 His appearance was like lightning, and his clothes were white as snow. 4 The guards were so afraid that they trembled and became like dead men.

5 The angel spoke to the women. "You must not be afraid," he said. "I know you are looking for Jesus, who was crucified. 6 He is not here; he has been raised, just as he said. Come here and see the place where he was lying. 7 Go quickly now, and tell his disciples, 'He has been raised from death, and now he is going to Galilee ahead of you; there you will see him!' Remember what I have told you."

8 So they left the tomb in a hurry, afraid and yet filled with joy, and ran to tell his disciples.

9 Suddenly Jesus met them and said, "Peace be with you." They came up to him, took hold of his feet, and worshiped him. 10 "Do not be afraid," Jesus said to them. "Go and tell my brothers to go to Galilee, and there they will see me."

The Report of the Guard

11 While the women went on their way, some of the soldiers guarding the tomb went back to the city and told the chief priests everything that had happened. 12 The chief priests met with the elders and made their plan; they gave a large sum of money to the soldiers 13 and said, "You are to say that his disciples came during the night and stole his body while you were asleep. 14 And if the Governor should hear of this, we will convince him that you are innocent, and you will have nothing to worry about."

15 The guards took the money and did what they were told to do. And so that is the report spread around by the Jews to this very day.

Jesus Appears to His Disciples

16 The eleven disciples went to the hill in Galilee where Jesus had told them to go. 17 When they saw him, they worshiped him, even though some of them doubted. 18 Jesus drew near and said to them, "I have been given all authority in heaven and on earth. 19 Go, then, to all peoples everywhere and make them my disciples: baptize them in the name of the Father, the Son, and the Holy Spirit, 20 and teach them to obey everything I have commanded you. And I will be with you always, to the end of the age."

Learn more on page 205.

The **GOSPEL** according to **MARK**

The Gospel of Mark was written by John Mark, a follower of Christ in the early Church, closely connected to Peter, and first mentioned in the Book of Acts as taking a mission trip with Barnabus and Paul. The home of John Mark's mother Mary served as a meeting place for the disciples in Jerusalem.

Using what was told to him by Peter about what Jesus said and did, **John Mark wrote to Gentile believers in Rome** who were not familiar with the customs associated with the Jewish faith. He explains Jewish traditions, defines Aramaic words and focuses on persecution and martyrdom for the faith. John Mark himself was martyred shortly after writing his Gospel. There is an urgency to his words that foreshadows that these believers may not have much time left.

The Gospel of Mark is **the shortest of all four Gospels** and is brief, quick and right-to-the-point in its retelling of the life, suffering, Death and Resurrection of Christ for our forgiveness and salvation. It is known for **using the word "immediately"** often, with very little transition from one episode to another.

What's the story?

John Mark skips the birth of Jesus all together and **begins with Jesus' ministry,** when Jesus is baptized in the Jordan by John the Baptist and Jesus journeys in the wilderness for 40 days, where he is tempted by Satan.

In Mark, Jesus' ministry begins in Galilee, where he calls his first disciples. He preaches, performs miracles, and heals people in and around Capernaum. His ministry grows as Jesus calls his 12 Apostles, speaks parables, heals more people and sends out six teams of disciples. Jesus spreads his message to the regions of Phoenica, the Decapolis and Caesarea Philippi, teaching and healing many.

The Passion narrative rounds out Mark's Gospel with descriptions of Palm Sunday, the clearing of the Temple, the anointing of Jesus, the Lord's Supper, and the arrest, trial and Death of Jesus. The account of the Resurrection of Jesus is so abrupt that **the Church has included an additional ending (or endings) in most Bibles (including this one).**

The GOSPEL according to MARK

Chapter 1

The Preaching of John the Baptist

1 This is the Good News about Jesus Christ, the Son of God. 2 It began as the prophet Isaiah had written:

"God said, 'I will send my messenger ahead of you
    to open the way for you.'
3 Someone is shouting in the desert,
    'Get the road ready for the Lord;
    make a straight path for him to travel!'"

4 So John appeared in the desert, baptizing and preaching. "Turn away from your sins and be baptized," he told the people, "and God will forgive your sins." 5 Many people from the province of Judea and the city of Jerusalem went out to hear John. They confessed their sins, and he baptized them in the Jordan River.

6 John wore clothes made of camel's hair, with a leather belt around his waist, and his food was locusts and wild honey. 7 He announced to the people, "The man who will come after me is much greater than I am. I am not good enough even to bend down and untie his sandals. 8 I baptize you with water, but he will baptize you with the Holy Spirit."

The Baptism and Temptation of Jesus

9 Not long afterward Jesus came from Nazareth in the province of Galilee, and was baptized by John in the Jordan. 10 As soon as Jesus came up out of the water, he saw heaven opening and the Spirit coming down on him like a dove. 11 And a voice came from heaven, "You are my own dear Son. I am pleased with you."

12 At once the Spirit made him go into the desert, 13 where he stayed forty days, being tempted by Satan. Wild animals were there also, but angels came and helped him.

Jesus Calls Four Fishermen

14 After John had been put in prison, Jesus went to Galilee and preached the Good News from God. 15 "The right time has come," he said, "and the Kingdom of God is near! Turn away from your sins and believe the Good News!"

16 As Jesus walked along the shore of Lake Galilee, he saw two fishermen, Simon and his brother Andrew, catching fish with a net. 17 Jesus said to them, "Come with me, and I will teach you to catch people." 18 At once they left their nets and went with him.

19 He went a little farther on and saw two other brothers, James and John, the sons of Zebedee. They were in their boat getting their nets ready. 20 As soon as Jesus saw them, he called them; they left their father Zebedee in the boat with the hired men and went with Jesus.

A Man with an Evil Spirit

21 Jesus and his disciples came to the town of Capernaum, and on the next Sabbath Jesus went to the synagogue and began to teach. 22 The people who heard him were amazed at the way he taught, for he wasn't like the teachers of the Law; instead, he taught with authority.

23 Just then a man with an evil spirit came into the synagogue and screamed, 24 "What do you want with us, Jesus of Nazareth? Are you here to destroy us? I know who you are—you are God's holy messenger!"

25 Jesus ordered the spirit, "Be quiet, and come out of the man!"

26 The evil spirit shook the man hard, gave a loud scream, and came out of him. 27 The people were all so amazed that they started saying to one another, "What is this? Is it some kind of new teaching? This man has authority to give orders to the evil spirits, and they obey him!"

28 And so the news about Jesus spread quickly everywhere in the province of Galilee.

Jesus Heals Many People

29 Jesus and his disciples, including James and John, left the synagogue and went straight to the home of Simon and Andrew. 30 Simon's mother-in-law was sick in bed with a fever, and as soon as Jesus arrived, he was told about her. 31 He went to her, took her by the hand, and helped her up. The fever left her, and she began to wait on them.

32 After the sun had set and evening had come, people brought to Jesus all the sick and those who had demons. 33 All the people of the town gathered in front of the house. 34 Jesus healed many who were sick with all kinds of diseases and drove out many demons. He would not let the demons say anything, because they knew who he was.

Jesus Preaches in Galilee

35 Very early the next morning, long before daylight, Jesus got up and left the house. He went out of town to a lonely place, where he prayed. 36 But Simon and his companions went out searching for him, 37 and when they found him, they said, "Everyone is looking for you."

38 But Jesus answered, "We must go on to the other villages around here. I have to preach in them also, because that is why I came."

39 So he traveled all over Galilee, preaching in the synagogues and driving out demons.

Jesus Heals a Man

40 A man suffering from a dreaded skin disease came to Jesus, knelt down, and begged him for help. "If you want to," he said, "you can make me clean."

41 Jesus was filled with pity, and reached out and touched him. "I do want to," he answered. "Be clean!" 42 At once the disease left the man, and he was clean. 43 Then Jesus spoke sternly to him and sent him away at once, 44 after saying to him, "Listen, don't tell anyone about this. But go straight to the priest and let him examine you; then in order to prove to everyone that you are cured, offer the sacrifice that Moses ordered."

45 But the man went away and began to spread the news everywhere. Indeed, he talked so much that Jesus could not go into a town publicly. Instead, he stayed out in lonely places, and people came to him from everywhere.

Chapter 2

Jesus Heals a Paralyzed Man

1 A few days later Jesus went back to Capernaum, and the news spread that he was at home. 2 So many people came together that there was no room left, not even out in front of the door. Jesus was preaching the message to them 3 when four men arrived, carrying a paralyzed man to Jesus. 4 Because of the crowd, however, they could not get the man to him. So they made a hole in the roof right above the place where Jesus was. When they had made an opening, they let the man down, lying on his mat. 5 Seeing how much faith they had, Jesus said to the paralyzed man, "My son, your sins are forgiven."

6 Some teachers of the Law who were sitting there thought to themselves, 7 "How does he dare talk like this? This is blasphemy! God is the only one who can forgive sins!"

8 At once Jesus knew what they were thinking, so he said to them, "Why do you think such things? 9 Is it easier to say to this paralyzed man, 'Your sins are forgiven,' or to say, 'Get up, pick up your mat, and walk'? 10 I will prove to you, then, that the Son of Man has authority on earth

Learn more on page 1

to forgive sins." So he said to the paralyzed man, [11] "I tell you, get up, pick up your mat, and go home!"

[12] While they all watched, the man got up, picked up his mat, and hurried away. They were all completely amazed and praised God, saying, "We have never seen anything like this!"

Jesus Calls Levi

[13] Jesus went back again to the shore of Lake Galilee. A crowd came to him, and he started teaching them. [14] As he walked along, he saw a tax collector, Levi son of Alphaeus, sitting in his office. Jesus said to him, "Follow me." Levi got up and followed him.

[15] Later on Jesus was having a meal in Levi's house. A large number of tax collectors and other outcasts was following Jesus, and many of them joined him and his disciples at the table. [16] Some teachers of the Law, who were Pharisees, saw that Jesus was eating with these outcasts and tax collectors, so they asked his disciples, "Why does he eat with such people?"

[17] Jesus heard them and answered, "People who are well do not need a doctor, but only those who are sick. I have not come to call respectable people, but outcasts."

The Question about Fasting

[18] On one occasion the followers of John the Baptist and the Pharisees were fasting. Some people came to Jesus and asked him, "Why is it that the disciples of John the Baptist and the disciples of the Pharisees fast, but yours do not?"

[19] Jesus answered, "Do you expect the guests at a wedding party to go without food? Of course not! As long as the bridegroom is with them, they will not do that. [20] But the day will come when the bridegroom will be taken away from them, and then they will fast.

[21] "No one uses a piece of new cloth to patch up an old coat, because the new patch will shrink and tear off some of the old cloth, making an even bigger hole. [22] Nor does anyone pour new wine into used wineskins, because the wine will burst the skins, and both the wine and the skins will be ruined. Instead, new wine must be poured into fresh wineskins."

The Question about the Sabbath

[23] Jesus was walking through some wheat fields on a Sabbath. As his disciples walked along with him, they began to pick the heads of wheat. [24] So the Pharisees said to Jesus, "Look, it is against our Law for your disciples to do that on the Sabbath!"

[25] Jesus answered, "Have you never read what David did that time when he needed something to eat? He and his men were hungry, [26] so he went into the house of God and ate the bread offered to God. This happened when Abiathar was the High Priest. According to our Law only the priests may eat this bread—but David ate it and even gave it to his men."

[27] And Jesus concluded, "The Sabbath was made for the good of human beings; they were not made for the Sabbath. [28] So the Son of Man is Lord even of the Sabbath."

Chapter 3
The Man with a Paralyzed Hand

[1] Then Jesus went back to the synagogue, where there was a man who had a paralyzed hand. [2] Some people were there who wanted to accuse Jesus of doing wrong; so they watched him closely to see whether he would cure the man on the Sabbath. [3] Jesus said to the man, "Come up here to the front." [4] Then he asked the people, "What does our Law allow us to do on the Sabbath? To help or to harm? To save someone's life or to destroy it?"

But they did not say a thing. [5] Jesus was angry as he looked around at them, but at the same time he felt sorry for them, because they were so stubborn and wrong. Then he said to the man, "Stretch out your hand." He stretched it out, and it became well again. [6] So the Pharisees left the synagogue and met at once with some members of Herod's party, and they made plans to kill Jesus.

A Crowd by the Lake

7 Jesus and his disciples went away to Lake Galilee, and a large crowd followed him. They had come from Galilee, from Judea, 8 from Jerusalem, from the territory of Idumea, from the territory on the east side of the Jordan, and from the region around the cities of Tyre and Sidon. All these people came to Jesus because they had heard of the things he was doing. 9 The crowd was so large that Jesus told his disciples to get a boat ready for him, so that the people would not crush him. 10 He had healed many people, and all the sick kept pushing their way to him in order to touch him. 11 And whenever the people who had evil spirits in them saw him, they would fall down before him and scream, "You are the Son of God!"

12 Jesus sternly ordered the evil spirits not to tell anyone who he was.

Jesus Chooses the Twelve Apostles

13 Then Jesus went up a hill and called to himself the men he wanted. They came to him, 14 and he chose twelve, whom he named apostles. "I have chosen you to be with me," he told them. "I will also send you out to preach, 15 and you will have authority to drive out demons."

16 These are the twelve he chose: Simon (Jesus gave him the name Peter); 17 James and his brother John, the sons of Zebedee (Jesus gave them the name Boanerges, which means "Men of Thunder"); 18 Andrew, Philip, Bartholomew, Matthew, Thomas, James son of Alphaeus, Thaddaeus, Simon the Patriot, 19 and Judas Iscariot, who betrayed Jesus.

Jesus and Beelzebul

20 Then Jesus went home. Again such a large crowd gathered that Jesus and his disciples had no time to eat. 21 When his family heard about it, they set out to take charge of him, because people were saying, "He's gone mad!"

22 Some teachers of the Law who had come from Jerusalem were saying, "He has Beelzebul in him! It is the chief of the demons who gives him the power to drive them out."

23 So Jesus called them to him and spoke to them in parables: "How can Satan drive out Satan? 24 If a country divides itself into groups which fight each other, that country will fall apart. 25 If a family divides itself into groups which fight each other, that family will fall apart. 26 So if Satan's kingdom divides into groups, it cannot last, but will fall apart and come to an end.

27 "No one can break into a strong man's house and take away his belongings unless he first ties up the strong man; then he can plunder his house.

28 "I assure you that people can be forgiven all their sins and all the evil things they may say. 29 But whoever says evil things against the Holy Spirit will never be forgiven, because he has committed an eternal sin." (30 Jesus said this because some people were saying, "He has an evil spirit in him.")

Jesus' Mother and Brothers

31 Then Jesus' mother and brothers arrived. They stood outside the house and sent in a message, asking for him. 32 A crowd was sitting around Jesus, and they said to him, "Look, your mother and your brothers and sisters are outside, and they want you."

33 Jesus answered, "Who is my mother? Who are my brothers?" 34 He looked at the people sitting around him and said, "Look! Here are my mother and my brothers! 35 Whoever does what God wants is my brother, my sister, my mother."

Chapter 4
The Parable of the Sower

1 Again Jesus began to teach beside Lake Galilee. The crowd that gathered around him was so large that he got into a boat and sat in it. The boat was out in the water, and the crowd stood on the shore at the water's edge. 2 He used parables to teach them many things, saying to them:

³ "Listen! Once there was a man who went out to sow grain. ⁴ As he scattered the seed in the field, some of it fell along the path, and the birds came and ate it up. ⁵ Some of it fell on rocky ground, where there was little soil. The seeds soon sprouted, because the soil wasn't deep. ⁶ Then, when the sun came up, it burned the young plants; and because the roots had not grown deep enough, the plants soon dried up. ⁷ Some of the seed fell among thorn bushes, which grew up and choked the plants, and they didn't bear grain. ⁸ But some seeds fell in good soil, and the plants sprouted, grew, and bore grain: some had thirty grains, others sixty, and others one hundred."

⁹ And Jesus concluded, "Listen, then, if you have ears!"

The Purpose of the Parables

¹⁰ When Jesus was alone, some of those who had heard him came to him with the twelve disciples and asked him to explain the parables. ¹¹ "You have been given the secret of the Kingdom of God," Jesus answered. "But the others, who are on the outside, hear all things by means of parables, ¹² so that,

'They may look and look,
   yet not see;
they may listen and listen,
   yet not understand.
For if they did, they would turn to God,
   and he would forgive them.'"

Jesus Explains the Parable of the Sower

¹³ Then Jesus asked them, "Don't you understand this parable? How, then, will you ever understand any parable? ¹⁴ The sower sows God's message. ¹⁵ Some people are like the seeds that fall along the path; as soon as they hear the message, Satan comes and takes it away. ¹⁶ Other people are like the seeds that fall on rocky ground. As soon as they hear the message, they receive it gladly. ¹⁷ But it does not sink deep into them, and they don't last long. So when trouble or persecution comes because of the message, they give up at once. ¹⁸ Other people are like the seeds sown among the thorn bushes. These are the ones who hear the message, ¹⁹ but the worries about this life, the love for riches, and all other kinds of desires crowd in and choke the message, and they don't bear fruit. ²⁰ But other people are like seeds sown in good soil. They hear the message, accept it, and bear fruit: some thirty, some sixty, and some one hundred."

A Lamp under a Bowl

²¹ Jesus continued, "Does anyone ever bring in a lamp and put it under a bowl or under the bed? Isn't it put on the lampstand? ²² Whatever is hidden away will be brought out into the open, and whatever is covered up will be uncovered. ²³ Listen, then, if you have ears!"

²⁴ He also said to them, "Pay attention to what you hear! The same rules you use to judge others will be used by God to judge you—but with even greater severity. ²⁵ Those who have something will be given more, and those who have nothing will have taken away from them even the little they have."

The Parable of the Growing Seed

²⁶ Jesus went on to say, "The Kingdom of God is like this. A man scatters seed in his field. ²⁷ He sleeps at night, is up and about during the day, and all the while the seeds are sprouting and growing. Yet he does not know how it happens. ²⁸ The soil itself makes the plants grow and bear fruit; first the tender stalk appears, then the head, and finally the head full of grain. ²⁹ When the grain is ripe, the man starts cutting it with his sickle, because harvest time has come.

The Parable of the Mustard Seed

³⁰ "What shall we say the Kingdom of God is like?" asked Jesus. "What parable shall we use to explain it? ³¹ It is like this. A man takes a mustard seed, the smallest seed in the world, and plants it in the ground. ³² After a while it grows

up and becomes the biggest of all plants. It puts out such large branches that the birds come and make their nests in its shade."

³³ Jesus preached his message to the people, using many other parables like these; he told them as much as they could understand. ³⁴ He would not speak to them without using parables, but when he was alone with his disciples, he would explain everything to them.

Learn more on page 168.

Jesus Calms a Storm

³⁵ On the evening of that same day Jesus said to his disciples, "Let us go across to the other side of the lake." ³⁶ So they left the crowd; the disciples got into the boat in which Jesus was already sitting, and they took him with them. Other boats were there too. ³⁷ Suddenly a strong wind blew up, and the waves began to spill over into the boat, so that it was about to fill with water. ³⁸ Jesus was in the back of the boat, sleeping with his head on a pillow. The disciples woke him up and said, "Teacher, don't you care that we are about to die?"

³⁹ Jesus stood up and commanded the wind, "Be quiet!" and he said to the waves, "Be still!" The wind died down, and there was a great calm. ⁴⁰ Then Jesus said to his disciples, "Why are you frightened? Do you still have no faith?"

⁴¹ But they were terribly afraid and began to say to one another, "Who is this man? Even the wind and the waves obey him!"

Chapter 5
Jesus Heals a Man with Evil Spirits

¹ Jesus and his disciples arrived on the other side of Lake Galilee, in the territory of Gerasa. ² As soon as Jesus got out of the boat, he was met by a man who came out of the burial caves there. This man had an evil spirit in him ³ and lived among the tombs. Nobody could keep him tied with chains any more; ⁴ many times his feet and his hands had been tied, but every time he broke the chains and smashed the irons on his feet. He was too strong for anyone to control him. ⁵ Day and night he wandered among the tombs and through the hills, screaming and cutting himself with stones.

⁶ He was some distance away when he saw Jesus; so he ran, fell on his knees before him, ⁷ and screamed in a loud voice, "Jesus, Son of the Most High God! What do you want with me? For God's sake, I beg you, don't punish me!" (⁸ He said this because Jesus was saying, "Evil spirit, come out of this man!")

⁹ So Jesus asked him, "What is your name?"

The man answered, "My name is 'Mob'—there are so many of us!" ¹⁰ And he kept begging Jesus not to send the evil spirits out of that region.

¹¹ There was a large herd of pigs near by, feeding on a hillside. ¹² So the spirits begged Jesus, "Send us to the pigs, and let us go into them." ¹³ He let them go, and the evil spirits went out of the man and entered the pigs. The whole herd—about two thousand pigs in all—rushed down the side of the cliff into the lake and was drowned.

¹⁴ The men who had been taking care of the pigs ran away and spread the news in the town and among the farms. People went out to see what had happened, ¹⁵ and when they came to Jesus, they saw the man who used to have the mob of demons in him. He was sitting there, clothed and in his right mind; and they were all afraid. ¹⁶ Those who had seen it told the people what had happened to the man with the demons, and about the pigs.

¹⁷ So they asked Jesus to leave their territory.

¹⁸ As Jesus was getting into the boat, the man who had had the demons begged him, "Let me go with you!"

¹⁹ But Jesus would not let him. Instead, he told him, "Go back home to your family and tell them how much the Lord has done for you and how kind he has been to you."

²⁰ So the man left and went all through the Ten Towns, telling what Jesus had done for him. And all who heard it were amazed.

Jairus' Daughter and the Woman Who Touched Jesus' Cloak

²¹ Jesus went back across to the other side of the lake. There at the lakeside a large crowd gathered around him. ²² Jairus, an official of the local synagogue, arrived, and when he saw Jesus, he threw himself down at his feet ²³ and begged him earnestly, "My little daughter is very sick. Please come and place your hands on her, so that she will get well and live!"

²⁴ Then Jesus started off with him. So many people were going along with Jesus that they were crowding him from every side.

²⁵ There was a woman who had suffered terribly from severe bleeding for twelve years, ²⁶ even though she had been treated by many doctors. She had spent all her money, but instead of getting better she got worse all the time. ²⁷ She had heard about Jesus, so she came in the crowd behind him, ²⁸ saying to herself, "If I just touch his clothes, I will get well."

²⁹ She touched his cloak, and her bleeding stopped at once; and she had the feeling inside herself that she was healed of her trouble. ³⁰ At once Jesus knew that power had gone out of him, so he turned around in the crowd and asked, "Who touched my clothes?"

³¹ His disciples answered, "You see how the people are crowding you; why do you ask who touched you?"

³² But Jesus kept looking around to see who had done it. ³³ The woman realized what had happened to her, so she came, trembling with fear, knelt at his feet, and told him the whole truth. ³⁴ Jesus said to her, "My daughter, your faith has made you well. Go in peace, and be healed of your trouble."

³⁵ While Jesus was saying this, some messengers came from Jairus' house and told him, "Your daughter has died. Why bother the Teacher any longer?"

³⁶ Jesus paid no attention to what they said, but told him, "Don't be afraid, only believe." ³⁷ Then he did not let anyone else go on with him except Peter and James and his brother John. ³⁸ They arrived at Jairus' house, where Jesus saw the confusion and heard all the loud crying and wailing. ³⁹ He went in and said to them, "Why all this confusion? Why are you crying? The child is not dead—she is only sleeping!"

Learn more on page 171.

⁴⁰ They started making fun of him, so he put them all out, took the child's father and mother and his three disciples, and went into the room where the child was lying. ⁴¹ He took her by the hand and said to her, *"Talitha, koum,"* which means, "Little girl, I tell you to get up!"

⁴² She got up at once and started walking around. (She was twelve years old.) When this happened, they were completely amazed. ⁴³ But Jesus gave them strict orders not to tell anyone, and he said, "Give her something to eat."

Chapter 6
Jesus Is Rejected at Nazareth

¹ Jesus left that place and went back to his hometown, followed by his disciples. ² On the Sabbath he began to teach in the synagogue. Many people were there; and when they heard him, they were all amazed. "Where did he get all this?" they asked. "What wisdom is this that has been given him? How does he perform miracles? ³ Isn't he the carpenter, the son of Mary, and the brother of James, Joseph, Judas, and Simon? Aren't his sisters living

here?" And so they rejected him.

4 Jesus said to them, "Prophets are respected everywhere except in their own hometown and by their relatives and their family."

5 He was not able to perform any miracles there, except that he placed his hands on a few sick people and healed them. 6 He was greatly surprised, because the people did not have faith.

Jesus Sends Out the Twelve Disciples

Then Jesus went to the villages around there, teaching the people. 7 He called the twelve disciples together and sent them out two by two. He gave them authority over the evil spirits 8 and ordered them, "Don't take anything with you on the trip except a walking stick—no bread, no beggar's bag, no money in your pockets. 9 Wear sandals, but don't carry an extra shirt." 10 He also told them, "Wherever you are welcomed, stay in the same house until you leave that place. 11 If you come to a town where people do not welcome you or will not listen to you, leave it and shake the dust off your feet. That will be a warning to them!"

12 So they went out and preached that people should turn away from their sins. 13 They drove out many demons, and rubbed olive oil on many sick people and healed them.

The Death of John the Baptist

14 Now King Herod heard about all this, because Jesus' reputation had spread everywhere. Some people were saying, "John the Baptist has come back to life! That is why he has this power to perform miracles."

15 Others, however, said, "He is Elijah."

Others said, "He is a prophet, like one of the prophets of long ago."

16 When Herod heard it, he said, "He is John the Baptist! I had his head cut off, but he has come back to life!"

17 Herod himself had ordered John's arrest, and he had him tied up and put in prison. Herod did this because of Herodias, whom he had married, even though she was the wife of his brother Philip. 18 John the Baptist kept telling Herod, "It isn't right for you to marry your brother's wife!"

19 So Herodias held a grudge against John and wanted to kill him, but she could not because of Herod. 20 Herod was afraid of John because he knew that John was a good and holy man, and so he kept him safe. He liked to listen to him, even though he became greatly disturbed every time he heard him.

21 Finally Herodias got her chance. It was on Herod's birthday, when he gave a feast for all the top government officials, the military chiefs, and the leading citizens of Galilee. 22 The daughter of Herodias came in and danced, and pleased Herod and his guests. So the king said to the girl, "What would you like to have? I will give you anything you want." 23 With many vows he said to her, "I swear that I will give you anything you ask for, even as much as half my kingdom!"

24 So the girl went out and asked her mother, "What shall I ask for?"

"The head of John the Baptist," she answered.

25 The girl hurried back at once to the king and demanded, "I want you to give me here and now the head of John the Baptist on a plate!"

26 This made the king very sad, but he could not refuse her because of the vows he had made in front of all his guests. 27 So he sent off a guard at once with orders to bring John's head. The guard left, went to the prison, and cut John's head off; 28 then he brought it on a plate and gave it to the girl, who gave it to her mother. 29 When John's disciples heard about this, they came and got his body, and buried it.

Jesus Feeds Five Thousand

30 The apostles returned and met with Jesus, and told him all they had done and taught. 31 There were so many people coming and going that Jesus and his disciples didn't even have time to eat. So he said to them, "Let

us go off by ourselves to some place where we will be alone and you can rest a while." 32 So they started out in a boat by themselves to a lonely place.

33 Many people, however, saw them leave and knew at once who they were; so they went from all the towns and ran ahead by land and arrived at the place ahead of Jesus and his disciples. 34 When Jesus got out of the boat, he saw this large crowd, and his heart was filled with pity for them, because they were like sheep without a shepherd. So he began to teach them many things. 35 When it was getting late, his disciples came to him and said, "It is already very late, and this is a lonely place. 36 Send the people away, and let them go to the nearby farms and villages in order to buy themselves something to eat."

37 "You yourselves give them something to eat," Jesus answered.

They asked, "Do you want us to go and spend two hundred silver coins on bread in order to feed them?"

38 So Jesus asked them, "How much bread do you have? Go and see."

When they found out, they told him, "Five loaves and also two fish."

39 Jesus then told his disciples to make all the people divide into groups and sit down on the green grass. 40 So the people sat down in rows, in groups of a hundred and groups of fifty. 41 Then Jesus took the five loaves and the two fish, looked up to heaven, and gave thanks to God. He broke the loaves and gave them to his disciples to distribute to the people. He also divided the two fish among them all. 42 Everyone ate and had enough. 43 Then the disciples took up twelve baskets full of what was left of the bread and the fish. 44 The number of men who were fed was five thousand.

Jesus Walks on the Water

45 At once Jesus made his disciples get into the boat and go ahead of him to Bethsaida, on the other side of the lake, while he sent the crowd away. 46 After saying good-bye to the people, he went away to a hill to pray. 47 When evening came, the boat was in the middle of the lake, while Jesus was alone on land. 48 He saw that his disciples were straining at the oars, because they were rowing against the wind; so sometime between three and six o'clock in the morning, he came to them, walking on the water. He was going to pass them by, 49 but they saw him walking on the water. "It's a ghost!" they thought, and screamed. 50 They were all terrified when they saw him.

Jesus spoke to them at once, "Courage!" he said. "It is I. Don't be afraid!" 51 Then he got into the boat with them, and the wind died down. The disciples were completely amazed, 52 because they had not understood the real meaning of the feeding of the five thousand; their minds could not grasp it.

Jesus Heals the Sick in Gennesaret

53 They crossed the lake and came to land at Gennesaret, where they tied up the boat. 54 As they left the boat, people recognized Jesus at once. 55 So they ran throughout the whole region; and wherever they heard he was, they brought to him the sick lying on their mats. 56 And everywhere Jesus went, to villages, towns, or farms, people would take their sick to the marketplaces and beg him to let the sick at least touch the edge of his cloak. And all who touched it were made well.

Chapter 7
The Teaching of the Ancestors

1 Some Pharisees and teachers of the Law who had come from Jerusalem gathered around Jesus. 2 They noticed that some of his disciples were eating their food with hands that were ritually unclean—that is, they had

not washed them in the way the Pharisees said people should.

(³ For the Pharisees, as well as the rest of the Jews, follow the teaching they received from their ancestors: they do not eat unless they wash their hands in the proper way; ⁴ nor do they eat anything that comes from the market unless they wash it first. And they follow many other rules which they have received, such as the proper way to wash cups, pots, copper bowls, and beds.)

⁵ So the Pharisees and the teachers of the Law asked Jesus, "Why is it that your disciples do not follow the teaching handed down by our ancestors, but instead eat with ritually unclean hands?"

⁶ Jesus answered them, "How right Isaiah was when he prophesied about you! You are hypocrites, just as he wrote:

'These people, says God, honor me with their words,
    but their heart is really far away from me.
⁷ It is no use for them to worship me,
    because they teach human rules
    as though they were my laws!'

⁸ "You put aside God's command and obey human teachings."

⁹ And Jesus continued, "You have a clever way of rejecting God's law in order to uphold your own teaching. ¹⁰ For Moses commanded, 'Respect your father and your mother,' and, 'If you curse your father or your mother, you are to be put to death.' ¹¹ But you teach that if people have something they could use to help their father or mother, but say, 'This is Corban' (which means, it belongs to God), ¹² they are excused from helping their father or mother. ¹³ In this way the teaching you pass on to others cancels out the word of God. And there are many other things like this that you do."

The Things That Make a Person Unclean
¹⁴ Then Jesus called the crowd to him once more and said to them, "Listen to me, all of you, and understand. ¹⁵ There is nothing that goes into you from the outside which can make you ritually unclean. Rather, it is what comes out of you that makes you unclean."

¹⁷ When he left the crowd and went into the house, his disciples asked him to explain this saying. ¹⁸ "You are no more intelligent than the others," Jesus said to them. "Don't you understand? Nothing that goes into you from the outside can really make you unclean, ¹⁹ because it does not go into your heart but into your stomach and then goes on out of the body." (In saying this, Jesus declared that all foods are fit to be eaten.)

²⁰ And he went on to say, "It is what comes out of you that makes you unclean. ²¹ For from the inside, from your heart, come the evil ideas which lead you to do immoral things, to rob, kill, ²² commit adultery, be greedy, and do all sorts of evil things; deceit, indecency, jealousy, slander, pride, and folly— ²³ all these evil things come from inside you and make you unclean."

A Woman's Faith
²⁴ Then Jesus left and went away to the territory near the city of Tyre. He went into a house and did not want anyone to know he was there, but he could not stay hidden. ²⁵ A woman, whose daughter had an evil spirit in her, heard about Jesus and came to him at once and fell at his feet. ²⁶ The woman was a Gentile, born in the region of Phoenicia in Syria. She begged Jesus to drive the demon out of her daughter. ²⁷ But Jesus answered, "Let us first feed the children. It isn't right to take the children's food and throw it to the dogs."

²⁸ "Sir," she answered, "even the dogs under the table eat the children's leftovers!"

²⁹ So Jesus said to her, "Because of that answer, go back home, where you will find that the demon has gone out of your daughter!"

³⁰ She went home and found her child lying on the bed; the demon had indeed gone out of her.

Jesus Heals a Deaf-Mute

³¹ Jesus then left the neighborhood of Tyre and went on through Sidon to Lake Galilee, going by way of the territory of the Ten Towns. ³² Some people brought him a man who was deaf and could hardly speak, and they begged Jesus to place his hands on him. ³³ So Jesus took him off alone, away from the crowd, put his fingers in the man's ears, spat, and touched the man's tongue. ³⁴ Then Jesus looked up to heaven, gave a deep groan, and said to the man, *"Ephphatna,"* which means, "Open up!"

³⁵ At once the man was able to hear, his speech impediment was removed, and he began to talk without any trouble. ³⁵ Then Jesus ordered the people not to speak of it to anyone; but the more he ordered them not to, the more they told it. ³⁷ And all who heard were completely amazed. "How well he does everything!" they exclaimed. "He even causes the deaf to hear and the dumb to speak!"

Chapter 8

Jesus Feeds Four Thousand People

¹ Not long afterward another large crowd came together. When the people had nothing left to eat, Jesus called the disciples to him and said, ² "I feel sorry for these people, because they have been with me for three days and now have nothing to eat. ³ If I send them home without feeding them, they will faint as they go, because some of them have come a long way."

⁴ His disciples asked him, "Where in this desert can anyone find enough food to feed all these people?"

⁵ "How much bread do you have?" Jesus asked.

"Seven loaves," they answered.

⁶ He ordered the crowd to sit down on the ground. Then he took the seven loaves, gave thanks to God, broke them, and gave them to his disciples to distribute to the crowd; and the disciples did so. ⁷ They also had a few small fish. Jesus gave thanks for these and told the disciples to distribute them too. ⁸⁻⁹ Everybody ate and had enough—there were about four thousand people. Then the disciples took up seven baskets full of pieces left over. Jesus sent the people away ¹⁰ and at once got into a boat with his disciples and went to the district of Dalmanutha.

The Pharisees Ask for a Miracle

¹¹ Some Pharisees came to Jesus and started to argue with him. They wanted to trap him, so they asked him to perform a miracle to show that God approved of him. ¹² But Jesus gave a deep groan and said, "Why do the people of this day ask for a miracle? No, I tell you! No such proof will be given to these people!"

¹³ He left them, got back into the boat, and started across to the other side of the lake.

The Yeast of the Pharisees and of Herod

¹⁴ The disciples had forgotten to bring enough bread and had only one loaf with them in the boat. ¹⁵ "Take care," Jesus warned them, "and be on your guard against the yeast of the Pharisees and the yeast of Herod."

¹⁶ They started discussing among themselves: "He says this because we don't have any bread."

¹⁷ Jesus knew what they were saying, so he asked them, "Why are you discussing about not having any bread? Don't you know or understand yet? Are your minds so dull? ¹⁸ You have eyes—can't you see? You have ears—can't you hear? Don't you remember ¹⁹ when I broke the five loaves for the five thousand people? How many baskets full of leftover pieces did you take up?"

"Twelve," they answered.

²⁰ "And when I broke the seven loaves for the four thousand people," asked Jesus, "how many baskets full of leftover pieces did you take up?"

"Seven," they answered.

²¹ "And you still don't understand?" he asked them.

Jesus Heals a Blind Man at Bethsaida

²² They came to Bethsaida, where some people brought a blind man to Jesus and begged him to touch him. ²³ Jesus took the blind man by the hand and led him out of the village. After spitting on the man's eyes, Jesus placed his hands on him and asked him, "Can you see anything?"

²⁴ The man looked up and said, "Yes, I can see people, but they look like trees walking around."

²⁵ Jesus again placed his hands on the man's eyes. This time the man looked intently, his eyesight returned, and he saw everything clearly. ²⁶ Jesus then sent him home with the order, "Don't go back into the village."

Peter's Declaration about Jesus

²⁷ Then Jesus and his disciples went away to the villages near Caesarea Philippi. On the way he asked them, "Tell me, who do people say I am?"

²⁸ "Some say that you are John the Baptist," they answered; "others say that you are Elijah, while others say that you are one of the prophets."

²⁹ "What about you?" he asked them. "Who do you say I am?"

Peter answered, "You are the Messiah."

³⁰ Then Jesus ordered them, "Do not tell anyone about me."

Jesus Speaks about His Suffering and Death

³¹ Then Jesus began to teach his disciples: "The Son of Man must suffer much and be rejected by the elders, the chief priests, and the teachers of the Law. He will be put to death, but three days later he will rise to life." ³² He made this very clear to them. So Peter took him aside and began to rebuke him. ³³ But Jesus turned around, looked at his disciples, and rebuked Peter. "Get away from me, Satan," he said. "Your thoughts don't come from God but from human nature!"

³⁴ Then Jesus called the crowd and his disciples to him. "If any of you want to come with me," he told them, "you must forget yourself, carry your cross, and follow me. ³⁵ For if you want to save your own life, you will lose it; but if you lose your life for me and for the gospel, you will save it. ³⁶ Do you gain anything if you win the whole world but lose your life? Of course not! ³⁷ There is nothing you can give to regain your life. ³⁸ If you are ashamed of me and of my teaching in this godless and wicked day, then the Son of Man will be ashamed of you when he comes in the glory of his Father with the holy angels."

Chapter 9

¹ And he went on to say, "I tell you, there are some here who will not die until they have seen the Kingdom of God come with power."

The Transfiguration

² Six days later Jesus took with him Peter, James, and John, and led them up a high mountain, where they were alone. As they looked on, a change came over Jesus, ³ and his clothes became shining white—whiter than anyone in the world could wash them. ⁴ Then the three disciples saw Elijah and Moses talking with Jesus. ⁵ Peter spoke up and said to Jesus, "Teacher, how good it is that we are here! We will make three tents, one for you, one for Moses, and one for Elijah." ⁶ He and the others were so frightened that he did not know what to say.

⁷ Then a cloud appeared and covered them with its shadow, and a voice came from the cloud, "This is my own dear Son—listen to him!" ⁸ They took a quick look around but did not see anyone else; only Jesus was with them.

⁹ As they came down the mountain, Jesus ordered them, "Don't tell anyone what you have seen, until the Son of

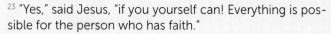

Man has risen from death."

¹⁰ They obeyed his order, but among themselves they started discussing the matter, "What does this 'rising from death' mean?" ¹¹ And they asked Jesus, "Why do the teachers of the Law say that Elijah has to come first?"

¹² His answer was, "Elijah is indeed coming first in order to get everything ready. Yet why do the Scriptures say that the Son of Man will suffer much and be rejected? ¹³ I tell you, however, that Elijah has already come and that people treated him just as they pleased, as the Scriptures say about him."

Jesus Heals a Boy with an Evil Spirit

¹⁴ When they joined the rest of the disciples, they saw a large crowd around them and some teachers of the Law arguing with them. ¹⁵ When the people saw Jesus, they were greatly surprised, and ran to him and greeted him. ¹⁶ Jesus asked his disciples, "What are you arguing with them about?"

¹⁷ A man in the crowd answered, "Teacher, I brought my son to you, because he has an evil spirit in him and cannot talk. ¹⁸ Whenever the spirit attacks him, it throws him to the ground, and he foams at the mouth, grits his teeth, and becomes stiff all over. I asked your disciples to drive the spirit out, but they could not."

¹⁹ Jesus said to them, "How unbelieving you people are! How long must I stay with you? How long do I have to put up with you? Bring the boy to me!" ²⁰ They brought him to Jesus.

As soon as the spirit saw Jesus, it threw the boy into a fit, so that he fell on the ground and rolled around, foaming at the mouth. ²¹ "How long has he been like this?" Jesus asked the father.

"Ever since he was a child," he replied. ²² "Many times the evil spirit has tried to kill him by throwing him in the fire and into water. Have pity on us and help us, if you possibly can!"

²³ "Yes," said Jesus, "if you yourself can! Everything is possible for the person who has faith."

²⁴ The father at once cried out, "I do have faith, but not enough. Help me have more!"

²⁵ Jesus noticed that the crowd was closing in on them, so he gave a command to the evil spirit. "Deaf and dumb spirit," he said, "I order you to come out of the boy and never go into him again!"

²⁶ The spirit screamed, threw the boy into a bad fit, and came out. The boy looked like a corpse, and everyone said, "He is dead!" ²⁷ But Jesus took the boy by the hand and helped him rise, and he stood up.

²⁸ After Jesus had gone indoors, his disciples asked him privately, "Why couldn't we drive the spirit out?"

²⁹ "Only prayer can drive this kind out," answered Jesus; "nothing else can."

Jesus Speaks Again about His Death

³⁰ Jesus and his disciples left that place and went on through Galilee. Jesus did not want anyone to know where he was, ³¹ because he was teaching his disciples: "The Son of Man will be handed over to those who will kill him. Three days later, however, he will rise to life."

³² But they did not understand what this teaching meant, and they were afraid to ask him.

Who Is the Greatest?

³³ They came to Capernaum, and after going indoors Jesus asked his disciples, "What were you arguing about on the road?"

³⁴ But they would not answer him, because on the road they had been arguing among themselves about who was the greatest. ³⁵ Jesus sat down, called the twelve disciples, and said to them, "Whoever wants to be first must place

himself last of all and be the servant of all." [36] Then he took a child and had him stand in front of them. He put his arms around him and said to them, [37] "Whoever welcomes in my name one of these children, welcomes me; and whoever welcomes me, welcomes not only me but also the one who sent me."

Whoever Is Not Against Us Is for Us

[38] John said to him, "Teacher, we saw a man who was driving out demons in your name, and we told him to stop, because he doesn't belong to our group."

[39] "Do not try to stop him," Jesus told them, "because no one who performs a miracle in my name will be able soon afterward to say evil things about me. [40] For whoever is not against us is for us. [41] I assure you that anyone who gives you a drink of water because you belong to me will certainly receive a reward.

Temptations to Sin

[42] "If anyone should cause one of these little ones to lose faith in me, it would be better for that person to have a large millstone tied around the neck and be thrown into the sea. [43] So if your hand makes you lose your faith, cut it off! It is better for you to enter life without a hand than to keep both hands and go off to hell, to the fire that never goes out. [45] And if your foot makes you lose your faith, cut it off! It is better for you to enter life without a foot than to keep both feet and be thrown into hell. [47] And if your eye makes you lose your faith, take it out! It is better for you to enter the Kingdom of God with only one eye than to keep both eyes and be thrown into hell. [48] There 'the worms that eat them never die, and the fire that burns them is never put out.'

[49] "Everyone will be purified by fire as a sacrifice is purified by salt.

[50] "Salt is good; but if it loses its saltiness, how can you make it salty again?

"Have the salt of friendship among yourselves, and live in peace with one another."

Chapter 10

Jesus Teaches about Divorce

[1] Then Jesus left that place, went to the province of Judea, and crossed the Jordan River. Crowds came flocking to him again, and he taught them, as he always did.

[2] Some Pharisees came to him and tried to trap him. "Tell us," they asked, "does our Law allow a man to divorce his wife?"

[3] Jesus answered with a question, "What law did Moses give you?"

[4] Their answer was, "Moses gave permission for a man to write a divorce notice and send his wife away."

[5] Jesus said to them, "Moses wrote this law for you because you are so hard to teach. [6] But in the beginning, at the time of creation, 'God made them male and female,' as the scripture says. [7] 'And for this reason a man will leave his father and mother and unite with his wife, [8] and the two will become one.' So they are no longer two, but one. [9] No human being must separate, then, what God has joined together."

[10] When they went back into the house, the disciples asked Jesus about this matter. [11] He said to them, "A man who divorces his wife and marries another woman commits adultery against his wife. [12] In the same way, a woman who divorces her husband and marries another man commits adultery."

Jesus Blesses Little Children

[13] Some people brought children to Jesus for him to place his hands on them, but the disciples scolded the people. [14] When Jesus noticed this, he was angry and said to his disciples, "Let the children come to me, and do not stop them, because the Kingdom of God belongs to such as these.

Learn more on page 186.

[15] I assure you that whoever does not receive the Kingdom of God like a child will never enter it." [16] Then he took the children in his arms, placed his hands on each of them, and blessed them.

The Rich Man

[17] As Jesus was starting on his way again, a man ran up, knelt before him, and asked him, "Good Teacher, what must I do to receive eternal life?"

[18] "Why do you call me good?" Jesus asked him. "No one is good except God alone. [19] You know the commandments: 'Do not commit murder; do not commit adultery; do not steal; do not accuse anyone falsely; do not cheat; respect your father and your mother.'"

[20] "Teacher," the man said, "ever since I was young, I have obeyed all these commandments."

[21] Jesus looked straight at him with love and said, "You need only one thing. Go and sell all you have and give the money to the poor, and you will have riches in heaven; then come and follow me." [22] When the man heard this, gloom spread over his face, and he went away sad, because he was very rich.

[23] Jesus looked around at his disciples and said to them, "How hard it will be for rich people to enter the Kingdom of God!"

[24] The disciples were shocked at these words, but Jesus went on to say, "My children, how hard it is to enter the Kingdom of God! [25] It is much harder for a rich person to enter the Kingdom of God than for a camel to go through the eye of a needle."

[26] At this the disciples were completely amazed and asked one another, "Who, then, can be saved?"

[27] Jesus looked straight at them and answered, "This is impossible for human beings but not for God; everything is possible for God."

[28] Then Peter spoke up, "Look, we have left everything and followed you."

[29] "Yes," Jesus said to them, "and I tell you that those who leave home or brothers or sisters or mother or father or children or fields for me and for the gospel, [30] will receive much more in this present age. They will receive a hundred times more houses, brothers, sisters, mothers, children, and fields—and persecutions as well; and in the age to come they will receive eternal life. [31] But many who are now first will be last, and many who are now last will be first."

Jesus Speaks a Third Time about His Death

[32] Jesus and his disciples were now on the road going up to Jerusalem. Jesus was going ahead of the disciples, who were filled with alarm; the people who followed behind were afraid. Once again Jesus took the twelve disciples aside and spoke of the things that were going to happen to him. [33] "Listen," he told them, "we are going up to Jerusalem where the Son of Man will be handed over to the chief priests and the teachers of the Law. They will condemn him to death and then hand him over to the Gentiles, [34] who will make fun of him, spit on him, whip him, and kill him; but three days later he will rise to life."

The Request of James and John

[35] Then James and John, the sons of Zebedee, came to Jesus. "Teacher," they said, "there is something we want you to do for us."

[36] "What is it?" Jesus asked them.

[37] They answered, "When you sit on your throne in your glorious Kingdom, we want you to let us sit with you, one at your right and one at your left."

[38] Jesus said to them, "You don't know what you are asking for. Can you drink the cup of suffering that I must drink? Can you be baptized in the way I must be baptized?"

[39] "We can," they answered.

Jesus said to them, "You will indeed drink the cup I must drink and be baptized in the way I must be baptized. 40 But I do not have the right to choose who will sit at my right and my left. It is God who will give these places to those for whom he has prepared them."

41 When the other ten disciples heard about it, they became angry with James and John. 42 So Jesus called them all together to him and said, "You know that those who are considered rulers of the heathen have power over them, and the leaders have complete authority.

43 This, however, is not the way it is among you. If one of you wants to be great, you must be the servant of the rest; 44 and if one of you wants to be first, you must be the slave of all. 45 For even the Son of Man did not come to be served; he came to serve and to give his life to redeem many people."

Jesus Heals Blind Bartimaeus

46 They came to Jericho, and as Jesus was leaving with his disciples and a large crowd, a blind beggar named Bartimaeus son of Timaeus was sitting by the road.

47 When he heard that it was Jesus of Nazareth, he began to shout, "Jesus! Son of David! Have mercy on me!"

48 Many of the people scolded him and told him to be quiet. But he shouted even more loudly, "Son of David, have mercy on me!"

49 Jesus stopped and said, "Call him."

So they called the blind man. "Cheer up!" they said. "Get up, he is calling you."

50 So he threw off his cloak, jumped up, and came to Jesus.

51 "What do you want me to do for you?" Jesus asked him.

"Teacher," the blind man answered, "I want to see again."

52 "Go," Jesus told him, "your faith has made you well."

At once he was able to see and followed Jesus on the road.

Chapter 11
The Triumphant Entry into Jerusalem

1 As they approached Jerusalem, near the towns of Bethphage and Bethany, they came to the Mount of Olives. Jesus sent two of his disciples on ahead 2 with these instructions: "Go to the village there ahead of you. As soon as you get there, you will find a colt tied up that has never been ridden. Untie it and bring it here. 3 And if someone asks you why you are doing that, say that the Master needs it and will send it back at once."

4 So they went and found a colt out in the street, tied to the door of a house. As they were untying it, 5 some of the bystanders asked them, "What are you doing, untying that colt?"

6 They answered just as Jesus had told them, and the crowd let them go. 7 They brought the colt to Jesus, threw their cloaks over the animal, and Jesus got on. 8 Many people spread their cloaks on the road, while others cut branches in the field and spread them on the road. 9 The people who were in front and those who followed behind began to shout, "Praise God! God bless him who comes in the name of the Lord! 10 God bless the coming kingdom of King David, our father! Praise be to God!"

11 Jesus entered Jerusalem, went into the Temple, and looked around at everything. But since it was already late in the day, he went out to Bethany with the twelve disciples.

Jesus Curses the Fig Tree

12 The next day, as they were coming back from Bethany, Jesus was hungry. 13 He saw in the distance a fig tree covered with leaves, so he went to see if he could find any figs on it. But when he came to it, he found only

leaves, because it was not the right time for figs. 14 Jesus said to the fig tree, "No one shall ever eat figs from you again!"

And his disciples heard him.

Jesus Goes to the Temple
15 When they arrived in Jerusalem, Jesus went to the Temple and began to drive out all those who were buying and selling. He overturned the tables of the moneychangers and the stools of those who sold pigeons, 16 and he would not let anyone carry anything through the Temple courtyards. 17 He then taught the people: "It is written in the Scriptures that God said, 'My Temple will be called a house of prayer for the people of all nations.' But you have turned it into a hideout for thieves!"

18 The chief priests and the teachers of the Law heard of this, so they began looking for some way to kill Jesus. They were afraid of him, because the whole crowd was amazed at his teaching.

19 When evening came, Jesus and his disciples left the city.

The Lesson from the Fig Tree
20 Early next morning, as they walked along the road, they saw the fig tree. It was dead all the way down to its roots. 21 Peter remembered what had happened and said to Jesus, "Look, Teacher, the fig tree you cursed has died!"

22 Jesus answered them, "Have faith in God. 23 I assure you that whoever tells this hill to get up and throw itself in the sea and does not doubt in his heart, but believes that what he says will happen, it will be done for him. 24 For this reason I tell you: When you pray and ask for something, believe that you have received it, and you will be given whatever you ask for. 25 And when you stand and pray, forgive anything you may have against anyone, so that your Father in heaven will forgive the wrongs you have done." 26 If you do not forgive others, your Father in heaven will not forgive the wrongs you have done.

The Question about Jesus' Authority
27 They arrived once again in Jerusalem. As Jesus was walking in the Temple, the chief priests, the teachers of the Law, and the elders came to him 28 and asked him, "What right do you have to do these things? Who gave you such right?"

29 Jesus answered them, "I will ask you just one question, and if you give me an answer, I will tell you what right I have to do these things. 30 Tell me, where did John's right to baptize come from: was it from God or from human beings?"

31 They started to argue among themselves: "What shall we say? If we answer, 'From God,' he will say, 'Why, then, did you not believe John?' 32 But if we say, 'From human beings ...'" (They were afraid of the people, because everyone was convinced that John had been a prophet.) 33 So their answer to Jesus was, "We don't know."

Jesus said to them, "Neither will I tell you, then, by what right I do these things."

Chapter 12
The Parable of the Tenants in the Vineyard
1 Then Jesus spoke to them in parables: "Once there was a man who planted a vineyard, put a fence around it, dug a hole for the wine press, and built a watchtower. Then he rented the vineyard to tenants and left home on a trip. 2 When the time came to gather the grapes, he sent a slave to the tenants to receive from them his share of the harvest. 3 The tenants grabbed the slave, beat him, and sent him back without a thing. 4 Then the owner sent another slave; the tenants beat him over the head and treated him shamefully. 5 The owner sent another slave,

and they killed him; and they treated many others the same way, beating some and killing others. [6] The only one left to send was the man's own dear son. Last of all, then, he sent his son to the tenants. 'I am sure they will respect my son,' he said. [7] But those tenants said to one another, 'This is the owner's son. Come on, let's kill him, and his property will be ours!' [8] So they grabbed the son and killed him and threw his body out of the vineyard.

[9] "What, then, will the owner of the vineyard do?" asked Jesus. "He will come and kill those tenants and turn the vineyard over to others. [10] Surely you have read this scripture?

'The stone which the builders rejected as worthless turned out to be the most important of all. [11] This was done by the Lord; what a wonderful sight it is!'"

[12] The Jewish leaders tried to arrest Jesus, because they knew that he had told this parable against them. But they were afraid of the crowd, so they left him and went away.

The Question about Paying Taxes

[13] Some Pharisees and some members of Herod's party were sent to Jesus to trap him with questions. [14] They came to him and said, "Teacher, we know that you tell the truth, without worrying about what people think. You pay no attention to anyone's status, but teach the truth about God's will for people. Tell us, is it against our Law to pay taxes to the Roman Emperor? Should we pay them or not?"

[15] But Jesus saw through their trick and answered, "Why are you trying to trap me? Bring a silver coin, and let me see it."

[16] They brought him one, and he asked, "Whose face and name are these?"

"The Emperor's," they answered.

[17] So Jesus said, "Well, then, pay to the Emperor what belongs to the Emperor, and pay to God what belongs to God."

And they were amazed at Jesus.

The Question about Rising from Death

[18] Then some Sadducees, who say that people will not rise from death, came to Jesus and said, [19] "Teacher, Moses wrote this law for us: 'If a man dies and leaves a wife but no children, that man's brother must marry the widow so that they can have children who will be considered the dead man's children.' [20] Once there were seven brothers; the oldest got married and died without having children. [21] Then the second one married the woman, and he also died without having children. The same thing happened to the third brother, [22] and then to the rest: all seven brothers married the woman and died without having children. Last of all, the woman died. [23] Now, when all the dead rise to life on the day of resurrection, whose wife will she be? All seven of them had married her."

[24] Jesus answered them, "How wrong you are! And do you know why? It is because you don't know the Scriptures or God's power. [25] For when the dead rise to life, they will be like the angels in heaven and will not marry. [26] Now, as for the dead being raised: haven't you ever read in the Book of Moses the passage about the burning bush? There it is written that God said to Moses, 'I am the God of Abraham, the God of Isaac, and the God of Jacob.' [27] He is the God of the living, not of the dead. You are completely wrong!"

The Great Commandment

[28] A teacher of the Law was there who heard the discussion. He saw that Jesus had given the Sadducees a good answer, so he came to him with a question: "Which commandment is the most important of all?"

Learn more on page 190.

29 Jesus replied, "The most important one is this: 'Listen, Israel! The Lord our God is the only Lord. 30 Love the Lord your God with all your heart, with all your soul, with all your mind, and with all your strength.' 31 The second most important commandment is this: 'Love your neighbor as you love yourself.' There is no other commandment more important than these two."

32 The teacher of the Law said to Jesus, "Well done, Teacher! It is true, as you say, that only the Lord is God and that there is no other god but he. 33 And you must love God with all your heart and with all your mind and with all your strength; and you must love your neighbor as you love yourself. It is more important to obey these two commandments than to offer on the altar animals and other sacrifices to God."

34 Jesus noticed how wise his answer was, and so he told him, "You are not far from the Kingdom of God."

After this nobody dared to ask Jesus any more questions.

The Question about the Messiah
35 As Jesus was teaching in the Temple, he asked the question, "How can the teachers of the Law say that the Messiah will be the descendant of David? 36 The Holy Spirit inspired David to say:

'The Lord said to my Lord:
    Sit here at my right side
    until I put your enemies under your feet.'

37 David himself called him 'Lord'; so how can the Messiah be David's descendant?"

Jesus Warns against the Teachers of the Law
A large crowd was listening to Jesus gladly. 38 As he taught them, he said, "Watch out for the teachers of the Law, who like to walk around in their long robes and be greeted with respect in the marketplace, 39 who choose the reserved seats in the synagogues and the best places at feasts. 40 They take advantage of widows and rob them of their homes, and then make a show of saying long prayers. Their punishment will be all the worse!"

The Widow's Offering
41 As Jesus sat near the Temple treasury, he watched the people as they dropped in their money. Many rich men dropped in a lot of money; 42 then a poor widow came along and dropped in two little copper coins, worth about a penny. 43 He called his disciples together and said to them, "I tell you that this poor widow put more in the offering box than all the others. 44 For the others put in what they had to spare of their riches; but she, poor as she is, put in all she had—she gave all she had to live on."

Chapter 13
Jesus Speaks of the Destruction of the Temple
1 As Jesus was leaving the Temple, one of his disciples said, "Look, Teacher! What wonderful stones and buildings!"

2 Jesus answered, "You see these great buildings? Not a single stone here will be left in its place; every one of them will be thrown down."

Troubles and Persecutions
3 Jesus was sitting on the Mount of Olives, across from the Temple, when Peter, James, John, and Andrew came to him in private. 4 "Tell us when this will be," they said, "and tell us what will happen to show that the time has come for all these things to take place."

5 Jesus said to them, "Watch out, and don't let anyone fool you. 6 Many men, claiming to speak for me, will come and say, 'I am he!' and they will fool many people. 7 And don't be troubled when you hear the noise of battles close by and news of battles far away. Such things must happen, but they do not mean that the end has

come. [8] Countries will fight each other; kingdoms will attack one another. There will be earthquakes everywhere, and there will be famines. These things are like the first pains of childbirth.

[9] "You yourselves must watch out. You will be arrested and taken to court. You will be beaten in the synagogues; you will stand before rulers and kings for my sake to tell them the Good News. [10] But before the end comes, the gospel must be preached to all peoples. [11] And when you are arrested and taken to court, do not worry ahead of time about what you are going to say; when the time comes, say whatever is then given to you. For the words you speak will not be yours; they will come from the Holy Spirit. [12] Men will hand over their own brothers to be put to death, and fathers will do the same to their children. Children will turn against their parents and have them put to death. [13] Everyone will hate you because of me. But whoever holds out to the end will be saved.

The Awful Horror

[14] "You will see 'The Awful Horror' standing in the place where he should not be." (Note to the reader: understand what this means!) "Then those who are in Judea must run away to the hills. [15] Someone who is on the roof of a house must not lose time by going down into the house to get anything to take along. [16] Someone who is in the field must not go back to the house for a cloak. [17] How terrible it will be in those days for women who are pregnant and for mothers with little babies! [18] Pray to God that these things will not happen in the winter! [19] For the trouble of those days will be far worse than any the world has ever known from the very beginning when God created the world until the present time. Nor will there ever be anything like it again. [20] But the Lord has reduced the number of those days; if he had not, nobody would survive. For the sake of his chosen people, however, he has reduced those days.

[21] "Then, if anyone says to you, 'Look, here is the Messiah!' or, 'Look, there he is!'—do not believe it. [22] For false Messiahs and false prophets will appear. They will perform miracles and wonders in order to deceive even God's chosen people, if possible. [23] Be on your guard! I have told you everything ahead of time.

The Coming of the Son of Man

[24] "In the days after that time of trouble the sun will grow dark, the moon will no longer shine, [25] the stars will fall from heaven, and the powers in space will be driven from their courses. [26] Then the Son of Man will appear, coming in the clouds with great power and glory. [27] He will send the angels out to the four corners of the earth to gather God's chosen people from one end of the world to the other.

The Lesson of the Fig Tree

[28] "Let the fig tree teach you a lesson. When its branches become green and tender and it starts putting out leaves, you know that summer is near. [29] In the same way, when you see these things happening, you will know that the time is near, ready to begin. [30] Remember that all these things will happen before the people now living have all died. [31] Heaven and earth will pass away, but my words will never pass away.

No One Knows the Day or Hour

[32] "No one knows, however, when that day or hour will come—neither the angels in heaven, nor the Son; only the Father knows. [33] Be on watch, be alert, for you do not know when the time will come. [34] It will be like a man who goes away from home on a trip and leaves his servants in charge, after giving to each one his own work to do and after telling the doorkeeper to keep watch. [35] Watch, then, because you do not know when the master of the house is coming—it might be in the evening or at midnight or before dawn or at sunrise. [36] If he comes suddenly, he must not find you asleep. [37] What I say to you, then, I say to all: Watch!"

Chapter 14

The Plot against Jesus

1 It was now two days before the Festival of Passover and Unleavened Bread. The chief priests and the teachers of the Law were looking for a way to arrest Jesus secretly and put him to death. 2 "We must not do it during the festival," they said, "or the people might riot."

Jesus Is Anointed at Bethany

3 Jesus was in Bethany at the house of Simon, a man who had suffered from a dreaded skin disease. While Jesus was eating, a woman came in with an alabaster jar full of a very expensive perfume made of pure nard. She broke the jar and poured the perfume on Jesus' head. 4 Some of the people there became angry and said to one another, "What was the use of wasting the perfume? 5 It could have been sold for more than three hundred silver coins and the money given to the poor!" And they criticized her harshly.

6 But Jesus said, "Leave her alone! Why are you bothering her? She has done a fine and beautiful thing for me. 7 You will always have poor people with you, and any time you want to, you can help them. But you will not always have me. 8 She did what she could; she poured perfume on my body to prepare it ahead of time for burial. 9 Now, I assure you that wherever the gospel is preached all over the world, what she has done will be told in memory of her."

Judas Agrees to Betray Jesus

10 Then Judas Iscariot, one of the twelve disciples, went off to the chief priests in order to betray Jesus to them. 11 They were pleased to hear what he had to say, and promised to give him money. So Judas started looking for a good chance to hand Jesus over to them.

Jesus Eats the Passover Meal with His Disciples

12 On the first day of the Festival of Unleavened Bread, the day the lambs for the Passover meal were killed, Jesus' disciples asked him, "Where do you want us to go and get the Passover meal ready for you?"

13 Then Jesus sent two of them with these instructions: "Go into the city, and a man carrying a jar of water will meet you. Follow him 14 to the house he enters, and say to the owner of the house: 'The Teacher says, Where is the room where my disciples and I will eat the Passover meal?' 15 Then he will show you a large upstairs room, fixed up and furnished, where you will get everything ready for us."

16 The disciples left, went to the city, and found everything just as Jesus had told them; and they prepared the Passover meal.

17 When it was evening, Jesus came with the twelve disciples. 18 While they were at the table eating, Jesus said, "I tell you that one of you will betray me—one who is eating with me."

19 The disciples were upset and began to ask him, one after the other, "Surely you don't mean me, do you?"

20 Jesus answered, "It will be one of you twelve, one who dips his bread in the dish with me. 21 The Son of Man will die as the Scriptures say he will; but how terrible for that man who will betray the Son of Man! It would have been better for that man if he had never been born!"

The Lord's Supper

22 While they were eating, Jesus took a piece of bread, gave a prayer of thanks, broke it, and gave it to his disciples. "Take it," he said, "this is my body."

23 Then he took a cup, gave thanks to God, and handed it to them; and they all drank from it. 24 Jesus said, "This is my blood which is poured out for many, my blood which seals God's covenant. 25 I tell you, I will never again drink this wine until the day I drink the new wine in the Kingdom of God."

26 Then they sang a hymn and went out to the Mount of Olives.

Jesus Predicts Peter's Denial

27 Jesus said to them, "All of you will run away and leave me, for the scripture says, 'God will kill the shepherd, and the sheep will all be scattered.' 28 But after I am raised to life, I will go to Galilee ahead of you."

29 Peter answered, "I will never leave you, even though all the rest do!"

30 Jesus said to Peter, "I tell you that before the rooster crows two times tonight, you will say three times that you do not know me."

31 Peter answered even more strongly, "I will never say that, even if I have to die with you!"

And all the other disciples said the same thing.

Jesus Prays in Gethsemane

32 They came to a place called Gethsemane, and Jesus said to his disciples, "Sit here while I pray." 33 He took Peter, James, and John with him. Distress and anguish came over him, 34 and he said to them, "The sorrow in my heart is so great that it almost crushes me. Stay here and keep watch."

35 He went a little farther on, threw himself on the ground, and prayed that, if possible, he might not have to go through that time of suffering. 36 "Father," he prayed, "my Father! All things are possible for you. Take this cup of suffering away from me. Yet not what I want, but what you want."

37 Then he returned and found the three disciples asleep. He said to Peter, "Simon, are you asleep? Weren't you able to stay awake for even one hour?" 38 And he said to them, "Keep watch, and pray that you will not fall into temptation. The spirit is willing, but the flesh is weak."

39 He went away once more and prayed, saying the same words. 40 Then he came back to the disciples and found them asleep; they could not keep their eyes open. And they did not know what to say to him.

41 When he came back the third time, he said to them, "Are you still sleeping and resting? Enough! The hour has come! Look, the Son of Man is now being handed over to the power of sinners. 42 Get up, let us go. Look, here is the man who is betraying me!"

The Arrest of Jesus

43 Jesus was still speaking when Judas, one of the twelve disciples, arrived. With him was a crowd armed with swords and clubs and sent by the chief priests, the teachers of the Law, and the elders. 44 The traitor had given the crowd a signal: "The man I kiss is the one you want. Arrest him and take him away under guard."

45 As soon as Judas arrived, he went up to Jesus and said, "Teacher!" and kissed him. 46 So they arrested Jesus and held him tight. 47 But one of those standing there drew his sword and struck at the High Priest's slave, cutting off his ear. 48 Then Jesus spoke up and said to them, "Did you have to come with swords and clubs to capture me, as though I were an outlaw? 49 Day after day I was with you teaching in the Temple, and you did not arrest me. But the Scriptures must come true."

50 Then all the disciples left him and ran away.

51 A certain young man, dressed only in a linen cloth, was following Jesus. They tried to arrest him, 52 but he ran away naked, leaving the cloth behind.

Jesus Before the Council

53 Then Jesus was taken to the High Priest's house, where all the chief priests, the elders, and the teachers of the Law were gathering. 54 Peter followed from a distance and went into the courtyard of the High Priest's house. There he sat down with the guards, keeping

himself warm by the fire. [55] The chief priests and the whole Council tried to find some evidence against Jesus in order to put him to death, but they could not find any. [56] Many witnesses told lies against Jesus, but their stories did not agree.

[57] Then some men stood up and told this lie against Jesus: [58] "We heard him say, 'I will tear down this Temple which men have made, and after three days I will build one that is not made by men.'" [59] Not even they, however, could make their stories agree.

[60] The High Priest stood up in front of them all and questioned Jesus, "Have you no answer to the accusation they bring against you?"

[61] But Jesus kept quiet and would not say a word. Again the High Priest questioned him, "Are you the Messiah, the Son of the Blessed God?"

[62] "I am," answered Jesus, "and you will all see the Son of Man seated at the right side of the Almighty and coming with the clouds of heaven!"

[63] The High Priest tore his robes and said, "We don't need any more witnesses! [64] You heard his blasphemy. What is your decision?"

They all voted against him: he was guilty and should be put to death.

[65] Some of them began to spit on Jesus, and they blindfolded him and hit him. "Guess who hit you!" they said. And the guards took him and slapped him.

Peter Denies Jesus

[66] Peter was still down in the courtyard when one of the High Priest's servant women came by. [67] When she saw Peter warming himself, she looked straight at him and said, "You, too, were with Jesus of Nazareth."

[68] But he denied it. "I don't know ... I don't understand what you are talking about," he answered, and went out into the passageway. Just then a rooster crowed.

[69] The servant woman saw him there and began to repeat to the bystanders, "He is one of them!" [70] But Peter denied it again.

A little while later the bystanders accused Peter again, "You can't deny that you are one of them, because you, too, are from Galilee."

[71] Then Peter said, "I swear that I am telling the truth! May God punish me if I am not! I do not know the man you are talking about!"

[72] Just then a rooster crowed a second time, and Peter remembered how Jesus had said to him, "Before the rooster crows two times, you will say three times that you do not know me." And he broke down and cried.

Chapter 15
Jesus before Pilate

[1] Early in the morning the chief priests met hurriedly with the elders, the teachers of the Law, and the whole Council, and made their plans. They put Jesus in chains, led him away, and handed him over to Pilate. [2] Pilate questioned him, "Are you the king of the Jews?"

Jesus answered, "So you say."

[3] The chief priests were accusing Jesus of many things, [4] so Pilate questioned him again, "Aren't you going to answer? Listen to all their accusations!"

[5] Again Jesus refused to say a word, and Pilate was amazed.

Jesus Is Sentenced to Death

[6] At every Passover Festival Pilate was in the habit of setting free any one prisoner the people asked for. [7] At that time a man named Barabbas was in prison with the rebels who had committed murder in the riot. [8] When the crowd gathered and began to ask Pilate for the usual favor, [9] he asked them, "Do you want me to set free for you the king of the Jews?" [10] He knew very well that the chief priests had handed Jesus over to him because they were jealous.

11 But the chief priests stirred up the crowd to ask, instead, that Pilate set Barabbas free for them. 12 Pilate spoke again to the crowd, "What, then, do you want me to do with the one you call the king of the Jews?"

13 They shouted back, "Crucify him!"

14 "But what crime has he committed?" Pilate asked.

They shouted all the louder, "Crucify him!"

15 Pilate wanted to please the crowd, so he set Barabbas free for them. Then he had Jesus whipped and handed him over to be crucified.

The Soldiers Make Fun of Jesus

16 The soldiers took Jesus inside to the courtyard of the governor's palace and called together the rest of the company. 17 They put a purple robe on Jesus, made a crown out of thorny branches, and put it on his head. 18 Then they began to salute him: "Long live the King of the Jews!" 19 They beat him over the head with a stick, spat on him, fell on their knees, and bowed down to him. 20 When they had finished making fun of him, they took off the purple robe and put his own clothes back on him. Then they led him out to crucify him.

Jesus Is Crucified

21 On the way they met a man named Simon, who was coming into the city from the country, and the soldiers forced him to carry Jesus' cross. (Simon was from Cyrene and was the father of Alexander and Rufus.) 22 They took Jesus to a place called Golgotha, which means "The Place of the Skull." 23 There they tried to give him wine mixed with a drug called myrrh, but Jesus would not drink it. 24 Then they crucified him and divided his clothes among themselves, throwing dice to see who would get which piece of clothing. 25 It was nine o'clock in the morning when they crucified him. 26 The notice of the accusation against him said: "The King of the Jews." 27 They also crucified two bandits with Jesus, one on his right and the other on his left. 28 In this way the scripture came true which says, "He shared the fate of criminals."

29 People passing by shook their heads and hurled insults at Jesus: "Aha! You were going to tear down the Temple and build it back up in three days! 30 Now come down from the cross and save yourself!"

31 In the same way the chief priests and the teachers of the Law made fun of Jesus, saying to one another, "He saved others, but he cannot save himself! 32 Let us see the Messiah, the king of Israel, come down from the cross now, and we will believe in him!"

And the two who were crucified with Jesus insulted him also.

The Death of Jesus

33 At noon the whole country was covered with darkness, which lasted for three hours. 34 At three o'clock Jesus cried out with a loud shout, *"Eloi, Eloi, lema sabachthani?"* which means, "My God, my God, why did you abandon me?"

35 Some of the people there heard him and said, "Listen, he is calling for Elijah!" 36 One of them ran up with a sponge, soaked it in cheap wine, and put it on the end of a stick. Then he held it up to Jesus' lips and said, "Wait! Let us see if Elijah is coming to bring him down from the cross!"

37 With a loud cry Jesus died.

38 The curtain hanging in the Temple was torn in two, from top to bottom. 39 The army officer who was standing there in front of the cross saw how Jesus had died. "This man was really the Son of God!" he said.

40 Some women were there, looking on from a distance. Among them were Mary Magdalene, Mary the mother of the younger James and of Joseph, and Salome. 41 They had followed Jesus while he was in Galilee and had helped him. Many other women who had come to Jerusalem with him were there also.

The Burial of Jesus

42-43 It was toward evening when Joseph of Arimathea arrived. He was a respected member of the Council, who was waiting for the coming of the Kingdom of God. It was Preparation day (that is, the day before the Sabbath), so Joseph went boldly into the presence of Pilate and asked him for the body of Jesus. 44 Pilate was surprised to hear that Jesus was already dead. He called the army officer and asked him if Jesus had been dead a long time. 45 After hearing the officer's report, Pilate told Joseph he could have the body. 46 Joseph bought a linen sheet, took the body down, wrapped it in the sheet, and placed it in a tomb which had been dug out of solid rock. Then he rolled a large stone across the entrance to the tomb. 47 Mary Magdalene and Mary the mother of Joseph were watching and saw where the body of Jesus was placed.

Chapter 16
The Resurrection

1 After the Sabbath was over, Mary Magdalene, Mary the mother of James, and Salome bought spices to go and anoint the body of Jesus. 2 Very early on Sunday morning, at sunrise, they went to the tomb. 3-4 On the way they said to one another, "Who will roll away the stone for us from the entrance to the tomb?" (It was a very large stone.) Then they looked up and saw that the stone had already been rolled back. 5 So they entered the tomb, where they saw a young man sitting at the right, wearing a white robe—and they were alarmed.

6 "Don't be alarmed," he said. "I know you are looking for Jesus of Nazareth, who was crucified. He is not here—he

has been raised! Look, here is the place where he was placed. 7 Now go and give this message to his disciples, including Peter: 'He is going to Galilee ahead of you; there you will see him, just as he told you.'"

8 So they went out and ran from the tomb, distressed and terrified. They said nothing to anyone, because they were afraid.

AN OLD ENDING TO THE GOSPEL
Jesus Appears to Mary Magdalene

[9 After Jesus rose from death early on Sunday, he appeared first to Mary Magdalene, from whom he had driven out seven demons. 10 She went and told his companions. They were mourning and crying; 11 and when they heard her say that Jesus was alive and that she had seen him, they did not believe her.

Jesus Appears to Two Followers

12 After this, Jesus appeared in a different manner to two of them while they were on their way to the country. 13 They returned and told the others, but these would not believe it.

Jesus Appears to the Eleven

14 Last of all, Jesus appeared to the eleven disciples as they were eating. He scolded them, because they did not have faith and because they were too stubborn to believe those who had seen him alive. 15 He said to them, "Go throughout the whole world and preach the gospel to all people. 16 Whoever believes and is baptized will be saved; whoever does not believe will be condemned. 17 Believers will be given the power to perform miracles: they will drive out demons in my name; they will speak in strange tongues; 18 if they pick up snakes or drink any poison, they will not be harmed; they will place their hands on sick people, and these will get well."

Jesus Is Taken Up to Heaven

19 After the Lord Jesus had talked with them, he was taken up to heaven and sat at the right side of God. 20 The disciples went and preached everywhere, and the Lord worked with them and proved that their preaching was true by the miracles that were performed.]

ANOTHER OLD ENDING

[9 The women went to Peter and his friends and gave them a brief account of all they had been told. 10 After this, Jesus himself sent out through his disciples from the east to the west the sacred and everliving message of eternal salvation.]

The GOSPEL according to LUKE

The Gospel of Luke was written by Luke, who was a **doctor**, most likely a Greek Gentile and a frequent traveler on mission trips with Paul. The Gospel is written specifically to **Theophilus**, meaning **"one who loves God."** Theophilus is believed to be a wealthy Roman official who supported Luke's missionary work. Luke's writing of this Gospel is meant to show that Jesus came for all people, not just the Jewish nation.

More than any of the other Gospels, Luke covers the life of Jesus on earth from beginning to end, **from Birth to Ascension.** Luke is also distinct in its emphasis on prayer, its concern for women, its interest in the poor, its sympathy for sinners, its focus on family, its repeated use of the term "the Son of Man," its dealing with the Holy Spirit and its large number of parables (the most among the Gospels at 28).

Luke makes it clear that **he relied on eyewitness accounts** from those who were there when Jesus was alive on this earth. Many consider that he must have spoken to Jesus' mother Mary and the disciples for a large portion of his writings. Luke seems to be much more detailed in his description of many of Jesus' healing miracles because of his training as a doctor.

What's the story?

The **births of John the Baptist and Jesus** are intertwined in the opening chapters of Luke, with Zechariah and Elizabeth welcoming their son John in their old age shortly before Mary and Joseph greeted Jesus in Bethlehem.

Luke presents a period of preparation for Jesus' ministry with John the Baptist announcing the way for Jesus and baptizing him in the Jordan River. Jesus' family tree is listed here, followed by the account of Jesus' temptation in the wilderness. Like in the other Synoptic Gospels, Jesus' ministry begins in Galilee, extends to Judea and ends in Perea. Luke includes many longer speeches from Jesus.

The last part of Luke's Gospel **expands more on Jesus' last days on earth** than Matthew and Mark do. Jesus' Palm Sunday entry into Jerusalem, the cleansing of the Temple, the Last Supper, the praying in Gethsemane, and the arrest, trial, Death and Resurrection narratives are followed by post-Resurrection appearances and by Jesus' Ascension. **Luke is also the writer of Acts**, which details the events of the early Church as it spreads the message of Jesus.

The GOSPEL according to LUKE

Chapter 1
Introduction

[1] Dear Theophilus:

Many people have done their best to write a report of the things that have taken place among us. [2] They wrote what we have been told by those who saw these things from the beginning and who proclaimed the message. [3] And so, Your Excellency, because I have carefully studied all these matters from their beginning, I thought it would be good to write an orderly account for you. [4] I do this so that you will know the full truth about everything which you have been taught.

The Birth of John the Baptist Is Announced

[5] During the time when Herod was king of Judea, there was a priest named Zechariah, who belonged to the priestly order of Abijah. His wife's name was Elizabeth; she also belonged to a priestly family. [6] They both lived good lives in God's sight and obeyed fully all the Lord's laws and commands. [7] They had no children because Elizabeth could not have any, and she and Zechariah were both very old.

[8] One day Zechariah was doing his work as a priest in the Temple, taking his turn in the daily service. [9] According to the custom followed by the priests, he was chosen by lot to burn incense on the altar. So he went into the Temple of the Lord, [10] while the crowd of people outside prayed during the hour when the incense was burned. [11] An angel of the Lord appeared to him, standing at the right side of the altar where the incense was burned. [12] When Zechariah saw him, he was alarmed and felt afraid. [13] But the angel said to him, "Don't be afraid, Zechariah! God has heard your prayer, and your wife Elizabeth will bear you a son. You are to name him John. [14] How glad and happy you will be, and how happy many others will be when he is born! [15] John will be great in the Lord's sight. He must not drink any wine or strong drink. From his very birth he will be filled with the Holy Spirit, [16] and he will bring back many of the people of Israel to the Lord their God. [17] He will go ahead of the Lord, strong and mighty like the prophet Elijah. He will bring fathers and children together again; he will turn disobedient people back to the way of thinking of the righteous; he will get the Lord's people ready for him."

[18] Zechariah said to the angel, "How shall I know if this is so? I am an old man, and my wife is old also."

[19] "I am Gabriel," the angel answered. "I stand in the presence of God, who sent me to speak to you and tell you this good news. [20] But you have not believed my message, which will come true at the right time. Because you have not believed, you will be unable to speak; you will remain silent until the day my promise to you comes true."

[21] In the meantime the people were waiting for Zechariah and wondering why he was spending such a long time in the Temple. [22] When he came out, he could not speak to them, and so they knew that he had seen a vision in the Temple. Unable to say a word, he made signs to them with his hands.

[23] When his period of service in the Temple was over, Zechariah went back home. [24] Some time later his wife Elizabeth became pregnant and did not leave the house for five months. [25] "Now at last the Lord has helped me," she said. "He has taken away my public disgrace!"

The Birth of Jesus Is Announced

[26] In the sixth month of Elizabeth's pregnancy God sent the angel Gabriel to a town in Galilee named Nazareth. [27] He had a message for a young woman promised in marriage to a man named Joseph, who was a descendant of King David. Her name was Mary. [28] The angel came to her and said, "Peace be with you!

Learn more on page 155.

The Lord is with you and has greatly blessed you!"

29 Mary was deeply troubled by the angel's message, and she wondered what his words meant. 30 The angel said to her, "Don't be afraid, Mary; God has been gracious to you. 31 You will become pregnant and give birth to a son, and you will name him Jesus. 32 He will be great and will be called the Son of the Most High God. The Lord God will make him a king, as his ancestor David was, 33 and he will be the king of the descendants of Jacob forever; his kingdom will never end!"

34 Mary said to the angel, "I am a virgin. How, then, can this be?"

35 The angel answered, "The Holy Spirit will come on you, and God's power will rest upon you. For this reason the holy child will be called the Son of God. 36 Remember your relative Elizabeth. It is said that she cannot have children, but she herself is now six months pregnant, even though she is very old. 37 For there is nothing that God cannot do."

38 "I am the Lord's servant," said Mary; "may it happen to me as you have said." And the angel left her.

Mary Visits Elizabeth

39 Soon afterward Mary got ready and hurried off to a town in the hill country of Judea. 40 She went into Zechariah's house and greeted Elizabeth. 41 When Elizabeth heard Mary's greeting, the baby moved within her. Elizabeth was filled with the Holy Spirit 42 and said in a loud voice, "You are the most blessed of all women, and blessed is the child you will bear! 43 Why should this great thing happen to me, that my Lord's mother comes to visit me? 44 For as soon as I heard your greeting, the baby within me jumped with gladness. 45 How happy you are to believe that the Lord's message to you will come true!"

Mary's Song of Praise

46 Mary said,

"My heart praises the Lord;

47 my soul is glad because of God my Savior,
48 for he has remembered me, his lowly servant!
From now on all people will call me happy,
49 because of the great things the Mighty God has done for me.
His name is holy;
50 from one generation to another he shows mercy to those who honor him.
51 He has stretched out his mighty arm and scattered the proud with all their plans.
52 He has brought down mighty kings from their thrones, and lifted up the lowly.
53 He has filled the hungry with good things, and sent the rich away with empty hands.
54 He has kept the promise he made to our ancestors, and has come to the help of his servant Israel.
55 He has remembered to show mercy to Abraham and to all his descendants forever!"

56 Mary stayed about three months with Elizabeth and then went back home.

The Birth of John the Baptist

57 The time came for Elizabeth to have her baby, and she gave birth to a son. 58 Her neighbors and relatives heard how wonderfully good the Lord had been to her, and they all rejoiced with her.

Learn more c
page 15

59 When the baby was a week old, they came to circumcise him, and they were going to name him Zechariah, after his father. 60 But his mother said, "No! His name is to be John."

61 They said to her, "But you don't have any relative with that name!" 62 Then they made signs to his father, asking him what name he would like the boy to have.

63 Zechariah asked for a writing pad and wrote, "His name

is John." How surprised they all were! 64 At that moment Zechariah was able to speak again, and he started praising God. 65 The neighbors were all filled with fear, and the news about these things spread through all the hill country of Judea. 66 Everyone who heard of it thought about it and asked, "What is this child going to be?" For it was plain that the Lord's power was upon him.

Zechariah's Prophecy

67 John's father Zechariah was filled with the Holy Spirit, and he spoke God's message:

68 "Let us praise the Lord, the God of Israel!
      He has come to the help of his people and has set
      them free.
69 He has provided for us a mighty Savior,
      a descendant of his servant David.
70 He promised through his holy prophets long ago
      71 that he would save us from our enemies,
      from the power of all those who hate us.
72 He said he would show mercy to our ancestors
      and remember his sacred covenant.
73-74 With a solemn oath to our ancestor Abraham
      he promised to rescue us from our enemies
      and allow us to serve him without fear,
75 so that we might be holy and righteous before him
      all the days of our life.
76 "You, my child, will be called
      a prophet of the Most High God.
      You will go ahead of the Lord
      to prepare his road for him,
77 to tell his people that they will be saved
      by having their sins forgiven.
78 Our God is merciful and tender.
      He will cause the bright dawn of salvation to rise on us
      79 and to shine from heaven on all those who live in
      the dark shadow of death,
      to guide our steps into the path of peace."

80 The child grew and developed in body and spirit. He lived in the desert until the day when he appeared publicly to the people of Israel.

Chapter 2
The Birth of Jesus

1 At that time Emperor Augustus ordered a census to be taken throughout the Roman Empire. 2 When this first census took place, Quirinius was the governor of Syria. 3 Everyone, then, went to register himself, each to his own hometown.

4 Joseph went from the town of Nazareth in Galilee to the town of Bethlehem in Judea, the birthplace of King David. Joseph went there because he was a descendant of David. 5 He went to register with Mary, who was promised in marriage to him. She was pregnant, 6 and while they were in Bethlehem, the time came for her to have her baby. 7 She gave birth to her first son, wrapped him in cloths and laid him in a manger—there was no room for them to stay in the inn.

Learn more on page 157.

The Shepherds and the Angels

8 There were some shepherds in that part of the country who were spending the night in the fields, taking care of their flocks. 9 An angel of the Lord appeared to them, and the glory of the Lord shone over them. They were terribly afraid, 10 but the angel said to them, "Don't be afraid! I am here with good news for you, which will bring great joy to all the people. 11 This very day in David's town your Savior was born—Christ the Lord! 12 And this is what will prove it to you: you will find a baby wrapped in cloths and lying in a manger."

13 Suddenly a great army of heaven's angels appeared with the angel, singing praises to God:

14 "Glory to God in the highest heaven,
      and peace on earth to those with whom
      he is pleased!"

15 When the angels went away from them back into heaven, the shepherds said to one another, "Let's go to Bethlehem and see this thing that has happened, which the Lord has told us."

16 So they hurried off and found Mary and Joseph and saw the baby lying in the manger. 17 When the shepherds saw him, they told them what the angel had said about the child. 18 All who heard it were amazed at what the shepherds said. 19 Mary remembered all these things and thought deeply about them. 20 The shepherds went back, singing praises to God for all they had heard and seen; it had been just as the angel had told them.

Jesus Is Named
21 A week later, when the time came for the baby to be circumcised, he was named Jesus, the name which the angel had given him before he had been conceived.

Jesus Is Presented in the Temple
22 The time came for Joseph and Mary to perform the ceremony of purification, as the Law of Moses commanded. So they took the child to Jerusalem to present him to the Lord, 23 as it is written in the law of the Lord: "Every first-born male is to be dedicated to the Lord." 24 They also went to offer a sacrifice of a pair of doves or two young pigeons, as required by the law of the Lord.

25 At that time there was a man named Simeon living in Jerusalem. He was a good, God-fearing man and was waiting for Israel to be saved. The Holy Spirit was with him 26 and had assured him that he would not die before he had seen the Lord's promised Messiah. 27 Led by the Spirit, Simeon went into the Temple. When the parents brought the child Jesus into the Temple to do for him what the Law required, 28 Simeon took the child in his arms and gave thanks to God:

29 "Now, Lord, you have kept your promise,
and you may let your servant go in peace.
30 With my own eyes I have seen your salvation,
31 which you have prepared in the presence
of all peoples:
32 A light to reveal your will to the Gentiles
and bring glory to your people Israel."

Le
more
page 1

33 The child's father and mother were amazed at the things Simeon said about him. 34 Simeon blessed them and said to Mary, his mother, "This child is chosen by God for the destruction and the salvation of many in Israel. He will be a sign from God which many people will speak against 35 and so reveal their secret thoughts. And sorrow, like a sharp sword, will break your own heart."

36-37 There was a very old prophet, a widow named Anna, daughter of Phanuel of the tribe of Asher. She had been married for only seven years and was now eighty-four years old. She never left the Temple; day and night she worshiped God, fasting and praying. 38 That very same hour she arrived and gave thanks to God and spoke about the child to all who were waiting for God to set Jerusalem free.

The Return to Nazareth
39 When Joseph and Mary had finished doing all that was required by the Law of the Lord, they returned to their hometown of Nazareth in Galilee. 40 The child grew and became strong; he was full of wisdom, and God's blessings were upon him.

Learn more on page 1

The Boy Jesus in the Temple

⁴¹ Every year the parents of Jesus went to Jerusalem for the Passover Festival. ⁴² When Jesus was twelve years old, they went to the festival as usual. ⁴³ When the festival was over, they started back home, but the boy Jesus stayed in Jerusalem. His parents did not know this;

⁴⁴ they thought that he was with the group, so they traveled a whole day and then started looking for him among their relatives and friends. ⁴⁵ They did not find him, so they went back to Jerusalem looking for him. ⁴⁶ On the third day they found him in the Temple, sitting with the Jewish teachers, listening to them and asking questions. ⁴⁷ All who heard him were amazed at his intelligent answers. ⁴⁸ His parents were astonished when they saw him, and his mother said to him, "Son, why have you done this to us? Your father and I have been terribly worried trying to find you."

⁴⁹ He answered them, "Why did you have to look for me? Didn't you know that I had to be in my Father's house?" ⁵⁰ But they did not understand his answer.

⁵¹ So Jesus went back with them to Nazareth, where he was obedient to them. His mother treasured all these things in her heart. ⁵² Jesus grew both in body and in wisdom, gaining favor with God and people.

Chapter 3
The Preaching of John the Baptist

¹ It was the fifteenth year of the rule of Emperor Tiberius; Pontius Pilate was governor of Judea, Herod was ruler of Galilee, and his brother Philip was ruler of the territory of Iturea and Trachonitis; Lysanias was ruler of Abilene, ² and Annas and Caiaphas were High Priests. At that time the word of God came to John son of Zechariah in the desert. ³ So John went throughout the whole territory of the Jordan River, preaching, "Turn away from your sins and be baptized, and God will forgive your sins." ⁴ As it is written in the book of the prophet Isaiah:

"Someone is shouting in the desert:
   'Get the road ready for the Lord;
make a straight path for him to travel!
⁵ Every valley must be filled up,
   every hill and mountain leveled off.
The winding roads must be made straight,
   and the rough paths made smooth.
⁶ The whole human race will see God's salvation!'"

⁷ Crowds of people came out to John to be baptized by him. "You snakes!" he said to them. "Who told you that you could escape from the punishment God is about to send? ⁸ Do those things that will show that you have turned from your sins. And don't start saying among yourselves that Abraham is your ancestor. I tell you that God can take these rocks and make descendants for Abraham! ⁹ The ax is ready to cut down the trees at the roots; every tree that does not bear good fruit will be cut down and thrown in the fire."

¹⁰ The people asked him, "What are we to do, then?"

¹¹ He answered, "Whoever has two shirts must give one to the man who has none, and whoever has food must share it."

¹² Some tax collectors came to be baptized, and they asked him, "Teacher, what are we to do?"

¹³ "Don't collect more than is legal," he told them.

¹⁴ Some soldiers also asked him, "What about us? What are we to do?"

He said to them, "Don't take money from anyone by force or accuse anyone falsely. Be content with your pay."

¹⁵ People's hopes began to rise, and they began to wonder whether John perhaps might be the Messiah. ¹⁶ So John said to all of them, "I baptize you with water, but someone is coming who is much greater than I am. I am not good enough even to untie his sandals. He will baptize you with the Holy Spirit and fire. ¹⁷ He has his winnowing shovel with him, to thresh out all the grain and gather the wheat into his barn; but he will burn the chaff in a fire that never goes out."

¹⁸ In many different ways John preached the Good News to the people and urged them to change their ways. ¹⁹ But John reprimanded Governor Herod, because he had married Herodias, his brother's wife, and had done many other evil things. ²⁰ Then Herod did an even worse thing by putting John in prison.

The Baptism of Jesus
²¹ After all the people had been baptized, Jesus also was baptized. While he was praying, heaven was opened, ²² and the Holy Spirit came down upon him in bodily form like a dove. And a voice came from heaven, "You are my own dear Son. I am pleased with you."

The Ancestors of Jesus
²³ When Jesus began his work, he was about thirty years old. He was the son, so people thought, of Joseph, who was the son of Heli, ²⁴ the son of Matthat, the son of Levi, the son of Melchi, the son of Jannai, the son of Joseph, ²⁵ the son of Mattathias, the son of Amos, the son of Nahum, the son of Esli, the son of Naggai, ²⁶ the son of Maath, the son of Mattathias, the son of Semein, the son of Josech, the son of Joda, ²⁷ the son of Joanan, the son of Rhesa, the son of Zerubbabel, the son of Shealtiel, the son of Neri, ²⁸ the son of Melchi, the son of Addi, the son of Cosam, the son of Elmadam, the son of Er, ²⁹ the son of Joshua, the son of Eliezer, the son of Jorim, the son of Matthat, the son of Levi, ³⁰ the son of Simeon, the son of Judah, the son of Joseph, the son of Jonam, the son of Eliakim, ³¹ the son of Melea, the son of Menna, the son of Mattatha, the son of Nathan, the son of David, ³² the son of Jesse, the son of Obed, the son of Boaz, the son of Salmon, the son of Nahshon, ³³ the son of Amminadab, the son of Admin, the son of Arni, the son of Hezron, the son of Perez, the son of Judah, ³⁴ the son of Jacob, the son of Isaac, the son of Abraham, the son of Terah, the son of Nahor, ³⁵ the son of Serug, the son of Reu, the son of Peleg, the son of Eber, the son of Shelah, ³⁶ the son of Cainan, the son of Arphaxad, the son of Shem, the son of Noah, the son of Lamech, ³⁷ the son of Methuselah, the son of Enoch, the son of Jared, the son of Mahalaleel, the son of Kenan, ³⁸ the son of Enosh, the son of Seth, the son of Adam, the son of God.

Chapter 4
The Temptation of Jesus
¹ Jesus returned from the Jordan full of the Holy Spirit and was led by the Spirit into the desert, ² where he was tempted by the Devil for forty days. In all that time he ate nothing, so that he was hungry when it was over.

³ The Devil said to him, "If you are God's Son, order this stone to turn into bread."

⁴ But Jesus answered, "The scripture says, 'Human beings cannot live on bread alone.'"

⁵ Then the Devil took him up and showed him in a second all the kingdoms of the world. ⁶ "I will give you all this power and all this wealth," the Devil told him. "It has all been handed over to me, and I can give it to anyone I choose. ⁷ All this will be yours, then, if you worship me."

⁸ Jesus answered, "The scripture says, 'Worship the Lord your God and serve only him!'"

9 Then the Devil took him to Jerusalem and set him on the highest point of the Temple, and said to him, "If you are God's Son, throw yourself down from here. 10 For the scripture says, 'God will order his angels to take good care of you.' 11 It also says, 'They will hold you up with their hands so that not even your feet will be hurt on the stones.'"

12 But Jesus answered, "The scripture says, 'Do not put the Lord your God to the test.'"

13 When the Devil finished tempting Jesus in every way, he left him for a while.

Jesus Begins His Work in Galilee

14 Then Jesus returned to Galilee, and the power of the Holy Spirit was with him. The news about him spread throughout all that territory. 15 He taught in the synagogues and was praised by everyone.

Jesus Is Rejected at Nazareth

16 Then Jesus went to Nazareth, where he had been brought up, and on the Sabbath he went as usual to the synagogue. He stood up to read the Scriptures 17 and was handed the book of the prophet Isaiah. He unrolled the scroll and found the place where it is written,

18 "The Spirit of the Lord is upon me,
    because he has chosen me to bring good news
    to the poor.
He has sent me to proclaim liberty to the captives
    and recovery of sight to the blind,
to set free the oppressed
        19 and announce that the time has come
    when the Lord will save his people."

20 Jesus rolled up the scroll, gave it back to the attendant, and sat down. All the people in the synagogue had their eyes fixed on him, 21 as he said to them, "This passage of scripture has come true today, as you heard it being read."

22 They were all well impressed with him and marveled at the eloquent words that he spoke. They said, "Isn't he the son of Joseph?"

23 He said to them, "I am sure that you will quote this proverb to me, 'Doctor, heal yourself.' You will also tell me to do here in my hometown the same things you heard were done in Capernaum. 24 I tell you this," Jesus added, "prophets are never welcomed in their hometown. 25 Listen to me: it is true that there were many widows in Israel during the time of Elijah, when there was no rain for three and a half years and a severe famine spread throughout the whole land. 26 Yet Elijah was not sent to anyone in Israel, but only to a widow living in Zarephath in the territory of Sidon. 27 And there were many people suffering from a dreaded skin disease who lived in Israel during the time of the prophet Elisha; yet not one of them was healed, but only Naaman the Syrian."

28 When the people in the synagogue heard this, they were filled with anger. 29 They rose up, dragged Jesus out of town, and took him to the top of the hill on which their town was built. They meant to throw him over the cliff, 30 but he walked through the middle of the crowd and went his way.

A Man with an Evil Spirit

31 Then Jesus went to Capernaum, a town in Galilee, where he taught the people on the Sabbath. 32 They were all amazed at the way he taught, because he spoke with authority. 33 In the synagogue was a man who had the spirit of an evil demon in him; he screamed out in a loud voice, 34 "Ah! What do you want with us, Jesus of Nazareth? Are you here to destroy us? I know who you are: you are God's holy messenger!"

[35] Jesus ordered the spirit, "Be quiet and come out of the man!" The demon threw the man down in front of them and went out of him without doing him any harm.

[36] The people were all amazed and said to one another, "What kind of words are these? With authority and power this man gives orders to the evil spirits, and they come out!" [37] And the report about Jesus spread everywhere in that region.

Jesus Heals Many People
[38] Jesus left the synagogue and went to Simon's home. Simon's mother-in-law was sick with a high fever, and they spoke to Jesus about her. [39] He went and stood at her bedside and ordered the fever to leave her. The fever left her, and she got up at once and began to wait on them.

[40] After sunset all who had friends who were sick with various diseases brought them to Jesus; he placed his hands on every one of them and healed them all. [41] Demons also went out from many people, screaming, "You are the Son of God!"

Jesus gave the demons an order and would not let them speak, because they knew he was the Messiah.

Jesus Preaches in the Synagogues
[42] At daybreak Jesus left the town and went off to a lonely place. The people started looking for him, and when they found him, they tried to keep him from leaving. [43] But he said to them, "I must preach the Good News about the Kingdom of God in other towns also, because that is what God sent me to do."

[44] So he preached in the synagogues throughout the country.

Chapter 5
Jesus Calls the First Disciples
[1] One day Jesus was standing on the shore of Lake Gennesaret while the people pushed their way up to

Learn more on page 165.

him to listen to the word of God. [2] He saw two boats pulled up on the beach; the fishermen had left them and were washing the nets. [3] Jesus got into one of the boats—it belonged to Simon—and asked him to push off a little from the shore. Jesus sat in the boat and taught the crowd.

[4] When he finished speaking, he said to Simon, "Push the boat out further to the deep water, and you and your partners let down your nets for a catch."

[5] "Master," Simon answered, "we worked hard all night long and caught nothing. But if you say so, I will let down the nets." [6] They let them down and caught such a large number of fish that the nets were about to break. [7] So they motioned to their partners in the other boat to come and help them. They came and filled both boats so full of fish that the boats were about to sink. [8] When Simon Peter saw what had happened, he fell on his knees before Jesus and said, "Go away from me, Lord! I am a sinful man!"

[9] He and the others with him were all amazed at the large number of fish they had caught. [10] The same was true of Simon's partners, James and John, the sons of Zebedee. Jesus said to Simon, "Don't be afraid; from now on you will be catching people."

[11] They pulled the boats up on the beach, left everything, and followed Jesus.

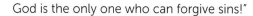

Jesus Heals a Man

12 Once Jesus was in a town where there was a man who was suffering from a dreaded skin disease. When he saw Jesus, he threw himself down and begged him, "Sir, if you want to, you can make me clean!"

13 Jesus reached out and touched him. "I do want to," he answered. "Be clean!" At once the disease left the man. 14 Jesus ordered him, "Don't tell anyone, but go straight to the priest and let him examine you; then to prove to everyone that you are cured, offer the sacrifice as Moses ordered."

15 But the news about Jesus spread all the more widely, and crowds of people came to hear him and be healed from their diseases. 16 But he would go away to lonely places, where he prayed.

Jesus Heals a Paralyzed Man

17 One day when Jesus was teaching, some Pharisees and teachers of the Law were sitting there who had come from every town in Galilee and Judea and from Jerusalem. The power of the Lord was present for Jesus to heal the sick. 18 Some men came carrying a paralyzed man on a bed, and they tried to carry him into the house and put him in front of Jesus. 19 Because of the crowd, however, they could find no way to take him in. So they carried him up on the roof, made an opening in the tiles, and let

him down on his bed into the middle of the group in front of Jesus. 20 When Jesus saw how much faith they had, he said to the man, "Your sins are forgiven, my friend."

21 The teachers of the Law and the Pharisees began to say to themselves, "Who is this man who speaks such blasphemy!

God is the only one who can forgive sins!"

22 Jesus knew their thoughts and said to them, "Why do you think such things? 23 Is it easier to say, 'Your sins are forgiven you,' or to say, 'Get up and walk'? 24 I will prove to you, then, that the Son of Man has authority on earth to forgive sins." So he said to the paralyzed man, "I tell you, get up, pick up your bed, and go home!"

25 At once the man got up in front of them all, took the bed he had been lying on, and went home, praising God. 26 They were all completely amazed! Full of fear, they praised God, saying, "What marvelous things we have seen today!"

Jesus Calls Levi

27 After this, Jesus went out and saw a tax collector named Levi, sitting in his office. Jesus said to him, "Follow me." 28 Levi got up, left everything, and followed him.

29 Then Levi had a big feast in his house for Jesus, and among the guests was a large number of tax collectors and other people. 30 Some Pharisees and some teachers of the Law who belonged to their group complained to Jesus' disciples. "Why do you eat and drink with tax collectors and other outcasts?" they asked.

31 Jesus answered them, "People who are well do not need a doctor, but only those who are sick. 32 I have not come to call respectable people to repent, but outcasts."

The Question about Fasting

33 Some people said to Jesus, "The disciples of John fast frequently and offer prayers, and the disciples of the Pharisees do the same; but your disciples eat and drink."

34 Jesus answered, "Do you think you can make the guests at a wedding party go without food as long as the bridegroom is with them? Of course not! 35 But the day will come when the bridegroom will be taken away from them, and then they will fast."

36 Jesus also told them this parable: "You don't tear a piece off a new coat to patch up an old coat. If you do,

you will have torn the new coat, and the piece of new cloth will not match the old. ³⁷ Nor do you pour new wine into used wineskins, because the new wine will burst the skins, the wine will pour out, and the skins will be ruined. ³⁸ Instead, new wine must be poured into fresh wineskins! ³⁹ And you don't want new wine after drinking old wine. 'The old is better,' you say."

Chapter 6

The Question about the Sabbath

¹ Jesus was walking through some wheat fields on a Sabbath. His disciples began to pick the heads of wheat, rub them in their hands, and eat the grain. ² Some Pharisees asked, "Why are you doing what our Law says you cannot do on the Sabbath?"

³ Jesus answered them, "Haven't you read what David did when he and his men were hungry? ⁴ He went into the house of God, took the bread offered to God, ate it, and gave it also to his men. Yet it is against our Law for anyone except the priests to eat that bread."

⁵ And Jesus concluded, "The Son of Man is Lord of the Sabbath."

The Man with a Paralyzed Hand

⁶ On another Sabbath Jesus went into a synagogue and taught. A man was there whose right hand was paralyzed. ⁷ Some teachers of the Law and some Pharisees wanted a reason to accuse Jesus of doing wrong, so they watched him closely to see if he would heal on the Sabbath. ⁸ But Jesus knew their thoughts and said to the man, "Stand up and come here to the front." The man got up and stood there. ⁹ Then Jesus said to them, "I ask you: What does our Law allow us to do on the Sabbath? To help or to harm? To save someone's life or destroy it?" ¹⁰ He looked around at them all; then he said to the man, "Stretch out your hand." He did so, and his hand became well again.

¹¹ They were filled with rage and began to discuss among themselves what they could do to Jesus.

Jesus Chooses the Twelve Apostles

¹² At that time Jesus went up a hill to pray and spent the whole night there praying to God. ¹³ When day came, he called his disciples to him and chose twelve of them, whom he named apostles: ¹⁴ Simon (whom he named Peter) and his brother Andrew; James and John, Philip and Bartholomew, ¹⁵ Matthew and Thomas, James son of Alphaeus, and Simon (who was called the Patriot), ¹⁶ Judas son of James, and Judas Iscariot, who became the traitor.

Jesus Teaches and Heals

¹⁷ When Jesus had come down from the hill with the apostles, he stood on a level place with a large number of his disciples. A large crowd of people was there from all over Judea and from Jerusalem and from the coast cities of Tyre and Sidon; ¹⁸ they had come to hear him and to be healed of their diseases. Those who were troubled by evil spirits also came and were healed. ¹⁹ All the people tried to touch him, for power was going out from him and healing them all.

Happiness and Sorrow

²⁰ Jesus looked at his disciples and said,

"Happy are you poor;
    the Kingdom of God is yours!
²¹ "Happy are you who are hungry now;
    you will be filled!
"Happy are you who weep now;
    you will laugh!

22 "Happy are you when people hate you, reject you, insult you, and say that you are evil, all because of the Son of Man! 23 Be glad when that happens and dance for joy, because a great reward is kept for you in heaven. For their ancestors did the very same things to the prophets.

24 "But how terrible for you who are rich now;
    you have had your easy life!
25 "How terrible for you who are full now;
    you will go hungry!
"How terrible for you who laugh now;
    you will mourn and weep!

26 "How terrible when all people speak well of you; their ancestors said the very same things about the false prophets.

Love for Enemies

27 "But I tell you who hear me: Love your enemies, do good to those who hate you, 28 bless those who curse you, and pray for those who mistreat you. 29 If anyone hits you on one cheek, let him hit the other one too; if someone takes your coat, let him have your shirt as well. 30 Give to everyone who asks you for something, and when someone takes what is yours, do not ask for it back. 31 Do for others just what you want them to do for you.

32 "If you love only the people who love you, why should you receive a blessing? Even sinners love those who love them! 33 And if you do good only to those who do good to you, why should you receive a blessing? Even sinners do that! 34 And if you lend only to those from whom you hope to get it back, why should you receive a blessing? Even sinners lend to sinners, to get back the same amount! 35 No! Love your enemies and do good to them; lend and expect nothing back. You will then have a great reward, and you will be children of the Most High God. For he is good to the ungrateful and the wicked. 36 Be merciful just as your Father is merciful.

Judging Others

37 "Do not judge others, and God will not judge you; do not condemn others, and God will not condemn you;

forgive others, and God will forgive you. 38 Give to others, and God will give to you. Indeed, you will receive a full measure, a generous helping, poured into your hands—all that you can hold. The measure you use for others is the one that God will use for you."

39 And Jesus told them this parable: "One blind man cannot lead another one; if he does, both will fall into a ditch. 40 No pupils are greater than their teacher; but all pupils, when they have completed their training, will be like their teacher.

41 "Why do you look at the speck in your brother's eye, but pay no attention to the log in your own eye? 42 How can you say to your brother, 'Please, brother, let me take that speck out of your eye,' yet cannot even see the log in your own eye? You hypocrite! First take the log out of your own eye, and then you will be able to see clearly to take the speck out of your brother's eye.

A Tree and Its Fruit

43 "A healthy tree does not bear bad fruit, nor does a poor tree bear good fruit. 44 Every tree is known by the fruit it bears; you do not pick figs from thorn bushes or gather grapes from bramble bushes. 45 A good person brings good out of the treasure of good things in his heart; a bad person brings bad out of his treasure of bad things. For the mouth speaks what the heart is full of.

The Two House Builders

46 "Why do you call me, 'Lord, Lord,' and yet don't do what I tell you? 47 Anyone who comes to me and listens to my words and obeys them—I will show you what he is like. 48 He is like a man who, in building his

house, dug deep and laid the foundation on rock. The river flooded over and hit that house but could not shake it, because it was well built. ⁴⁹ But anyone who hears my words and does not obey them is like a man who built his house without laying a foundation; when the flood hit that house it fell at once—and what a terrible crash that was!"

Chapter 7

Jesus Heals a Roman Officer's Servant

¹ When Jesus had finished saying all these things to the people, he went to Capernaum. ² A Roman officer there had a servant who was very dear to him; the man was sick and about to die. ³ When the officer heard about Jesus, he sent some Jewish elders to ask him to come and heal his servant. ⁴ They came to Jesus and begged him earnestly, "This man really deserves your help. ⁵ He loves our people and he himself built a synagogue for us."

⁶ So Jesus went with them. He was not far from the house when the officer sent friends to tell him, "Sir, don't trouble yourself. I do not deserve to have you come into my house, ⁷ neither do I consider myself worthy to come to you in person. Just give the order, and my servant will get well. ⁸ I, too, am a man placed under the authority of superior officers, and I have soldiers under me. I order this one, 'Go!' and he goes; I order that one, 'Come!' and he comes; and I order my slave, 'Do this!' and he does it."

⁹ Jesus was surprised when he heard this; he turned around and said to the crowd following him, "I tell you, I have never found faith like this, not even in Israel!"

¹⁰ The messengers went back to the officer's house and found his servant well.

Jesus Raises a Widow's Son

¹¹ Soon afterward Jesus went to a town named Nain, accompanied by his disciples and a large crowd. ¹² Just as he arrived at the gate of the town, a funeral procession was coming out. The dead man was the only son of a woman who was a widow, and a large crowd from the town was with her. ¹³ When the Lord saw her, his heart was filled with pity for her, and he said to her, "Don't cry." ¹⁴ Then he walked over and touched the coffin, and the men carrying it stopped. Jesus said, "Young man! Get up, I tell you!" ¹⁵ The dead man sat up and began to talk, and Jesus gave him back to his mother.

¹⁶ They all were filled with fear and praised God. "A great prophet has appeared among us!" they said; "God has come to save his people!"

¹⁷ This news about Jesus went out through all the country and the surrounding territory.

The Messengers from John the Baptist

¹⁸ When John's disciples told him about all these things, he called two of them ¹⁹ and sent them to the Lord to ask him, "Are you the one John said was going to come, or should we expect someone else?"

²⁰ When they came to Jesus, they said, "John the Baptist sent us to ask if you are the one he said was going to come, or should we expect someone else?"

²¹ At that very time Jesus healed many people from their sicknesses, diseases, and evil spirits, and gave sight to many blind people. ²² He answered John's messengers, "Go back and tell John what you have seen and heard: the blind can see, the lame can walk, those who suffer from dreaded skin diseases are made clean, the deaf can hear, the dead are raised to life, and the Good News is preached to the poor. ²³ How happy are those who have no doubts about me!"

²⁴ After John's messengers had left, Jesus began to speak about him to the crowds: "When you went out to John in the desert, what did you expect to see? A blade of grass bending in the wind? ²⁵ What did you go out to see? A man dressed up in fancy clothes? People who dress like that and live in luxury are found in palaces! ²⁶ Tell me, what did you go out to see? A prophet? Yes indeed, but you saw much more than a prophet. ²⁷ For John is the one of whom the scripture says: 'God said, I will send my messenger ahead of you to open the way for you.' ²⁸ I tell you," Jesus added, "John is greater than anyone who has

ever lived. But the one who is least in the Kingdom of God is greater than John."

29 All the people heard him; they and especially the tax collectors were the ones who had obeyed God's righteous demands and had been baptized by John. 30 But the Pharisees and the teachers of the Law rejected God's purpose for themselves and refused to be baptized by John.

31 Jesus continued, "Now to what can I compare the people of this day? What are they like? 32 They are like children sitting in the marketplace. One group shouts to the other, 'We played wedding music for you, but you wouldn't dance! We sang funeral songs, but you wouldn't cry!' 33 John the Baptist came, and he fasted and drank no wine, and you said, 'He has a demon in him!' 34 The Son of Man came, and he ate and drank, and you said, 'Look at this man! He is a glutton and wine drinker, a friend of tax collectors and other outcasts!' 35 God's wisdom, however, is shown to be true by all who accept it."

Jesus at the Home of Simon the Pharisee

36 A Pharisee invited Jesus to have dinner with him, and Jesus went to his house and sat down to eat. 37 In that town was a woman who lived a sinful life. She heard that Jesus was eating in the Pharisee's house, so she brought an alabaster jar full of perfume 38 and stood behind Jesus, by his feet, crying and wetting his feet with her tears. Then she dried his feet with her hair, kissed them, and poured the perfume on them. 39 When the Pharisee saw

this, he said to himself, "If this man really were a prophet, he would know who this woman is who is touching him; he would know what kind of sinful life she lives!"

40 Jesus spoke up and said to him, "Simon, I have something to tell you."

"Yes, Teacher," he said, "tell me."

41 "There were two men who owed money to a moneylender," Jesus began. "One owed him five hundred silver coins, and the other owed him fifty. 42 Neither of them could pay him back, so he canceled the debts of both. Which one, then, will love him more?"

43 "I suppose," answered Simon, "that it would be the one who was forgiven more."

"You are right," said Jesus. 44 Then he turned to the woman and said to Simon, "Do you see this woman? I came into your home, and you gave me no water for my feet, but she has washed my feet with her tears and dried them with her hair. 45 You did not welcome me with a kiss, but she has not stopped kissing my feet since I came. 46 You provided no olive oil for my head, but she has covered my feet with perfume. 47 I tell you, then, the great love she has shown proves that her many sins have been forgiven. But whoever has been forgiven little shows only a little love."

48 Then Jesus said to the woman, "Your sins are forgiven."

49 The others sitting at the table began to say to themselves, "Who is this, who even forgives sins?"

50 But Jesus said to the woman, "Your faith has saved you; go in peace"

Chapter 8
Women Who Accompanied Jesus

1 Some time later Jesus traveled through towns and villages, preaching the Good News about the Kingdom of God. The twelve disciples went with him, 2 and so did

some women who had been healed of evil spirits and diseases: Mary (who was called Magdalene), from whom seven demons had been driven out; ³ Joanna, whose husband Chuza was an officer in Herod's court; and Susanna, and many other women who used their own resources to help Jesus and his disciples.

The Parable of the Sower

⁴ People kept coming to Jesus from one town after another; and when a great crowd gathered, Jesus told this parable:

⁵ "Once there was a man who went out to sow grain. As he scattered the seed in the field, some of it fell along the path, where it was stepped on, and the birds ate it up. ⁶ Some of it fell on rocky ground, and when the plants sprouted, they dried up because the soil had no moisture. ⁷ Some of the seed fell among thorn bushes, which grew up with the plants and choked them. ⁸ And some seeds fell in good soil; the plants grew and bore grain, one hundred grains each."

And Jesus concluded, "Listen, then, if you have ears!"

The Purpose of the Parables

⁹ His disciples asked Jesus what this parable meant, ¹⁰ and he answered, "The knowledge of the secrets of the Kingdom of God has been given to you, but to the rest it comes by means of parables, so that they may look but not see, and listen but not understand.

Jesus Explains the Parable of the Sower

¹¹ "This is what the parable means: the seed is the word of God. ¹² The seeds that fell along the path stand for those who hear; but the Devil comes and takes the message away from their hearts in order to keep them from believing and being saved. ¹³ The seeds that fell on rocky ground stand for those who hear the message and receive it gladly. But it does not sink deep into them; they believe only for a while but when the time of testing comes, they fall away. ¹⁴ The seeds that fell among thorn bushes stand for those who hear; but the worries and riches and pleasures of this life crowd in and choke them, and their fruit never ripens. ¹⁵ The seeds that fell in good soil stand for those who hear the message and retain it in a good and obedient heart, and they persist until they bear fruit.

A Lamp Under a Bowl

¹⁶ "No one lights a lamp and covers it with a bowl or puts it under a bed. Instead, it is put on the lampstand, so that people will see the light as they come in.

¹⁷ "Whatever is hidden away will be brought out into the open, and whatever is covered up will be found and brought to light.

¹⁸ "Be careful, then, how you listen; because those who have something will be given more, but whoever has nothing will have taken away from them even the little they think they have."

Jesus' Mother and Brothers

¹⁹ Jesus' mother and brothers came to him, but were unable to join him because of the crowd. ²⁰ Someone said to Jesus, "Your mother and brothers are standing outside and want to see you."

²¹ Jesus said to them all, "My mother and brothers are those who hear the word of God and obey it."

Jesus Calms a Storm

²² One day Jesus got into a boat with his disciples and said to them, "Let us go across to the other side of the lake." So they started out. ²³ As they were sailing, Jesus fell asleep. Suddenly a strong wind blew down on the lake, and the boat began to fill with water, so that they were all in great danger. ²⁴ The disciples went to Jesus and woke him up, saying, "Master, Master! We are about to die!"

Jesus got up and gave an order to the wind and to the stormy water; they quieted down, and there was a great calm. 25 Then he said to the disciples, "Where is your faith?"

But they were amazed and afraid, and said to one another, "Who is this man? He gives orders to the winds and waves, and they obey him!"

Jesus Heals a Man with Demons

26 Jesus and his disciples sailed on over to the territory of Gerasa, which is across the lake from Galilee. 27 As Jesus stepped ashore, he was met by a man from the town who had demons in him. For a long time this man had gone without clothes and would not stay at home, but spent his time in the burial caves. 28 When he saw Jesus, he gave a loud cry, threw himself down at his feet, and shouted, "Jesus, Son of the Most High God! What do you want with me? I beg you, don't punish me!" 29 He said this because Jesus had ordered the evil spirit to go out of him. Many times it had seized him, and even though he was kept a prisoner, his hands and feet tied with chains, he would break the chains and be driven by the demon cut into the desert.

30 Jesus asked him, "What is your name?"

"My name is 'Mob,'" he answered—because many demons had gone into him. 31 The demons begged Jesus not to send them into the abyss.

32 There was a large herd of pigs near by, feeding on a hill-side. So the demons begged Jesus to let them go into the pigs, and he let them. 33 They went out of the man and into the pigs. The whole herd rushed down the side of the cliff into the lake and was drowned.

34 The men who had been taking care of the pigs saw what happened, so they ran off and spread the news in the town and among the farms. 35 People went out to see what had happened, and when they came to Jesus, they found the man from whom the demons had gone out sitting at the feet of Jesus, clothed and in his right mind; and they were all afraid. 36 Those who had seen it told the people how the man had been cured. 37 Then all the people from that territory asked Jesus to go away, because they were terribly afraid. So Jesus got into the boat and left. 38 The man from whom the demons had gone out begged Jesus, "Let me go with you."

But Jesus sent him away, saying, 39 "Go back home and tell what God has done for you."

The man went through the town, telling what Jesus had done for him.

Jairus' Daughter and the Woman Who Touched Jesus' Cloak

40 When Jesus returned to the other side of the lake, the people welcomed him, because they had all been waiting for him. 41 Then a man named Jairus arrived; he was an official in the local synagogue. He threw himself down at Jesus' feet and begged him to go to his home, 42 because his only daughter, who was twelve years old, was dying.

As Jesus went along, the people were crowding him from every side. 43 Among them was a woman who had suffered from severe bleeding for twelve years; she had spent all she had on doctors, but no one had been able to cure her. 44 She came up in the crowd behind Jesus and touched the edge of his cloak, and her bleeding stopped at once. 45 Jesus asked, "Who touched me?"

Everyone denied it, and Peter said, "Master, the people are all around you and crowding in on you."

46 But Jesus said, "Someone touched me, for I knew it when power went out of me." 47 The woman saw that she had been found out, so she came trembling and threw herself at Jesus' feet. There in front of everybody, she told him why she had touched him and how she had been

healed at once. [48] Jesus said to her, "My daughter, your faith has made you well. Go in peace."

[49] While Jesus was saying this, a messenger came from the official's house. "Your daughter has died," he told Jairus; "don't bother the Teacher any longer."

[50] But Jesus heard it and said to Jairus, "Don't be afraid; only believe, and she will be well."

[51] When he arrived at the house, he would not let anyone go in with him except Peter, John, and James, and the child's father and mother. [52] Everyone there was crying and mourning for the child. Jesus said, "Don't cry; the child is not dead—she is only sleeping!"

[53] They all made fun of him, because they knew that she was dead. [54] But Jesus took her by the hand and called out, "Get up, child!" [55] Her life returned, and she got up at once, and Jesus ordered them to give her something to eat. [56] Her parents were astounded, but Jesus commanded them not to tell anyone what had happened.

Chapter 9
Jesus Sends Out the Twelve Disciples

[1] Jesus called the twelve disciples together and gave them power and authority to drive out all demons and to cure diseases. [2] Then he sent them out to preach the Kingdom of God and to heal the sick, [3] after saying to them, "Take nothing with you for the trip: no walking stick, no beggar's bag, no food, no money, not even an extra shirt. [4] Wherever you are welcomed, stay in the same house until you leave that town; [5] wherever people don't welcome you, leave that town and shake the dust off your feet as a warning to them."

[6] The disciples left and traveled through all the villages, preaching the Good News and healing people everywhere.

Herod's Confusion

[7] When Herod, the ruler of Galilee, heard about all the things that were happening, he was very confused, because some people were saying that John the Baptist had come back to life. [8] Others were saying that Elijah had appeared, and still others that one of the prophets of long ago had come back to life. [9] Herod said, "I had John's head cut off; but who is this man I hear these things about?" And he kept trying to see Jesus.

Jesus Feeds Five Thousand

[10] The apostles came back and told Jesus everything they had done. He took them with him, and they went off by themselves to a town named Bethsaida. [11] When the crowds heard about it, they followed him. He welcomed them, spoke to them about the Kingdom of God, and healed those who needed it.

[12] When the sun was beginning to set, the twelve disciples came to him and said, "Send the people away so that they can go to the villages and farms around here and find food and lodging, because this is a lonely place."

[13] But Jesus said to them, "You yourselves give them something to eat."

They answered, "All we have are five loaves and two fish. Do you want us to go and buy food for this whole crowd?" [14] (There were about five thousand men there.)

Jesus said to his disciples, "Make the people sit down in groups of about fifty each."

[15] After the disciples had done so, [16] Jesus took the five loaves and two fish, looked up to heaven, thanked God for them, broke them, and gave them to the disciples to distribute to the people. [17] They all ate and had enough, and the disciples took up twelve baskets of what was left over.

Peter's Declaration about Jesus

18 One day when Jesus was praying alone, the disciples came to him. "Who do the crowds say I am?" he asked them.

19 "Some say that you are John the Baptist," they answered. "Others say that you are Elijah, while others say that one of the prophets of long ago has come back to life."

20 "What about you?" he asked them. "Who do you say I am?"

Peter answered, "You are God's Messiah."

Jesus Speaks about His Suffering and Death

21 Then Jesus gave them strict orders not to tell this to anyone. 22 He also told them, "The Son of Man must suffer much and be rejected by the elders, the chief priests, and the teachers of the Law. He will be put to death, but three days later he will be raised to life."

23 And he said to them all, "If you want to come with me, you must forget yourself, take up your cross every day, and follow me. 24 For if you want to save your own life, you will lose it, but if you lose your life for my sake, you will save it. 25 Will you gain anything if you win the whole world but are yourself lost or defeated? Of course not! 26 If you are ashamed of me and of my teaching, then the Son of Man will be ashamed of you when he comes in his glory and in the glory of the Father and of the holy angels. 27 I assure you that there are some here who will not die until they have seen the Kingdom of God."

The Transfiguration

28 About a week after he had said these things, Jesus took Peter, John, and James with him and went up a hill to pray. 29 While he was praying, his face changed its appearance, and his clothes

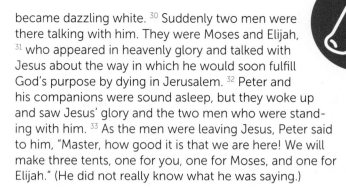

became dazzling white. 30 Suddenly two men were there talking with him. They were Moses and Elijah, 31 who appeared in heavenly glory and talked with Jesus about the way in which he would soon fulfill God's purpose by dying in Jerusalem. 32 Peter and his companions were sound asleep, but they woke up and saw Jesus' glory and the two men who were standing with him. 33 As the men were leaving Jesus, Peter said to him, "Master, how good it is that we are here! We will make three tents, one for you, one for Moses, and one for Elijah." (He did not really know what he was saying.)

34 While he was still speaking, a cloud appeared and covered them with its shadow; and the disciples were afraid as the cloud came over them. 35 A voice said from the cloud, "This is my Son, whom I have chosen— listen to him!"

36 When the voice stopped, there was Jesus all alone. The disciples kept quiet about all this and told no one at that time anything they had seen.

Jesus Heals a Boy with an Evil Spirit

37 The next day Jesus and the three disciples went down from the hill, and a large crowd met Jesus. 38 A man shouted from the crowd, "Teacher! I beg you, look at my son—my only son! 39 A spirit attacks him with a sudden shout and throws him into a fit, so that he foams at the mouth; it keeps on hurting him and will hardly let him go! 40 I begged your disciples to drive it out, but they couldn't."

41 Jesus answered, "How unbelieving and wrong you people are! How long must I stay with you? How long do I have to put up with you?" Then he said to the man, "Bring your son here."

42 As the boy was coming, the demon knocked him to the ground and threw him into a fit. Jesus gave a command to the evil spirit, healed the boy, and gave him back to his father. 43 All the people were amazed at the mighty power of God.

Learn more on page 175.

Jesus Speaks Again about His Death

The people were still marveling at everything Jesus was doing, when he said to his disciples, [44] "Don't forget what I am about to tell you! The Son of Man is going to be handed over to the power of human beings." [45] But the disciples did not know what this meant. It had been hidden from them so that they could not understand it, and they were afraid to ask him about the matter.

Who Is the Greatest?

[46] An argument broke out among the disciples as to which one of them was the greatest. [47] Jesus knew what they were thinking, so he took a child, stood him by his side, [48] and said to them, "Whoever welcomes this child in my name, welcomes me; and whoever welcomes me, also welcomes the one who sent me. For the one who is least among you all is the greatest."

Whoever Is Not Against You Is for You

[49] John spoke up, "Master, we saw a man driving out demons in your name, and we told him to stop, because he doesn't belong to our group."

[50] "Do not try to stop him," Jesus said to him and to the other disciples, "because whoever is not against you is for you."

A Samaritan Village Refuses to Receive Jesus

[51] As the time drew near when Jesus would be taken up to heaven, he made up his mind and set out on his way to Jerusalem. [52] He sent messengers ahead of him, who went into a village in Samaria to get everything ready for him. [53] But the people there would not receive him, because it was clear that he was on his way to Jerusalem. [54] When the disciples James and John saw this, they said, "Lord, do you want us to call fire down from heaven to destroy them?"

[55] Jesus turned and rebuked them. [56] Then Jesus and his disciples went on to another village.

The Would-Be Followers of Jesus

[57] As they went on their way, a man said to Jesus, "I will follow you wherever you go."

[58] Jesus said to him, "Foxes have holes, and birds have nests, but the Son of Man has no place to lie down and rest."

[59] He said to another man, "Follow me."

But that man said, "Sir, first let me go back and bury my father."

[60] Jesus answered, "Let the dead bury their own dead. You go and proclaim the Kingdom of God."

[61] Someone else said, "I will follow you, sir; but first let me go and say good-bye to my family."

[62] Jesus said to him, "Anyone who starts to plow and then keeps looking back is of no use for the Kingdom of God."

Chapter 10

Jesus Sends Out the Seventy-Two

[1] After this the Lord chose another seventy-two men and sent them out two by two, to go ahead of him to every town and place where he himself was about to go. [2] He said to them, "There is a large harvest, but few workers to gather it in. Pray to the owner of the harvest that he will send out workers to gather in his harvest.
[3] Go! I am sending you like lambs among wolves.
[4] Don't take a purse or a beggar's bag or shoes; don't stop to greet anyone on the road. [5] Whenever you go into a house, first say, 'Peace be with this house.' [6] If someone who is peace-loving lives there, let your greeting of peace remain on that person; if not, take back your greeting of peace. [7] Stay in that same house, eating and drinking whatever they offer you, for workers should be given their pay. Don't move around from one house

to another. [8] Whenever you go into a town and are made welcome, eat what is set before you, [9] heal the sick in that town, and say to the people there, 'The Kingdom of God has come near you.' [10] But whenever you go into a town and are not welcomed, go out in the streets and say, [11] 'Even the dust from your town that sticks to our feet we wipe off against you. But remember that the Kingdom of God has come near you!' [12] I assure you that on the Judgment Day God will show more mercy to Sodom than to that town!

The Unbelieving Towns
[13] "How terrible it will be for you, Chorazin! How terrible for you too, Bethsaida! If the miracles which were performed in you had been performed in Tyre and Sidon, the people there would have long ago sat down, put on sackcloth, and sprinkled ashes on themselves, to show that they had turned from their sins! [14] God will show more mercy on the Judgment Day to Tyre and Sidon than to you. [15] And as for you, Capernaum! Did you want to lift yourself up to heaven? You will be thrown down to hell!"

[16] Jesus said to his disciples, "Whoever listens to you listens to me; whoever rejects you rejects me; and whoever rejects me rejects the one who sent me."

The Return of the Seventy-Two
[17] The seventy-two men came back in great joy. "Lord," they said, "even the demons obeyed us when we gave them a command in your name!"

[18] Jesus answered them, "I saw Satan fall like lightning from heaven. [19] Listen! I have given you authority, so that you can walk on snakes and scorpions and overcome all the power of the Enemy, and nothing will hurt you. [20] But don't be glad because the evil spirits obey you; rather be glad because your names are written in heaven."

Jesus Rejoices
[21] At that time Jesus was filled with joy by the Holy Spirit and said, "Father, Lord of heaven and earth! I thank you because you have shown to the unlearned what you have hidden from the wise and learned. Yes, Father, this was

how you were pleased to have it happen.

[22] "My Father has given me all things. No one knows who the Son is except the Father, and no one knows who the Father is except the Son and those to whom the Son chooses to reveal him."

[23] Then Jesus turned to the disciples and said to them privately, "How fortunate you are to see the things you see! [24] I tell you that many prophets and kings wanted to see what you see, but they could not, and to hear what you hear, but they did not."

The Parable of the Good Samaritan
[25] A teacher of the Law came up and tried to trap Jesus. "Teacher," he asked, "what must I do to receive eternal life?"

[26] Jesus answered him, "What do the Scriptures say? How do you interpret them?"

[27] The man answered, "'Love the Lord your God with all your heart, with all your soul, with all your strength, and with all your mind'; and 'Love your neighbor as you love yourself.'"

[28] "You are right," Jesus replied; "do this and you will live."

[29] But the teacher of the Law wanted to justify himself, so he asked Jesus, "Who is my neighbor?"

[30] Jesus answered, "There was once a man who was going down from Jerusalem to Jericho when robbers attacked him, stripped him, and beat him up, leaving him half dead. [31] It so happened that a priest was going down that road; but when he saw the man, he walked on by on the other side. [32] In the

Learn more on page 176.

same way a Levite also came there, went over and looked at the man, and then walked on by on the other side. ³³ But a Samaritan who was traveling that way came upon the man, and when he saw him, his heart was filled with pity. ³⁴ He went over to him, poured oil and wine on his wounds and bandaged them; then he put the man on his own animal and took him to an inn, where he took care of him. ³⁵ The next day he took out two silver coins and gave them to the innkeeper. 'Take care of him,' he told the innkeeper, 'and when I come back this way, I will pay you whatever else you spend on him.'"

³⁶ And Jesus concluded, "In your opinion, which one of these three acted like a neighbor toward the man attacked by the robbers?"

³⁷ The teacher of the Law answered, "The one who was kind to him."

Jesus replied, "You go, then, and do the same."

Learn more on page 177.

Jesus Visits Martha and Mary

³⁸ As Jesus and his disciples went on their way, he came to a village where a woman named Martha welcomed him in her home. ³⁹ She had a sister named Mary, who sat down at the feet of the Lord and listened to his teaching. ⁴⁰ Martha was upset over all the work she had to do, so she came and said, "Lord, don't you care that my sister has left me to do all the work by myself? Tell her to come and help me!"

⁴¹ The Lord answered her, "Martha, Martha! You are worried and troubled over so many things, ⁴² but just one is needed. Mary has chosen the right thing, and it will not be taken away from her."

Chapter 11
Jesus' Teaching on Prayer

¹ One day Jesus was praying in a certain place. When he had finished, one of his disciples said to him, "Lord, teach us to pray, just as John taught his disciples."

² Jesus said to them, "When you pray, say this:

'Father:
May your holy name be honored;
    may your Kingdom come.
³ Give us day by day the food we need.
⁴ Forgive us our sins,
    for we forgive everyone who does us wrong.
And do not bring us to hard testing.'"

⁵ And Jesus said to his disciples, "Suppose one of you should go to a friend's house at midnight and say, 'Friend, let me borrow three loaves of bread. ⁶ A friend of mine who is on a trip has just come to my house, and I don't have any food for him!' ⁷ And suppose your friend should answer from inside, 'Don't bother me! The door is already locked, and my children and I are in bed. I can't get up and give you anything.' ⁸ Well, what then? I tell you that even if he will not get up and give you the bread because you are his friend, yet he will get up and give you everything you need because you are not ashamed to keep on asking. ⁹ And so I say to you: Ask, and you will receive; seek, and you will find; knock, and the door will be opened to you. ¹⁰ For those who ask will receive, and those who seek will find, and the door will be opened to anyone who knocks. ¹¹ Would any of you who are fathers give your son a snake when he asks for fish? ¹² Or would you give him a scorpion when he asks for an egg? ¹³ As bad as you are, you know how to give good things to your children. How much more, then, will the Father in heaven give the Holy Spirit to those who ask him!"

Jesus and Beelzebul

¹⁴ Jesus was driving out a demon that could not talk; and when the demon went out, the man began to talk. The crowds were amazed, ¹⁵ but some of the people said, "It

is Beelzebul, the chief of the demons, who gives him the power to drive them out."

[16] Others wanted to trap Jesus, so they asked him to perform a miracle to show that God approved of him. [17] But Jesus knew what they were thinking, so he said to them, "Any country that divides itself into groups which fight each other will not last very long; a family divided against itself falls apart. [18] So if Satan's kingdom has groups fighting each other, how can it last? You say that I drive out demons because Beelzebul gives me the power to do so. [19] If this is how I drive them out, how do your followers drive them out? Your own followers prove that you are wrong! [20] No, it is rather by means of God's power that I drive out demons, and this proves that the Kingdom of God has already come to you.

[21] "When a strong man, with all his weapons ready, guards his own house, all his belongings are safe. [22] But when a stronger man attacks him and defeats him, he carries away all the weapons the owner was depending on and divides up what he stole.

[23] "Anyone who is not for me is really against me; anyone who does not help me gather is really scattering.

The Return of the Evil Spirit
[24] "When an evil spirit goes out of a person, it travels over dry country looking for a place to rest. If it can't find one, it says to itself, 'I will go back to my house.' [25] So it goes back and finds the house clean and all fixed up. [26] Then it goes out and brings seven other spirits even worse than itself, and they come and live there. So when it is all over, that person is in worse shape than at the beginning."

True Happiness
[27] When Jesus had said this, a woman spoke up from the crowd and said to him, "How happy is the woman who bore you and nursed you!"

[28] But Jesus answered, "Rather, how happy are those who hear the word of God and obey it!"

The Demand for a Miracle
[29] As the people crowded around Jesus, he went on to say, "How evil are the people of this day! They ask for a miracle, but none will be given them except the miracle of Jonah. [30] In the same way that the prophet Jonah was a sign for the people of Nineveh, so the Son of Man will be a sign for the people of this day. [31] On the Judgment Day the Queen of Sheba will stand up and accuse the people of today, because she traveled all the way from her country to listen to King Solomon's wise teaching; and there is something here, I tell you, greater than Solomon. [32] On the Judgment Day the people of Nineveh will stand up and accuse you, because they turned from their sins when they heard Jonah preach; and I assure you that there is something here greater than Jonah!

The Light of the Body
[33] "No one lights a lamp and then hides it or puts it under a bowl; instead, it is put on the lampstand, so that people may see the light as they come in. [34] Your eyes are like a lamp for the body. When your eyes are sound, your whole body is full of light; but when your eyes are no good, your whole body will be in darkness. [35] Make certain, then, that the light in you is not darkness. [36] If your whole body is full of light, with no part of it in darkness, it will be bright all over, as when a lamp shines on you with its brightness."

Jesus Accuses the Pharisees and the Teachers of the Law
[37] When Jesus finished speaking, a Pharisee invited him to eat with him; so he went in and sat down to eat. [38] The Pharisee was surprised when he noticed that Jesus had not washed before eating. [39] So the Lord said to him, "Now then, you Pharisees clean the outside of your cup and plate, but inside you are full of violence and evil. [40] Fools! Did not God, who made the outside, also make the inside? [41] But give what is in your cups and plates to the poor, and everything will be ritually clean for you.

[42] "How terrible for you Pharisees! You give to God one

tenth of the seasoning herbs, such as mint and rue and all the other herbs, but you neglect justice and love for God. These you should practice, without neglecting the others.

[43] "How terrible for you Pharisees! You love the reserved seats in the synagogues and to be greeted with respect in the marketplaces. [44] How terrible for you! You are like unmarked graves which people walk on without knowing it."

[45] One of the teachers of the Law said to him, "Teacher, when you say this, you insult us too!"

[46] Jesus answered, "How terrible also for you teachers of the Law! You put onto people's backs loads which are hard to carry, but you yourselves will not stretch out a finger to help them carry those loads. [47] How terrible for you! You make fine tombs for the prophets—the very prophets your ancestors murdered. [48] You yourselves admit, then, that you approve of what your ancestors did; they murdered the prophets, and you build their tombs. [49] For this reason the Wisdom of God said, 'I will send them prophets and messengers; they will kill some of them and persecute others.' [50] So the people of this time will be punished for the murder of all the prophets killed since the creation of the world, [51] from the murder of Abel to the murder of Zechariah, who was killed between the altar and the Holy Place. Yes, I tell you, the people of this time will be punished for them all!

[52] "How terrible for you teachers of the Law! You have kept the key that opens the door to the house of knowledge; you yourselves will not go in, and you stop those who are trying to go in!"

[53] When Jesus left that place, the teachers of the Law and the Pharisees began to criticize him bitterly and ask him questions about many things, [54] trying to lay traps for him and catch him saying something wrong.

Chapter 12
A Warning against Hypocrisy
[1] As thousands of people crowded together, so that they were stepping on each other, Jesus said first to his disciples, "Be on guard against the yeast of the Pharisees—I mean their hypocrisy. [2] Whatever is covered up will be uncovered, and every secret will be made known. [3] So then, whatever you have said in the dark will be heard in broad daylight, and whatever you have whispered in private in a closed room will be shouted from the housetops.

Whom to Fear
[4] "I tell you, my friends, do not be afraid of those who kill the body but cannot afterward do anything worse. [5] I will show you whom to fear: fear God, who, after killing, has the authority to throw into hell. Believe me, he is the one you must fear!

[6] "Aren't five sparrows sold for two pennies? Yet not one sparrow is forgotten by God. [7] Even the hairs of your head have all been counted. So do not be afraid; you are worth much more than many sparrows!

Confessing and Rejecting Christ
[8] "I assure you that those who declare publicly that they belong to me, the Son of Man will do the same for them before the angels of God. [9] But those who reject me publicly, the Son of Man will also reject them before the angels of God.

[10] "Whoever says a word against the Son of Man can be forgiven; but whoever says evil things against the Holy Spirit will not be forgiven.

[11] "When they bring you to be tried in the synagogues or before governors or rulers, do not be worried about how you will defend yourself or what you will say. [12] For the Holy Spirit will teach you at that time what you should say."

The Parable of the Rich Fool
[13] A man in the crowd said to Jesus, "Teacher, tell my brother to divide with me the property our father left us."

[14] Jesus answered him, "Friend, who gave me the right to judge or to divide the property between you two?"

15 And he went on to say to them all, "Watch out and guard yourselves from every kind of greed; because your true life is not made up of the things you own, no matter how rich you may be."

16 Then Jesus told them this parable: "There was once a rich man who had land which bore good crops. 17 He began to think to himself, 'I don't have a place to keep all my crops. What can I do? 18 This is what I will do,' he told himself; 'I will tear down my barns and build bigger ones, where I will store the grain and all my other goods. 19 Then I will say to myself, Lucky man! You have all the good things you need for many years. Take life easy, eat, drink, and enjoy yourself!' 20 But God said to him, 'You fool! This very night you will have to give up your life; then who will get all these things you have kept for yourself?'"

21 And Jesus concluded, "This is how it is with those who pile up riches for themselves but are not rich in God's sight."

Trust in God

22 Then Jesus said to the disciples, "And so I tell you not to worry about the food you need to stay alive or about the clothes you need for your body. 23 Life is much more important than food, and the body much more important than clothes. 24 Look at the crows: they don't plant seeds or gather a harvest; they don't have storage rooms or barns; God feeds them! You are worth so much more than birds! 25 Can any of you live a bit longer by worrying about it? 26 If you can't manage even such a small thing, why worry about the other things? 27 Look how the wild flowers grow: they don't work or make clothes for themselves. But I tell you that not even King Solomon with all his wealth had clothes as beautiful as one of these flowers. 28 It is God who clothes the wild grass—grass that is here today and gone tomorrow, burned up in the oven.

Won't he be all the more sure to clothe you? What little faith you have!

29 "So don't be all upset, always concerned about what you will eat and drink. 30 (For the pagans of this world are always concerned about all these things.) Your Father knows that you need these things. 31 Instead, be concerned with his Kingdom, and he will provide you with these things.

Riches in Heaven

32 "Do not be afraid, little flock, for your Father is pleased to give you the Kingdom. 33 Sell all your belongings and give the money to the poor. Provide for yourselves purses that don't wear out, and save your riches in heaven, where they will never decrease, because no thief can get to them, and no moth can destroy them. 34 For your heart will always be where your riches are.

Watchful Servants

35 "Be ready for whatever comes, dressed for action and with your lamps lit, 36 like servants who are waiting for their master to come back from a wedding feast. When he comes and knocks, they will open the door for him at once. 37 How happy are those servants whose master finds them awake and ready when he returns! I tell you, he will take off his coat, have them sit down, and will wait on them. 38 How happy they are if he finds them ready, even if he should come at midnight or even later! 39 And you can be sure that if the owner of a house knew the time when the thief would come, he would not let the thief break into his house. 40 And you, too, must be ready, because the Son of Man will come at an hour when you are not expecting him."

The Faithful or the Unfaithful Servant

41 Peter said, "Lord, does this parable apply to us, or do you mean it for everyone?"

42 The Lord answered, "Who, then, is the faithful and wise servant? He is the one that his master will put in charge, to run the household and give the other servants their share of the food at the proper time. 43 How happy that

servant is if his master finds him doing this when he comes home! ⁴⁴ Indeed, I tell you, the master will put that servant in charge of all his property.

⁴⁵ But if that servant says to himself that his master is taking a long time to come back and if he begins to beat the other servants, both the men and the women, and eats and drinks and gets drunk, ⁴⁶ then the master will come back one day when the servant does not expect him and at a time he does not know. The master will cut him in pieces and make him share the fate of the disobedient.

⁴⁷ "The servant who knows what his master wants him to do, but does not get himself ready and do it, will be punished with a heavy whipping. ⁴⁸ But the servant who does not know what his master wants, and yet does something for which he deserves a whipping, will be punished with a light whipping. Much is required from the person to whom much is given; much more is required from the person to whom much more is given.

Jesus the Cause of Division

⁴⁹ "I came to set the earth on fire, and how I wish it were already kindled! ⁵⁰ I have a baptism to receive, and how distressed I am until it is over! ⁵¹ Do you suppose that I came to bring peace to the world? No, not peace, but division. ⁵² From now on a family of five will be divided, three against two and two against three. ⁵³ Fathers will be against their sons, and sons against their fathers; mothers will be against their daughters, and daughters against their mothers; mothers-in-law will be against their daughters-in-law, and daughters-in-law against their mothers-in-law."

Understanding the Time

⁵⁴ Jesus said also to the people, "When you see a cloud coming up in the west, at once you say that it is going to rain—and it does. ⁵⁵ And when you feel the south wind blowing, you say that it is going to get hot—and it does. ⁵⁶ Hypocrites! You can look at the earth and the sky and predict the weather; why, then, don't you know the meaning of this present time?

Settle with Your Opponent

⁵⁷ "Why do you not judge for yourselves the right thing to do? ⁵⁸ If someone brings a lawsuit against you and takes you to court, do your best to settle the dispute before you get to court. If you don't, you will be dragged before the judge, who will hand you over to the police, and you will be put in jail. ⁵⁹ There you will stay, I tell you, until you pay the last penny of your fine."

Chapter 13
Turn from Your Sins or Die

¹ At that time some people were there who told Jesus about the Galileans whom Pilate had killed while they were offering sacrifices to God. ² Jesus answered them, "Because those Galileans were killed in that way, do you think it proves that they were worse sinners than all other Galileans? ³ No indeed! And I tell you that if you do not turn from your sins, you will all die as they did. ⁴ What about those eighteen people in Siloam who were killed when the tower fell on them? Do you suppose this proves that they were worse than all the other people living in Jerusalem? ⁵ No indeed! And I tell you that if you do not turn from your sins, you will all die as they did."

The Parable of the Unfruitful Fig Tree

⁶ Then Jesus told them this parable: "There was once a man who had a fig tree growing in his vineyard. He went looking for figs on it but found none. ⁷ So he said to his gardener, 'Look, for three years I have been coming here looking for figs on this fig tree, and I haven't found any. Cut it down! Why should it go on using up the soil?' ⁸ But the gardener answered, 'Leave it alone, sir, just one more year; I will dig around it and put in some fertilizer. ⁹ Then if the tree bears figs next year, so much the better; if not, then you can have it cut down.'"

Jesus Heals a Crippled Woman on the Sabbath

¹⁰ One Sabbath Jesus was teaching in a synagogue. ¹¹ A woman there had an evil spirit that had kept her sick for eighteen years; she was bent over and could not straighten up at all. ¹² When Jesus saw her, he called out to her, "Woman, you are free from your sickness!" ¹³ He placed

his hands on her, and at once she straightened herself up and praised God.

14 The official of the synagogue was angry that Jesus had healed on the Sabbath, so he spoke up and said to the people, "There are six days in which we should work; so come during those days and be healed, but not on the Sabbath!"

15 The Lord answered him, "You hypocrites! Any one of you would untie your ox or your donkey from the stall and take it out to give it water on the Sabbath. 16 Now here is this descendant of Abraham whom Satan has kept in bonds for eighteen years; should she not be released on the Sabbath?" 17 His answer made his enemies ashamed of themselves, while the people rejoiced over all the wonderful things that he did.

The Parable of the Mustard Seed

18 Jesus asked, "What is the Kingdom of God like? What shall I compare it with? 19 It is like this. A man takes a mustard seed and plants it in his field. The plant grows and becomes a tree, and the birds make their nests in its branches."

The Parable of the Yeast

20 Again Jesus asked, "What shall I compare the Kingdom of God with? 21 It is like this. A woman takes some yeast and mixes it with a bushel of flour until the whole batch of dough rises."

The Narrow Door

22 Jesus went through towns and villages, teaching the people and making his way toward Jerusalem. 23 Someone asked him, "Sir, will just a few people be saved?"

Jesus answered them, 24 "Do your best to go in through the narrow door; because many people will surely try

to go in but will not be able. 25 The master of the house will get up and close the door; then when you stand outside and begin to knock on the door and say, 'Open the door for us, sir!' he will answer you, 'I don't know where you come from!' 26 Then you will answer, 'We ate and drank with you; you taught in our town!' 27 But he will say again, 'I don't know where you come from. Get away from me, all you wicked people!' 28 How you will cry and gnash your teeth when you see Abraham, Isaac, and Jacob, and all the prophets in the Kingdom of God, while you are thrown out! 29 People will come from the east and the west, from the north and the south, and sit down at the feast in the Kingdom of God. 30 Then those who are now last will be first, and those who are now first will be last."

Jesus' Love for Jerusalem

31 At that same time some Pharisees came to Jesus and said to him, "You must get out of here and go somewhere else, because Herod wants to kill you."

32 Jesus answered them, "Go and tell that fox: 'I am driving out demons and performing cures today and tomorrow, and on the third day I shall finish my work.' 33 Yet I must be on my way today, tomorrow, and the next day; it is not right for a prophet to be killed anywhere except in Jerusalem.

34 "Jerusalem, Jerusalem! You kill the prophets, you stone the messengers God has sent you! How many times I wanted to put my arms around all your people, just as a hen gathers her chicks under her wings, but you would not let me! 35 And so your Temple will be abandoned. I assure you that you will not see me until the time comes when you say, 'God bless him who comes in the name of the Lord.'"

Chapter 14
Jesus Heals a Sick Man

1 One Sabbath Jesus went to eat a meal at the home of one of the leading Pharisees; and people were watching Jesus closely. 2 A man whose legs and arms were swollen

came to Jesus, [3] and Jesus spoke up and asked the teachers of the Law and the Pharisees, "Does our Law allow healing on the Sabbath or not?"

[4] But they would not say a thing. Jesus took the man, healed him, and sent him away. [5] Then he said to them, "If any one of you had a child or an ox that happened to fall in a well on a Sabbath, would you not pull it out at once on the Sabbath itself?"

[6] But they were not able to answer him about this.

Humility and Hospitality

[7] Jesus noticed how some of the guests were choosing the best places, so he told this parable to all of them: [8] "When someone invites you to a wedding feast, do not sit down in the best place. It could happen that someone more important than you has been invited, [9] and your host, who invited both of you, would have to come and say to you, 'Let him have this place.' Then you would be embarrassed and have to sit in the lowest place. [10] Instead, when you are invited, go and sit in the lowest place, so that your host will come to you and say, 'Come on up, my friend, to a better place.' This will bring you honor in the presence of all the other guests. [11] For those who make themselves great will be humbled, and those who humble themselves will be made great."

[12] Then Jesus said to his host, "When you give a lunch or a dinner, do not invite your friends or your brothers or your relatives or your rich neighbors—for they will invite you back, and in this way you will be paid for what you did. [13] When you give a feast, invite the poor, the crippled, the lame, and the blind; [14] and you will be blessed, because they are not able to pay you back. God will repay you on the day the good people rise from death."

The Parable of the Great Feast

[15] When one of the guests sitting at the table heard this, he said to Jesus, "How happy are those who will sit down at the feast in the Kingdom of God!"

[16] Jesus said to him, "There was once a man who was giving a great feast to which he invited many people.

[17] When it was time for the feast, he sent his servant to tell his guests, 'Come, everything is ready!' [18] But they all began, one after another, to make excuses. The first one told the servant, 'I have bought a field and must go and look at it; please accept my apologies.' [19] Another one said, 'I have bought five pairs of oxen and am on my way to try them out; please accept my apologies.' [20] Another one said, 'I have just gotten married, and for that reason I cannot come.' [21] The servant went back and told all this to his master. The master was furious and said to his servant, 'Hurry out to the streets and alleys of the town, and bring back the poor, the crippled, the blind, and the lame.' [22] Soon the servant said, 'Your order has been carried out, sir, but there is room for more.' [23] So the master said to the servant, 'Go out to the country roads and lanes and make people come in, so that my house will be full. [24] I tell you all that none of those who were invited will taste my dinner!'"

The Cost of Being a Disciple

[25] Once when large crowds of people were going along with Jesus, he turned and said to them, [26] "Those who come to me cannot be my disciples unless they love me more than they love father and mother, wife and children, brothers and sisters, and themselves as well. [27] Those who do not carry their own cross and come after me cannot be my disciples. [28] If one of you is planning to build a tower, you sit down first and figure out what it will cost, to see if you have enough money to finish the job. [29] If you don't, you will not be able to finish the tower after laying the foundation; and all who see what happened will make

fun of you. [30] 'You began to build but can't finish the job!' they will say. [31] If a king goes out with ten thousand men to fight another king who comes against him with twenty thousand men, he will sit down first and decide if he is strong enough to face that other king. [32] If he isn't, he will send messengers to meet the other king to ask for terms of peace while he is still a long way off. [33] In the same way," concluded Jesus, "none of you can be my disciple unless you give up everything you have.

Worthless Salt

[34] "Salt is good, but if it loses its saltiness, there is no way to make it salty again. [35] It is no good for the soil or for the manure pile; it is thrown away. Listen, then, if you have ears!"

Chapter 15

The Lost Sheep

[1] One day when many tax collectors and other outcasts came to listen to Jesus, [2] the Pharisees and the teachers of the Law started grumbling, "This man welcomes outcasts and even eats with them!" [3] So Jesus told them this parable:

[4] "Suppose one of you has a hundred sheep and loses one of them—what do you do? You leave the other ninety-nine sheep in the pasture and go looking for the one that got lost until you find it. [5] When you find it, you are so happy that you put it on your shoulders [6] and carry it back home. Then you call your friends and neighbors together and say to them, 'I am so happy I found my lost sheep. Let us celebrate!' [7] In the same way, I tell you, there will be more joy in heaven over one sinner who repents than over ninety-nine respectable people who do not need to repent.

Learn more on page 182.

The Lost Coin

[8] "Or suppose a woman who has ten silver coins loses one of them—what does she do? She lights a lamp, sweeps her house, and looks carefully everywhere until she finds it. [9] When she finds it, she calls her friends and neighbors together, and says to them, 'I am so happy I found the coin I lost. Let us celebrate!' [10] In the same way, I tell you, the angels of God rejoice over one sinner who repents."

The Lost Son

[11] Jesus went on to say, "There was once a man who had two sons. [12] The younger one said to him, 'Father, give me my share of the property now.' So the man divided his property between his two sons. [13] After a few days the younger son sold his part of the property and left home with the money. He went to a country far away, where he wasted his money in reckless living. [14] He spent everything he had. Then a severe famine spread over that country, and he was left without a thing. [15] So he went to work for one of the citizens of that country, who sent him out to his farm to take care of the pigs. [16] He wished he could fill himself with the bean pods the pigs ate, but no one gave him anything to eat. [17] At last he came to his senses and said, 'All my father's hired workers have more than they can eat, and here I am about to starve! [18] I will get up and go to my father and say, "Father, I have sinned against God and against you. [19] I am no longer fit to be called your son; treat me as one of your hired workers."' [20] So he got up and started back to his father.

"He was still a long way from home when his father saw him; his heart was filled with pity, and he ran, threw his arms around his son, and kissed him. [21] 'Father,' the son said, 'I have sinned against God and against you. I am no longer fit to be called your son.' [22] But the father called to his servants. 'Hurry!' he said. 'Bring the best robe and put it on him. Put a ring on his finger and shoes on his feet. [23] Then go and get the prize calf and kill it, and let us celebrate with a feast! [24] For this son of mine was dead, but now he is alive; he was lost, but now he has been found.' And so the feasting began.

25 "In the meantime the older son was out in the field. On his way back, when he came close to the house, he heard the music and dancing. 26 So he called one of the servants and asked him, 'What's going on?' 27 'Your brother has come back home,' the servant answered, 'and your father has killed the prize calf, because he got him back safe and sound.' 28 The older brother was so angry that he would not go into the house; so his father came out and begged him to come in. 29 But he spoke back to his father, 'Look, all these years I have worked for you like a slave, and I have never disobeyed your orders. What have you given me? Not even a goat for me to have a feast with my friends! 30 But this son of yours wasted all your property on prostitutes, and when he comes back home, you kill the prize calf for him!' 31 'My son,' the father answered, 'you are always here with me, and everything I have is yours. 32 But we had to celebrate and be happy, because your brother was dead, but now he is alive; he was lost, but now he has been found.'"

Learn more on page 183.

Chapter 16
The Shrewd Manager

1 Jesus said to his disciples, "There was once a rich man who had a servant who managed his property. The rich man was told that the manager was wasting his master's money, 2 so he called him in and said, 'What is this I hear about you? Turn in a complete account of your handling of my property, because you cannot be my manager any longer.' 3 The servant said to himself, 'My master is going to dismiss me from my job. What shall I do? I am not strong enough to dig ditches, and I am ashamed to beg. 4 Now I know what I will do! Then when my job is gone, I shall have friends who will welcome me in their homes.' 5 So he called in all the people who were in debt to his master. He asked the first one, 'How much do you owe my master?' 6 'One hundred barrels of olive oil,' he answered. 'Here is your account,' the manager told him; 'sit down and write fifty.' 7 Then he asked another one, 'And you—how much do you owe?' 'A thousand bushels of wheat,' he answered. 'Here is your account,' the manager told him; 'write eight hundred.' 8 As a result the master of this dishonest manager praised him for doing such a shrewd thing; because the people of this world are much more shrewd in handling their affairs than the people who belong to the light."

9 And Jesus went on to say, "And so I tell you: make friends for yourselves with worldly wealth, so that when it gives out, you will be welcomed in the eternal home. 10 Whoever is faithful in small matters will be faithful in large ones; whoever is dishonest in small matters will be dishonest in large ones. 11 If, then, you have not been faithful in handling worldly wealth, how can you be trusted with true wealth? 12 And if you have not been faithful with what belongs to someone else, who will give you what belongs to you?

13 "No servant can be the slave of two masters; such a slave will hate one and love the other or will be loyal to one and despise the other. You cannot serve both God and money."

Some Sayings of Jesus

14 When the Pharisees heard all this, they made fun of Jesus, because they loved money. 15 Jesus said to them, "You are the ones who make yourselves look right in other people's sight, but God knows your hearts. For the things that are considered of great value by people are worth nothing in God's sight.

16 "The Law of Moses and the writings of the prophets were in effect up to the time of John the Baptist; since then the Good News about the Kingdom of God is being told, and everyone forces their way in. 17 But it is easier for heaven and earth to disappear than for the smallest detail of the Law to be done away with.

18 "Any man who divorces his wife and marries another woman commits adultery; and the man who marries a divorced woman commits adultery.

The Rich Man and Lazarus

19 "There was once a rich man who dressed in the most expensive clothes and lived in great luxury every day. 20 There was also a poor man named Lazarus, covered with sores, who used to be brought to the rich man's door, 21 hoping to eat the bits of food that fell from the rich man s table. Even the dogs would come and lick his sores. 22 The poor man died and was carried by the angels to sit beside Abraham at the feast in heaven. The rich man died and was buried, 23 and in Hades, where he was in great pain, he looked up and saw Abraham, far away, with Lazarus at his side. 24 So he called out, 'Father Abraham! Take pity on me, and send Lazarus to dip his finger in some water and cool off my tongue, because I am in great pain in this fire!' 25 But Abraham said, 'Remember, my son, that in your lifetime you were given all the good things, while Lazarus got all the bad things. But now he is enjoying himself here, while you are in pain. 26 Besides all that, there is a deep pit lying between us, so that those who want to cross over from here to you cannot do so, nor can anyone cross over to us from where you are.' 27 The rich man said, 'Then I beg you, father Abraham, send Lazarus to my father's house, 28 where I have five brothers. Let him go and warn them so that they, at least, will not come to this place of pain.' 29 Abraham said, 'Your brothers have Moses and the prophets to warn them; your brothers should listen to what they say.' 30 The rich man answered, 'That is not enough, father Abraham! But if someone were to rise from death and go to them, then they would turn from their sins.' 31 But Abraham said, 'If they will not listen to Moses and the prophets, they will not be convinced even if someone were to rise from death.'"

Chapter 17

Sin

1 Jesus said to his disciples, "Things that make people fall into sin are bound to happen, but how terrible for the one who makes them happen! 2 It would be better for him if a large millstone were tied around his neck and he were thrown into the sea than for him to cause one of these little ones to sin. 3 So watch what you do!

"If your brother sins, rebuke him, and if he repents, forgive him. 4 If he sins against you seven times in one day, and each time he comes to you saying, 'I repent,' you must forgive him."

Faith

5 The apostles said to the Lord, "Make our faith greater."

6 The Lord answered, "If you had faith as big as a mustard seed, you could say to this mulberry tree, 'Pull yourself up by the roots and plant yourself in the sea!' and it would obey you.

A Servant's Duty

7 "Suppose one of you has a servant who is plowing or looking after the sheep. When he comes in from the field, do you tell him to hurry along and eat his meal? 8 Of course not! Instead, you say to him, 'Get my supper ready, then put on your apron and wait on me while I eat and drink; after that you may have your meal.' 9 The servant does not deserve thanks for obeying orders, does he? 10 It is the same with you; when you have done all you have been told to do, say, 'We are ordinary servants; we have only done our duty.'"

earn more on page 184.

Jesus Heals Ten Men

[11] As Jesus made his way to Jerusalem, he went along the border between Samaria and Galilee. [12] He was going into a village when he was met by ten men suffering from a dreaded skin disease. They stood at a distance [13] and shouted, "Jesus! Master! Have pity on us!"

[14] Jesus saw them and said to them, "Go and let the priests examine you."

Learn more on page 185.

On the way they were made clean. [15] When one of them saw that he was healed, he came back, praising God in a loud voice. [16] He threw himself to the ground at Jesus' feet and thanked him. The man was a Samaritan. [17] Jesus spoke up, "There were ten who were healed; where are the other nine? [18] Why is this foreigner the only one who came back to give thanks to God?" [19] And Jesus said to him, "Get up and go; your faith has made you well."

The Coming of the Kingdom

[20] Some Pharisees asked Jesus when the Kingdom of God would come. His answer was, "The Kingdom of God does not come in such a way as to be seen. [21] No one will say, 'Look, here it is!' or, 'There it is!'; because the Kingdom of God is within you."

[22] Then he said to the disciples, "The time will come when you will wish you could see one of the days of the Son of Man, but you will not see it. [23] There will be those who will say to you, 'Look, over there!' or, 'Look, over here!' But don't go out looking for it. [24] As the lightning flashes across the sky and lights it up from one side to the other, so will the Son of Man be in his day. [25] But first he must suffer much and be rejected by the people of this day. [26] As it was in the time of Noah so shall it be in the days of the Son of Man. [27] Everybody kept on eating and drinking, and men and women married, up to the very day Noah went into the boat and the flood came and killed them all. [28] It will be as it was in the time of Lot. Everybody kept on eating and drinking, buying and selling, planting and building. [29] On the day Lot left Sodom, fire and sulfur rained down from heaven and killed them all. [30] That is how it will be on the day the Son of Man is revealed.

[31] "On that day someone who is on the roof of a house must not go down into the house to get any belongings; in the same way anyone who is out in the field must not go back to the house. [32] Remember Lot's wife! [33] Those who try to save their own life will lose it; those who lose their life will save it. [34] On that night, I tell you, there will be two people sleeping in the same bed: one will be taken away, the other will be left behind. [35] Two women will be grinding meal together: one will be taken away, the other will be left behind."

[37] The disciples asked him, "Where, Lord?"

Jesus answered, "Wherever there is a dead body, the vultures will gather."

Chapter 18
The Parable of the Widow and the Judge

[1] Then Jesus told his disciples a parable to teach them that they should always pray and never become discouraged. [2] "In a certain town there was a judge who neither feared God nor respected people. [3] And there was a widow in that same town who kept coming to him and pleading for her rights, saying, 'Help me against my opponent!' [4] For a long time the judge refused to act, but at last he said to himself, 'Even though I don't fear God or respect people, [5] yet because of all the trouble this widow is giving me, I will see to it that she gets her rights. If I don't, she will keep on coming and finally wear me out!'"

[6] And the Lord continued, "Listen to what that corrupt judge said. [7] Now, will God not judge in favor of his own people who cry to him day and night for help? Will he be slow to help them? [8] I tell you, he will judge in their favor

and do it quickly. But will the Son of Man find faith on earth when he comes?"

The Parable of the Pharisee and the Tax Collector

⁹ Jesus also told this parable to people who were sure of their own goodness and despised everybody else. ¹⁰ "Once there were two men who went up to the Temple to pray: one was a Pharisee, the other a tax collector. ¹¹ The Pharisee stood apart by himself and prayed, 'I thank you, God, that I am not greedy, dishonest, or an adulterer, like everybody else. I thank you that I am not like that tax collector over there. ¹² I fast two days a week, and I give you one tenth of all my income.' ¹³ But the tax collector stood at a distance and would not even raise his face to heaven, but beat on his breast and said, 'God, have pity on me, a sinner!' ¹⁴ I tell you," said Jesus, "the tax collector, and not the Pharisee, was in the right with God when he went home. For those who make themselves great will be humbled, and those who humble themselves will be made great."

Jesus Blesses Little Children

¹⁵ Some people brought their babies to Jesus for him to place his hands on them. The disciples saw them and scolded them for doing so, ¹⁶ but Jesus called the children to him and said, "Let the children come to me and do not stop them, because the Kingdom of God belongs to such as these. ¹⁷ Remember this! Whoever does not receive the Kingdom of God like a child will never enter it."

The Rich Man

¹⁸ A Jewish leader asked Jesus, "Good Teacher, what must I do to receive eternal life?"

¹⁹ "Why do you call me good?" Jesus asked him. "No one is good except God alone. ²⁰ You know the commandments: 'Do not commit adultery; do not commit murder; do not steal; do not accuse anyone falsely; respect your father and your mother.'"

²¹ The man replied, "Ever since I was young, I have obeyed all these commandments."

²² When Jesus heard this, he said to him, "There is still one more thing you need to do. Sell all you have and give the money to the poor, and you will have riches in heaven; then come and follow me." ²³ But when the man heard this, he became very sad, because he was very rich.

²⁴ Jesus saw that he was sad and said, "How hard it is for rich people to enter the Kingdom of God! ²⁵ It is much harder for a rich person to enter the Kingdom of God than for a camel to go through the eye of a needle."

²⁶ The people who heard him asked, "Who, then, can be saved?"

²⁷ Jesus answered, "What is humanly impossible is possible for God."

²⁸ Then Peter said, "Look! We have left our homes to follow you."

²⁹ "Yes," Jesus said to them, "and I assure you that anyone who leaves home or wife or brothers or parents or children for the sake of the Kingdom of God ³⁰ will receive much more in this present age and eternal life in the age to come."

Jesus Speaks a Third Time about His Death

³¹ Jesus took the twelve disciples aside and said to them, "Listen! We are going to Jerusalem where everything the prophets wrote about the Son of Man will come true. ³² He will be handed over to the Gentiles, who will make fun of him, insult him, and spit on him. ³³ They will whip him and kill him, but three days later he will rise to life."

³⁴ But the disciples did not understand any of these things; the meaning of the words was hidden from them, and they did not know what Jesus was talking about.

Jesus Heals a Blind Beggar

35 As Jesus was coming near Jericho, there was a blind man sitting by the road, begging. 36 When he heard the crowd passing by, he asked, "What is this?"

37 "Jesus of Nazareth is passing by," they told him.

38 He cried out, "Jesus! Son of David! Have mercy on me!"

39 The people in front scolded him and told him to be quiet. But he shouted even more loudly, "Son of David! Have mercy on me!"

40 So Jesus stopped and ordered the blind man to be brought to him. When he came near, Jesus asked him, 41 "What do you want me to do for you?"

"Sir," he answered, "I want to see again."

42 Jesus said to him, "Then see! Your faith has made you well."

43 At once he was able to see, and he followed Jesus, giving thanks to God. When the crowd saw it, they all praised God.

Chapter 19
Jesus and Zacchaeus

1 Jesus went on into Jericho and was passing through. 2 There was a chief tax collector there named Zacchaeus, who was rich. 3 He was trying to see who Jesus was, but he was a little man and could not see Jesus because of the crowd. 4 So he ran ahead of the crowd and climbed a sycamore tree to see Jesus, who was going to pass that way. 5 When Jesus came to that place,

he looked up and said to Zacchaeus, "Hurry down, Zacchaeus, because I must stay in your house today."

6 Zacchaeus hurried down and welcomed him with great joy. 7 All the people who saw it started grumbling, "This man has gone as a guest to the home of a sinner!"

8 Zacchaeus stood up and said to the Lord, "Listen, sir! I will give half my belongings to the poor, and if I have cheated anyone, I will pay back four times as much."

9 Jesus said to him, "Salvation has come to this house today, for this man, also, is a descendant of Abraham. 10 The Son of Man came to seek and to save the lost."

The Parable of the Gold Coins

11 While the people were listening to this, Jesus continued and told them a parable. He was now almost at Jerusalem, and they supposed that the Kingdom of God was just about to appear. 12 So he said, "There was once a man of high rank who was going to a country far away to be made king, after which he planned to come back home. 13 Before he left, he called his ten servants and gave them each a gold coin and told them, 'See what you can earn with this while I am gone.' 14 Now, his own people hated him, and so they sent messengers after him to say, 'We don't want this man to be our king.'

15 "The man was made king and came back. At once he ordered his servants to appear before him, in order to find out how much they had earned. 16 The first one came and said, 'Sir, I have earned ten gold coins with the one you gave me.' 17 'Well done,' he said; 'you are a good servant! Since you were faithful in small matters, I will put you in charge of ten cities.' 18 The second servant came and said, 'Sir, I have earned five gold coins with the one you gave me.' 19 To this one he said, 'You will be in charge of five cities.' 20 Another servant came and said, 'Sir, here is your gold coin; I kept it hidden in a handkerchief. 21 I was afraid of you, because you are a hard man. You take what is not yours and reap what you did not plant.' 22 He said to him, 'You bad servant! I will use your own words to condemn you! You know that I am a hard man, taking what is not

 Learn more on page 187.

mine and reaping what I have not planted. ²³ Well, then, why didn't you put my money in the bank? Then I would have received it back with interest when I returned.' ²⁴ Then he said to those who were standing there, 'Take the gold coin away from him and give it to the servant who has ten coins.' ²⁵ But they said to him, 'Sir, he already has ten coins!' ²⁶ 'I tell you,' he replied, 'that to those who have something, even more will be given; but those who have nothing, even the little that they have will be taken away from them. ²⁷ Now, as for those enemies of mine who did not want me to be their king, bring them here and kill them in my presence!'"

The Triumphant Approach to Jerusalem
²⁸ After Jesus said this, he went on in front of them toward Jerusalem. ²⁹ As he came near Bethphage and Bethany at the Mount of Olives, he sent two disciples ahead ³⁰ with these instructions: "Go to the village there ahead of you; as you go in, you will find a colt tied up that has never been ridden. Untie it and bring it here. ³¹ If someone asks you why you are untying it, tell him that the Master needs it."

³² They went on their way and found everything just as Jesus had told them. ³³ As they were untying the colt, its owners said to them, "Why are you untying it?"

³⁴ "The Master needs it," they answered, ³⁵ and they took the colt to Jesus. Then they threw their cloaks over the animal and helped Jesus get on. ³⁶ As he rode on, people spread their cloaks on the road.

³⁷ When he came near Jerusalem, at the place where the road went down the Mount of Olives, the large crowd of his disciples began to thank God and praise him in loud voices for all the great things that they had seen: ³⁸ "God bless the king who comes in the name of the Lord! Peace in heaven and glory to God!"

³⁹ Then some of the Pharisees in the crowd spoke to Jesus. "Teacher," they said, "command your disciples to be quiet!"

⁴⁰ Jesus answered, "I tell you that if they keep quiet, the stones themselves will start shouting."

Jesus Weeps over Jerusalem
⁴¹ He came closer to the city, and when he saw it, he wept over it, ⁴² saying, "If you only knew today what is needed for peace! But now you cannot see it! ⁴³ The time will come when your enemies will surround you with barricades, blockade you, and close in on you from every side. ⁴⁴ They will completely destroy you and the people within your walls; not a single stone will they leave in its place, because you did not recognize the time when God came to save you!"

Jesus Goes to the Temple
⁴⁵ Then Jesus went into the Temple and began to drive out the merchants, ⁴⁶ saying to them, "It is written in the Scriptures that God said, 'My Temple will be a house of prayer.' But you have turned it into a hideout for thieves!"

⁴⁷ Every day Jesus taught in the Temple. The chief priests, the teachers of the Law, and the leaders of the people wanted to kill him, ⁴⁸ but they

Learn more on page 189.

could not find a way to do it, because all the people kept listening to him, not wanting to miss a single word.

Chapter 20
The Question about Jesus' Authority
¹ One day when Jesus was in the Temple teaching the people and preaching the Good News, the chief priests and the teachers of the Law, together with the elders, came ² and said to him, "Tell us, what right do you have to do these things? Who gave you such right?"

³ Jesus answered them, "Now let me ask you a question. Tell me, ⁴ did John's right to baptize come from God or from human beings?"

5 They started to argue among themselves, "What shall we say? If we say, 'From God,' he will say, 'Why, then, did you not believe John?' 6 But if we say, 'From human beings,' this whole crowd here will stone us, because they are convinced that John was a prophet." 7 So they answered, "We don't know where it came from."

8 And Jesus said to them, "Neither will I tell you, then, by what right I do these things."

The Parable of the Tenants in the Vineyard

9 Then Jesus told the people this parable: "There was once a man who planted a vineyard, rented it out to tenants, and then left home for a long time. 10 When the time came to gather the grapes, he sent a slave to the tenants to receive from them his share of the harvest. But the tenants beat the slave and sent him back without a thing. 11 So he sent another slave; but the tenants beat him also, treated him shamefully, and sent him back without a thing. 12 Then he sent a third slave; the tenants wounded him, too, and threw him out. 13 Then the owner of the vineyard said, 'What shall I do? I will send my own dear son; surely they will respect him!' 14 But when the tenants saw him, they said to one another, 'This is the owner's son. Let's kill him, and his property will be ours!' 15 So they threw him out of the vineyard and killed him.

"What, then, will the owner of the vineyard do to the tenants?" Jesus asked. 16 "He will come and kill those men, and turn the vineyard over to other tenants."

When the people heard this, they said, "Surely not!"

17 Jesus looked at them and asked, "What, then, does this scripture mean?

'The stone which the builders rejected as worthless turned out to be the most important of all.'

18 Everyone who falls on that stone will be cut to pieces; and if that stone falls on someone, that person will be crushed to dust."

The Question about Paying Taxes

19 The teachers of the Law and the chief priests tried to arrest Jesus on the spot, because they knew that he had told this parable against them; but they were afraid of the people. 20 So they looked for an opportunity. They bribed some men to pretend they were sincere, and they sent them to trap Jesus with questions, so that they could hand him over to the authority and power of the Roman Governor. 21 These spies said to Jesus, "Teacher, we know that what you say and teach is right. We know that you pay no attention to anyone's status, but teach the truth about God's will for people. 22 Tell us, is it against our Law for us to pay taxes to the Roman Emperor, or not?"

23 But Jesus saw through their trick and said to them, 24 "Show me a silver coin. Whose face and name are these on it?"

"The Emperor's," they answered.

25 So Jesus said, "Well, then, pay to the Emperor what belongs to the Emperor, and pay to God what belongs to God."

26 There before the people they could not catch him in a thing, so they kept quiet, amazed at his answer.

The Question about Rising from Death

27 Then some Sadducees, who say that people will not rise from death, came to Jesus and said, 28 "Teacher, Moses wrote this law for us: 'If a man dies and leaves a wife but no children, that man's brother must marry the widow so that they can have children who will be

considered the dead man's children.' ²⁹ Once there were seven brothers; the oldest got married and died without having children. ³⁰ Then the second one married the woman, ³¹ and then the third. The same thing happened to all seven—they died without having children. ³² Last of all, the woman died. ³³ Now, on the day when the dead rise to life, whose wife will she be? All seven of them had married her."

³⁴ Jesus answered them, "The men and women of this age marry, ³⁵ but the men and women who are worthy to rise from death and live in the age to come will not then marry. ³⁶ They will be like angels and cannot die. They are the children of God, because they have risen from death. ³⁷ And Moses clearly proves that the dead are raised to life. In the passage about the burning bush he speaks of the Lord as 'the God of Abraham, the God of Isaac, and the God of Jacob.' ³⁸ He is the God of the living, not of the dead, for to him all are alive."

³⁹ Some of the teachers of the Law spoke up, "A good answer, Teacher!" ⁴⁰ For they did not dare ask him any more questions.

The Question about the Messiah
⁴¹ Jesus asked them, "How can it be said that the Messiah will be the descendant of David? ⁴² For David himself says in the book of Psalms,

'The Lord said to my Lord:
   Sit here at my right side
      ⁴³ until I put your enemies as a footstool
   under your feet.'

⁴⁴ David called him 'Lord'; how, then, can the Messiah be David's descendant?"

Jesus Warns against the Teachers of the Law
⁴⁵ As all the people listened to him, Jesus said to his disciples, ⁴⁶ "Be on your guard against the teachers of the Law, who like to walk around in their long robes and love to be greeted with respect in the marketplace; who choose the reserved seats in the synagogues and the best places at feasts; ⁴⁷ who take advantage of widows and rob them of their homes, and then make a show of saying long prayers! Their punishment will be all the worse!"

Chapter 21
The Widow's Offering
¹ Jesus looked around and saw rich people dropping their gifts in the Temple treasury, ² and he also saw a very poor widow dropping in two little copper coins.

³ He said, "I tell you that this poor widow put in more than all the others. ⁴ For the others offered their gifts from what they had to spare of their riches; but she, poor as she is, gave all she had to live on."

Jesus Speaks of the Destruction of the Temple
⁵ Some of the disciples were talking about the Temple, how beautiful it looked with its fine stones and the gifts offered to God. Jesus said, ⁶ "All this you see—the time will come when not a single stone here will be left in its place; every one will be thrown down."

Troubles and Persecutions
⁷ "Teacher," they asked, "when will this be? And what will happen in order to show that the time has come for it to take place?"

⁸ Jesus said, "Watch out; don't be fooled. Many men, claiming to speak for me, will come and say, 'I am he!' and, 'The time has come!' But don't follow them. ⁹ Don't be afraid when you hear of wars and revolutions; such things must happen first, but they do not mean that the end is near."

¹⁰ He went on to say, "Countries will fight each other;

kingdoms will attack one another. [11] There will be terrible earthquakes, famines, and plagues everywhere; there will be strange and terrifying things coming from the sky. [12] Before all these things take place, however, you will be arrested and persecuted; you will be handed over to be tried in synagogues and be put in prison; you will be brought before kings and rulers for my sake. [13] This will be your chance to tell the Good News. [14] Make up your minds ahead of time not to worry about how you will defend yourselves, [15] because I will give you such words and wisdom that none of your enemies will be able to refute or contradict what you say. [16] You will be handed over by your parents, your brothers, your relatives, and your friends; and some of you will be put to death. [17] Everyone will hate you because of me. [18] But not a single hair from your heads will be lost. [19] Stand firm, and you will save yourselves.

Jesus Speaks of the Destruction of Jerusalem

[20] "When you see Jerusalem surrounded by armies, then you will know that it will soon be destroyed. [21] Then those who are in Judea must run away to the hills; those who are in the city must leave, and those who are out in the country must not go into the city. [22] For those will be 'The Days of Punishment,' to make come true all that the Scriptures say. [23] How terrible it will be in those days for women who are pregnant and for mothers with little babies! Terrible distress will come upon this land, and God's punishment will fall on this people. [24] Some will be killed by the sword, and others will be taken as prisoners to all countries; and the heathen will trample over Jerusalem until their time is up.

The Coming of the Son of Man

[25] "There will be strange things happening to the sun, the moon, and the stars. On earth whole countries will be in despair, afraid of the roar of the sea and the raging tides. [26] People will faint from fear as they wait for what is coming over the whole earth, for the powers in space will be driven from their courses. [27] Then the Son of Man will appear, coming in a cloud with great power and glory.

[28] When these things begin to happen, stand up and raise your heads, because your salvation is near."

The Lesson of the Fig Tree

[29] Then Jesus told them this parable: "Think of the fig tree and all the other trees. [30] When you see their leaves beginning to appear, you know that summer is near. [31] In the same way, when you see these things happening, you will know that the Kingdom of God is about to come.

[32] "Remember that all these things will take place before the people now living have all died. [33] Heaven and earth will pass away, but my words will never pass away.

The Need to Watch

[34] "Be careful not to let yourselves become occupied with too much feasting and drinking and with the worries of this life, or that Day may suddenly catch you [35] like a trap. For it will come upon all people everywhere on earth. [36] Be on watch and pray always that you will have the strength to go safely through all those things that will happen and to stand before the Son of Man."

[37] Jesus spent those days teaching in the Temple, and when evening came, he would go out and spend the night on the Mount of Olives. [38] Early each morning all the people went to the Temple to listen to him.

Chapter 22
The Plot Against Jesus

[1] The time was near for the Festival of Unleavened Bread, which is called the Passover. [2] The chief priests and the teachers of the Law were afraid of the people, and so they were trying to find a way of putting Jesus to death secretly.

Judas Agrees to Betray Jesus

[3] Then Satan entered into Judas, called Iscariot, who was one of the twelve disciples. [4] So Judas went off and spoke with the chief priests and the officers of the Temple guard about how he could betray Jesus to them. [5] They were pleased and offered to pay him money. [6] Judas agreed to it and started looking for a good

chance to hand Jesus over to them without the people knowing about it.

Jesus Prepares to Eat the Passover Meal

[7] The day came during the Festival of Unleavened Bread when the lambs for the Passover meal were to be killed. [8] Jesus sent Peter and John with these instructions: "Go and get the Passover meal ready for us to eat."

[9] "Where do you want us to get it ready?" they asked him.

[10] He answered, "As you go into the city, a man carrying a jar of water will meet you. Follow him into the house that he enters, [11] and say to the owner of the house: 'The Teacher says to you, Where is the room where my disciples and I will eat the Passover meal?' [12] He will show you a large furnished room upstairs, where you will get everything ready."

[13] They went off and found everything just as Jesus had told them, and they prepared the Passover meal.

The Lord's Supper

[14] When the hour came, Jesus took his place at the table with the apostles. [15] He said to them, "I have wanted so much to eat this Passover meal with you before I suffer! [16] For I tell you, I will never eat it until it is given its full meaning in the Kingdom of God."

[17] Then Jesus took a cup, gave thanks to God, and said, "Take this and share it among yourselves. [18] I tell you that from now on I will not drink this wine until the Kingdom of God comes."

[19] Then he took a piece of bread, gave thanks to God, broke it, and gave it to them, saying, "This is my body, which is given for you. Do this in memory of me." [20] In the same way, he gave them the cup after the supper, saying, "This cup is God's new covenant sealed with my blood, which is poured out for you.

[21] "But, look! The one who betrays me is here at the table with me! [22] The Son of Man will die as God has decided, but how terrible for that man who betrays him!"

[23] Then they began to ask among themselves which one of them it could be who was going to do this.

The Argument about Greatness

[24] An argument broke out among the disciples as to which one of them should be thought of as the greatest. [25] Jesus said to them, "The kings of the pagans have power over their people, and the rulers claim the title 'Friends of the People.' [26] But this is not the way it is with you; rather, the greatest one among you must be like the youngest, and the leader must be like the servant. [27] Who is greater, the one who sits down to eat or the one who serves? The one who sits down, of course. But I am among you as one who serves.

[28] "You have stayed with me all through my trials; [29] and just as my Father has given me the right to rule, so I will give you the same right. [30] You will eat and drink at my table in my Kingdom, and you will sit on thrones to rule over the twelve tribes of Israel.

Jesus Predicts Peter's Denial

[31] "Simon, Simon! Listen! Satan has received permission to test all of you, to separate the good from the bad, as a farmer separates the wheat from the chaff. [32] But I have prayed for you, Simon, that your faith will not fail. And when you turn back to me, you must strengthen your brothers."

33 Peter answered, "Lord, I am ready to go to prison with you and to die with you!"

34 "I tell you, Peter," Jesus said, "the rooster will not crow tonight until you have said three times that you do not know me."

Purse, Bag, and Sword

35 Then Jesus asked his disciples, "When I sent you out that time without purse, bag, or shoes, did you lack anything?"

"Not a thing," they answered.

36 "But now," Jesus said, "whoever has a purse or a bag must take it; and whoever does not have a sword must sell his coat and buy one. 37 For I tell you that the scripture which says, 'He shared the fate of criminals,' must come true about me, because what was written about me is coming true."

38 The disciples said, "Look! Here are two swords, Lord!"

"That is enough!" he replied.

Learn more on page 197.

Jesus Prays on the Mount of Olives

39 Jesus left the city and went, as he usually did, to the Mount of Olives; and the disciples went with him. 40 When he arrived at the place, he said to them, "Pray that you will not fall into temptation."

41 Then he went off from them about the distance of a stone's throw and knelt down and prayed. 42 "Father," he said, "if you will, take this cup of suffering away from me. Not my will, however, but your will be done."

43 An angel from heaven appeared to him and strengthened him. 44 In great anguish he prayed even more fervently; his sweat was like drops of blood falling to the ground.

45 Rising from his prayer, he went back to the disciples and found them asleep, worn out by their grief. 46 He said to them, "Why are you sleeping? Get up and pray that you will not fall into temptation."

The Arrest of Jesus

47 Jesus was still speaking when a crowd arrived, led by Judas, one of the twelve disciples. He came up to Jesus to kiss him. 48 But Jesus said, "Judas, is it with a kiss that you betray the Son of Man?"

49 When the disciples who were with Jesus saw what was going to happen, they asked, "Shall we use our swords, Lord?" 50 And one of them struck the High Priest's slave and cut off his right ear.

51 But Jesus said, "Enough of this!" He touched the man's ear and healed him.

52 Then Jesus said to the chief priests and the officers of the Temple guard and the elders who had come there to get him, "Did you have to come with swords and clubs, as though I were an outlaw? 53 I was with you in the Temple every day, and you did not try to arrest me. But this is your hour to act, when the power of darkness rules."

Peter Denies Jesus

54 They arrested Jesus and took him away into the house of the High Priest; and Peter followed at a distance. 55 A fire had been lit in the center of the courtyard, and Peter joined those who were sitting around it. 56 When one of the servant women saw him sitting there at the fire, she looked straight at him and said, "This man too was with Jesus!"

57 But Peter denied it, "Woman, I don't even know him!"

58 After a little while a man noticed Peter and said, "You are one of them, too!"

But Peter answered, "Man, I am not!"

Learn more on page 198.

59 And about an hour later another man insisted strongly, "There isn't any doubt that this man was with Jesus, because he also is a Galilean!"

60 But Peter answered, "Man, I don't know what you are talking about!"

At once, while he was still speaking, a rooster crowed. 61 The Lord turned around and looked straight at Peter, and Peter remembered that the Lord had said to him, "Before the rooster crows tonight, you will say three times that you do not know me." 62 Peter went out and wept bitterly.

Jesus Is Mocked and Beaten
63 The men who were guarding Jesus made fun of him and beat him. 64 They blindfolded him and asked him, "Who hit you? Guess!" 65 And they said many other insulting things to him.

Jesus Before the Council
66 When day came, the elders, the chief priests, and the teachers of the Law met together, and Jesus was brought before the Council. 67 "Tell us," they said, "are you the Messiah?"

He answered, "If I tell you, you will not believe me; 68 and if I ask you a question, you will not answer. 69 But from now on the Son of Man will be seated at the right side of Almighty God."

70 They al. said, "Are you, then, the Son of God?"

He answered them, "You say that I am."

71 And they said, "We don't need any witnesses! We ourselves have heard what he said!"

Chapter 23
Jesus Before Pilate
1 The whole group rose up and took Jesus before Pilate, 2 where they began to accuse him: "We caught this man misleading our people, telling them not to pay taxes to the Emperor and claiming that he himself is the Messiah, a king."

3 Pilate asked him, "Are you the king of the Jews?"

"So you say," answered Jesus.

4 Then Pilate said to the chief priests and the crowds, "I find no reason to condemn this man."

5 But they insisted even more strongly, "With his teaching he is starting a riot among the people all through Judea. He began in Galilee and now has come here."

Jesus Before Herod
6 When Pilate heard this, he asked, "Is this man a Galilean?" 7 When he learned that Jesus was from the region ruled by Herod, he sent him to Herod, who was also in Jerusalem at that time. 8 Herod was very pleased when he saw Jesus, because he had heard about him and had been wanting to see him for a long time. He was hoping to see Jesus perform some miracle. 9 So Herod asked Jesus many questions, but Jesus made no answer. 10 The chief priests and the teachers of the Law stepped forward and made strong accusations against Jesus. 11 Herod and his soldiers made fun of Jesus and treated him with contempt; then they put a fine robe on him and sent him back to Pilate. 12 On that very day Herod and Pilate became friends; before this they had been enemies.

Jesus Is Sentenced to Death
13 Pilate called together the chief priests, the leaders, and the people, 14 and said to them, "You brought this man to me and said that he was misleading the people. Now, I have examined him here in your presence, and I have not found him guilty of any of the crimes you accuse him of. 15 Nor did Herod find him guilty, for he sent him back to us. There is nothing this man has done to deserve death.

¹⁶ So I will have him whipped and let him go."

¹⁸ The whole crowd cried out, "Kill him! Set Barabbas free for us!" (¹⁹ Barabbas had been put in prison for a riot that had taken place in the city, and for murder.)

²⁰ Pilate wanted to set Jesus free, so he appealed to the crowd again. ²¹ But they shouted back, "Crucify him! Crucify him!"

²² Pilate said to them the third time, "But what crime has he committed? I cannot find anything he has done to deserve death! I will have him whipped and set him free."

²³ But they kept on shouting at the top of their voices that Jesus should be crucified, and finally their shouting succeeded. ²⁴ So Pilate passed the sentence on Jesus that they were asking for. ²⁵ He set free the man they wanted, the one who had been put in prison for riot and murder, and he handed Jesus over for them to do as they wished.

Jesus Is Crucified

²⁶ The soldiers led Jesus away, and as they were going, they met a man from Cyrene named Simon who was coming into the city from the country. They seized him, put the cross on him, and made him carry it behind Jesus.

²⁷ A large crowd of people followed him; among them were some women who were weeping and wailing for him. ²⁸ Jesus turned to them and said, "Women of Jerusalem! Don't cry for me, but for yourselves and your children. ²⁹ For the days are coming when people will say, 'How lucky are the women who never had children, who never bore babies, who never nursed them!' ³⁰ That will be the time when people will say to the mountains, 'Fall on us!' and to the hills, 'Hide us!' ³¹ For if such things as these are done when the wood is green, what will happen when it is dry?"

³² Two other men, both of them criminals, were also led out to be put to death with Jesus. ³³ When they came to

the place called "The Skull," they crucified Jesus there, and the two criminals, one on his right and the other on his left. ³⁴ Jesus said, "Forgive them, Father! They don't know what they are doing."

They divided his clothes among themselves by throwing dice. ³⁵ The people stood there watching while the Jewish leaders made fun of him: "He saved others; let him save himself if he is the Messiah whom God has chosen!"

³⁶ The soldiers also made fun of him: they came up to him and offered him cheap wine, ³⁷ and said, "Save yourself if you are the king of the Jews!"

³⁸ Above him were written these words: "This is the King of the Jews."

³⁹ One of the criminals hanging there hurled insults at him: "Aren't you the Messiah? Save yourself and us!"

⁴⁰ The other one, however, rebuked him, saying, "Don't you fear God? You received the same sentence he did. ⁴¹ Ours, however, is only right, because we are getting what we deserve for what we did; but he has done no wrong." ⁴² And he said to Jesus, "Remember me, Jesus, when you come as King!"

⁴³ Jesus said to him, "I promise you that today you will be in Paradise with me."

The Death of Jesus

44-45 It was about twelve o'clock when the sun stopped shining and darkness covered the whole country until three o'clock; and the curtain hanging in the Temple was torn in two. **46** Jesus cried out in a loud voice, "Father! In your hands I place my spirit!" He said this and died.

47 The army officer saw what had happened, and he praised God, saying, "Certainly he was a good man!"

48 When the people who had gathered there to watch the spectacle saw what happened, they all went back home, beating their breasts in sorrow. **49** All those who knew Jesus personally, including the women who had followed him from Galilee, stood at a distance to watch.

The Burial of Jesus

50-51 There was a man named Joseph from Arimathea, a town in Judea. He was a good and honorable man, who was waiting for the coming of the Kingdom of God. Although he was a member of the Council, he had not agreed with their decision and action. **52** He went into the presence of Pilate and asked for the body of Jesus. **53** Then he took the body down, wrapped it in a linen sheet, and placed it in a tomb which had been dug out of solid rock and which had never been used. **54** It was Friday, and the Sabbath was about to begin.

55 The women who had followed Jesus from Galilee went with Joseph and saw the tomb and how Jesus' body was placed in it. **56** Then they went back home and prepared the spices and perfumes for the body.

On the Sabbath they rested, as the Law commanded.

Chapter 24
The Resurrection

1 Very early on Sunday morning the women went to the tomb, carrying the spices they had prepared. **2** They found the stone rolled away from the entrance to the tomb, **3** so they went in; but they did not find the body of the Lord Jesus. **4** They stood there puzzled about this, when suddenly two men in bright shining clothes stood by

them. **5** Full of fear, the women bowed down to the ground, as the men said to them, "Why are you looking among the dead for one who is alive? **6** He is not here; he has been raised. Remember what he said to you while he was in Galilee: **7** 'The Son of Man must be handed over to sinners, be crucified, and three days later rise to life.'"

8 Then the women remembered his words, **9** returned from the tomb, and told all these things to the eleven disciples and all the rest. **10** The women were Mary Magdalene, Joanna, and Mary the mother of James; they and the other women with them told these things to the apostles. **11** But the apostles thought that what the women said was nonsense, and they did not believe them. **12** But Peter got up and ran to the tomb; he bent down and saw the grave cloths but nothing else. Then he went back home amazed at what had happened.

The Walk to Emmaus

13 On that same day two of Jesus' followers were going to a village named Emmaus, about seven miles from Jerusalem, **14** and they were talking to each other about all the things that had happened. **15** As they talked and discussed, Jesus himself drew near and walked along with them; **16** they saw him, but somehow did not recognize him. **17** Jesus said to them, "What are you talking about to each other, as you walk along?"

They stood still, with sad faces. **18** One of them, named Cleopas, asked him, "Are you the only visitor in Jerusalem who doesn't know the things that have been happening there these last few days?"

19 "What things?" he asked.

Learn more on page 202.

"The things that happened to Jesus of Nazareth," they answered. "This man was a prophet and was considered by God and by all the people to be powerful in everything he said and did. ²⁰ Our chief priests and rulers handed him over to be sentenced to death, and he was crucified. ²¹ And we had hoped that he would be the one who was going to set Israel free! Besides all that, this is now the third day since it happened. ²² Some of the women of our group surprised us; they went at dawn to the tomb, ²³ but could not find his body. They came back saying they had seen a vision of angels who told them that he is alive. ²⁴ Some of our group went to the tomb and found it exactly as the women had said, but they did not see him."

²⁵ Then Jesus said to them, "How foolish you are, how slow you are to believe everything the prophets said! ²⁶ Was it not necessary for the Messiah to suffer these things and then to enter his glory?" ²⁷ And Jesus explained to them what was said about himself in all the Scriptures, beginning with the books of Moses and the writings of all the prophets.

²⁸ As they came near the village to which they were going, Jesus acted as if he were going farther; ²⁹ but they held him back, saying, "Stay with us; the day is almost over and it is getting dark." So he went in to stay with them. ³⁰ He sat down to eat with them, took the bread, and said the blessing; then he broke the bread and gave it to them. ³¹ Then their eyes were opened and they recognized him, but he disappeared from their sight. ³² They said to each other, "Wasn't it like a fire burning in us when he talked to us on the road and explained the Scriptures to us?"

³³ They got up at once and went back to Jerusalem, where they found the eleven disciples gathered together with the others ³⁴ and saying, "The Lord is risen indeed! He has appeared to Simon!"

³⁵ The two then explained to them what had happened on the road, and how they had recognized the Lord when he broke the bread.

Jesus Appears to His Disciples

³⁶ While the two were telling them this, suddenly the Lord himself stood among them and said to them, "Peace be with you."

³⁷ They were terrified, thinking that they were seeing a ghost. ³⁸ But he said to them, "Why are you alarmed? Why are these doubts coming up in your minds? ³⁹ Look at my hands and my feet, and see that it is I myself. Feel me, and you will know, for a ghost doesn't have flesh and bones, as you can see I have."

⁴⁰ He said this and showed them his hands and his feet. ⁴¹ They still could not believe, they were so full of joy and wonder; so he asked them, "Do you have anything here to eat?" ⁴² They gave him a piece of cooked fish, ⁴³ which he took and ate in their presence.

⁴⁴ Then he said to them, "These are the very things I told you about while I was still with you: everything written about me in the Law of Moses, the writings of the prophets, and the Psalms had to come true."

45 Then he opened their minds to understand the Scriptures, 46 and said to them, "This is what is written: the Messiah must suffer and must rise from death three days later, 47 and in his name the message about repentance and the forgiveness of sins must be preached to all nations, beginning in Jerusalem. 48 You are witnesses of these things. 49 And I myself will send upon you what my Father has promised. But you must wait in the city until the power from above comes down upon you.

Jesus Is Taken Up to Heaven

50 Then he led them out of the city as far as Bethany, where he raised his hands and blessed them. 51 As he was blessing them, he departed from them and was taken up into heaven. 52 They worshiped him and went back into Jerusalem, filled with great joy, 53 and spent all their time in the Temple giving thanks to God.

The **GOSPEL** according to **JOHN**

The Gospel of John is written by the disciple John, referred to in the Gospel itself as **"the one whom Jesus loved."** John was one of the three disciples (including Peter and James) whom Jesus set apart for special teaching and for unique experiences with him. John exhibits tremendous recall to add details not mentioned in the other Gospels. John is of Jewish descent, knows well Jewish customs and is well aware of the hostility between Samaritans and Jews.

Unlike the Synoptic Gospels which follow the story of Jesus chronologically, John's Gospel **reveals the story of Jesus in a more thematic way** with a series of events linked with symbolic proclamations that announce who Jesus is and uncover "signs" of his purpose and mission. John dwells on the connection between Jesus and God the Father and on the glory that is seen through Jesus. A series of **"I am" statements** from Jesus echo the fact that Jesus is God, the I Am of Old Testament Scripture. John clearly states that his Gospel was written so that the reader may know that **Jesus is the Christ, the Son of God,** and that by believing in him the reader may have life in his name.

What's the story?

The opening chapters of John's Gospel focus on the **Word of God being made flesh in Jesus.** Then the Gospel moves directly into a series of miracles (or "signs") that show the reader in a very personal way the identity of Christ. Questions about who Jesus is are scattered throughout this section.

Passion Week makes up the final third of the Gospel with the entry into Jerusalem, Jesus' farewell prayers, the Last Supper with many predictions by Jesus, the journey to Gethsemane with revelations by Christ about the place of his followers in the world, and Jesus' prayer for himself, his disciples and all believers. A descriptive account of Jesus' betrayal and arrest, trials, crucifixion, burial and Resurrection follow, with **references to John taking Jesus' mother Mary into his home** as his own mother, as Jesus asked of him from the Cross. **John is later running to the empty tomb** with Peter on Easter morning, seeing only the grave clothes there.

John ends with the Risen Jesus telling his disciples to tell the world about him. John explains that the "signs" and words in this Gospel were specifically chosen that all might believe in Jesus.

The GOSPEL according to JOHN

Chapter 1
The Word of Life

¹ In the beginning the Word already existed; the Word was with God, and the Word was God. ² From the very beginning the Word was with God. ³ Through him God made all things; not one thing in all creation was made without him. ⁴ The Word was the source of life, and this life brought light to people. ⁵ The light shines in the darkness, and the darkness has never put it out.

⁶ God sent his messenger, a man named John, ⁷ who came to tell people about the light, so that all should hear the message and believe. ⁸ He himself was not the light; he came to tell about the light. ⁹ This was the real light—the light that comes into the world and shines on all people.

¹⁰ The Word was in the world, and though God made the world through him, yet the world did not recognize him. ¹¹ He came to his own country, but his own people did not receive him. ¹² Some, however, did receive him and believed in him; so he gave them the right to become God's children. ¹³ They did not become God's children by natural means, that is, by being born as the children of a human father; God himself was their Father.

¹⁴ The Word became a human being and, full of grace and truth, lived among us. We saw his glory, the glory which he received as the Father's only Son.

¹⁵ John spoke about him. He cried out, "This is the one I was talking about when I said, 'He comes after me, but he is greater than I am, because he existed before I was born.'"

¹⁶ Out of the fullness of his grace he has blessed us all, giving us one blessing after another. ¹⁷ God gave the Law through Moses, but grace and truth came through Jesus Christ. ¹⁸ No one has ever seen God. The only Son, who is the same as God and is at the Father's side, he has made him known.

John the Baptist's Message

¹⁹ The Jewish authorities in Jerusalem sent some priests and Levites to John to ask him, "Who are you?"

²⁰ John did not refuse to answer, but spoke out openly and clearly, saying: "I am not the Messiah."

²¹ "Who are you, then?" they asked. "Are you Elijah?"

"No, I am not," John answered.

"Are you the Prophet?" they asked.

"No," he replied.

²² "Then tell us who you are," they said. "We have to take an answer back to those who sent us. What do you say about yourself?"

²³ John answered by quoting the prophet Isaiah:

"I am 'the voice of someone shouting in the desert:

Make a straight path for the Lord to travel!'"

²⁴ The messengers, who had been sent by the Pharisees, ²⁵ then asked John, "If you are not the Messiah nor Elijah nor the Prophet, why do you baptize?"

²⁶ John answered, "I baptize with water, but among you stands the one you do not know. ²⁷ He is coming after me, but I am not good enough even to untie his sandals."

²⁸ All this happened in Bethany on the east side of the Jordan River, where John was baptizing.

The Lamb of God

²⁹ The next day John saw Jesus coming to him, and said, "There is the Lamb of God, who takes away the sin of the world! ³⁰ This is the one I was talking about when I said, 'A man is coming after me, but he is greater than I am, because he existed be-

Learn more on page 161.

fore I was born.' [31] I did not know who he would be, but I came baptizing with water in order to make him known to the people of Israel."

[32] And John gave this testimony: "I saw the Spirit come down like a dove from heaven and stay on him. [33] I still did not know that he was the one, but God, who sent me to baptize with water, had said to me, 'You will see the Spirit come down and stay on a man; he is the one who baptizes with the Holy Spirit.' [34] I have seen it," said John, "and I tell you that he is the Son of God."

The First Disciples of Jesus

[35] The next day John was standing there again with two of his disciples, [36] when he saw Jesus walking by. "There is the Lamb of God!" he said.

[37] The two disciples heard him say this and went with Jesus. [38] Jesus turned, saw them following him, and asked, "What are you looking for?"

They answered, "Where do you live, Rabbi?" (This word means "Teacher.")

[39] "Come and see," he answered. (It was then about four o'clock in the afternoon.) So they went with him and saw where he lived, and spent the rest of that day with him.

[40] One of them was Andrew, Simon Peter's brother. [41] At once he found his brother Simon and told him, "We have found the Messiah." (This word means "Christ.") [42] Then he took Simon to Jesus.

Jesus looked at him and said, "Your name is Simon son of John, but you will be called Cephas." (This is the same as Peter and means "a rock.")

Jesus Calls Philip and Nathanael

[43] The next day Jesus decided to go to Galilee. He found Philip and said to him, "Come with me!" ([44] Philip was from Bethsaida, the town where Andrew and Peter lived.) [45] Philip found Nathanael and told him, "We have found the one whom Moses wrote about in the book of the Law and whom the prophets also wrote about. He is Jesus son of Joseph, from Nazareth."

[46] "Can anything good come from Nazareth?" Nathanael asked.

"Come and see," answered Philip.

[47] When Jesus saw Nathanael coming to him, he said about him, "Here is a real Israelite; there is nothing false in him!"

[48] Nathanael asked him, "How do you know me?"

Jesus answered, "I saw you when you were under the fig tree before Philip called you."

[49] "Teacher," answered Nathanael, "you are the Son of God! You are the King of Israel!"

[50] Jesus said, "Do you believe just because I told you I saw you when you were under the fig tree? You will see much greater things than this!" [51] And he said to them, "I am telling you the truth: you will see heaven open and God's angels going up and coming down on the Son of Man."

Chapter 2

The Wedding in Cana

[1] Two days later there was a wedding in the town of Cana in Galilee. Jesus' mother was there, [2] and Jesus and his disciples had also been invited to the wedding. [3] When the wine had given out, Jesus' mother said to him, "They are out of wine."

[4] "You must not tell me what to do," Jesus replied. "My time has not yet come."

[5] Jesus' mother then told the servants, "Do whatever he tells you."

[6] The Jews have rules about ritual washing, and for this

Learn more on page 164.

purpose six stone water jars were there, each one large enough to hold between twenty and thirty gallons. ⁷ Jesus said to the servants, "Fill these jars with water." They filled them to the brim, ⁸ and then he told them, "Now draw some water out and take it to the man in charge of the feast." They took him the water, ⁹ which now had turned into wine, and he tasted it. He did not know where this wine had come from (but, of course, the servants who had drawn out the water knew); so he called the bridegroom ¹⁰ and said to him, "Everyone else serves the best wine first, and after the guests have drunk a lot, he serves the ordinary wine. But you have kept the best wine until now!"

¹¹ Jesus performed this first miracle in Cana in Galilee; there he revealed his glory, and his disciples believed in him.

¹² After this, Jesus and his mother, brothers, and disciples went to Capernaum and stayed there a few days.

Jesus Goes to the Temple
¹³ It was almost time for the Passover Festival, so Jesus went to Jerusalem. ¹⁴ There in the Temple he found people selling cattle, sheep, and pigeons, and also the moneychangers sitting at their tables. ¹⁵ So he made a whip from cords and drove all the animals out of the Temple, both the sheep and the cattle; he overturned the tables of the moneychangers and scattered their coins; ¹⁶ and he ordered those who sold the pigeons, "Take them out of here! Stop making my Father's house a marketplace!" ¹⁷ His disciples remembered that the scripture says, "My devotion to your house, O God, burns in me like a fire."

¹⁸ The Jewish authorities came back at him with a question, "What miracle can you perform to show us that you have the right to do this?"

¹⁹ Jesus answered, "Tear down this Temple, and in three days I will build it again."

²⁰ "Are you going to build it again in three days?" they asked him. "It has taken forty-six years to build this Temple!"

²¹ But the temple Jesus was speaking about was his body. ²² So when he was raised from death, his disciples remembered that he had said this, and they believed the scripture and what Jesus had said.

Jesus' Knowledge of Human Nature
²³ While Jesus was in Jerusalem during the Passover Festival, many believed in him as they saw the miracles he performed. ²⁴ But Jesus did not trust himself to them, because he knew them all. ²⁵ There was no need for anyone to tell him about them, because he himself knew what was in their hearts.

Chapter 3
Jesus and Nicodemus
¹ There was a Jewish leader named Nicodemus, who belonged to the party of the Pharisees. ² One night he went to Jesus and said to him, "Rabbi, we know that you are a teacher sent by God. No one could perform the miracles you are doing unless God were with him."

³ Jesus answered, "I am telling you the truth: no one can see the Kingdom of God without being born again."

⁴ "How can a grown man be born again?" Nicodemus asked. "He certainly cannot enter his mother's womb and be born a second time!"

⁵ "I am telling you the truth," replied Jesus, "that no one can enter the Kingdom of God without being born of water and the Spirit. ⁶ A person is born physically of human parents, but is born spiritually of the Spirit. ⁷ Do not be surprised because I tell you that you must all be born again. ⁸ The wind blows wherever it wishes; you hear the sound it makes, but you do not know where it comes from or where it is going. It is like that with everyone who is born of the Spirit."

9 "How can this be?" asked Nicodemus.

10 Jesus answered, "You are a great teacher in Israel, and you don't know this? 11 I am telling you the truth: we speak of what we know and report what we have seen, yet none of you is willing to accept our message. 12 You do not believe me when I tell you about the things of this world; how will you ever believe me, then, when I tell you about the things of heaven? 13 And no one has ever gone up to heaven except the Son of Man, who came down from heaven."

14 As Moses lifted up the bronze snake on a pole in the desert, in the same way the Son of Man must be lifted up, 15 so that everyone who believes in him may have eternal life. 16 For God loved the world so much that he gave his only Son, so that everyone who believes in him may not die but have eternal life. 17 For God did not send his Son into the world to be its judge, but to be its savior.

18 Those who believe in the Son are not judged; but those who do not believe have already been judged, because they have not believed in God's only Son. 19 This is how the judgment works: the light has come into the world, but people love the darkness rather than the light, because their deeds are evil. 20 Those who do evil things hate the light and will not come to the light, because they do not want their evil deeds to be shown up. 21 But those who do what is true come to the light in order that the light may show that what they did was in obedience to God.

Jesus and John

22 After this, Jesus and his disciples went to the province of Judea, where he spent some time with them and baptized. 23 John also was baptizing in Aenon, not far from Salim, because there was plenty of water in that place.

People were going to him, and he was baptizing them. (24 This was before John had been put in prison.)

25 Some of John's disciples began arguing with a Jew about the matter of ritual washing. 26 So they went to John and told him, "Teacher, you remember the man who was with you on the east side of the Jordan, the one you spoke about? Well, he is baptizing now, and everyone is going to him!"

27 John answered, "No one can have anything unless God gives it. 28 You yourselves are my witnesses that I said, 'I am not the Messiah, but I have been sent ahead of him.' 29 The bridegroom is the one to whom the bride belongs; but the bridegroom's friend, who stands by and listens, is glad when he hears the bridegroom's voice. This is how my own happiness is made complete. 30 He must become more important while I become less important."

He Who Comes from Heaven

31 He who comes from above is greater than all. He who is from the earth belongs to the earth and speaks about earthly matters, but he who comes from heaven is above all. 32 He tells what he has seen and heard, yet no one accepts his message. 33 But whoever accepts his message confirms by this that God is truthful. 34 The one whom God has sent speaks God's words, because God gives him the fullness of his Spirit. 35 The Father loves his Son and has put everything in his power. 36 Whoever believes in the Son has eternal life; whoever disobeys the Son will not have life, but will remain under God's punishment.

Chapter 4
Jesus and the Samaritan Woman

1 The Pharisees heard that Jesus was winning and baptizing more disciples than John. (2 Actually, Jesus himself did not baptize anyone; only his disciples did.) 3 So when Jesus heard what was being said, he left Judea and went back to Galilee; 4 on his way there he had to go through Samaria.

5 In Samaria he came to a town named Sychar, which was

not far from the field that Jacob had given to his son Joseph. ⁶ Jacob's well was there, and Jesus, tired out by the trip, sat down by the well. It was about noon.

⁷ A Samaritan woman came to draw some water, and Jesus said to her, "Give me a drink of water." (⁸ His disciples had gone into town to buy food.)

⁹ The woman answered, "You are a Jew, and I am a Samaritan—so how can you ask me for a drink?" (Jews will not use the same cups and bowls that Samaritans use.)

¹⁰ Jesus answered, "If you only knew what God gives and who it is that is asking you for a drink, you would ask him, and he would give you life-giving water."

¹¹ "Sir," the woman said, "you don't have a bucket, and the well is deep. Where would you get that life-giving water? ¹² It was our ancestor Jacob who gave us this well; he and his children and his flocks all drank from it. You don't claim to be greater than Jacob, do you?"

¹³ Jesus answered, "Those who drink this water will get thirsty again, ¹⁴ but those who drink the water that I will give them will never be thirsty again. The water that I will give them will become in them a spring which will provide them with life-giving water and give them eternal life."

¹⁵ "Sir," the woman said, "give me that water! Then I will never be thirsty again, nor will I have to come here to draw water."

¹⁶ "Go and call your husband," Jesus told her, "and come back."

¹⁷ "I don't have a husband," she answered.

Jesus replied, "You are right when you say you don't have a husband. ¹⁸ You have been married to five men, and the man you live with now is not really your husband. You have told me the truth."

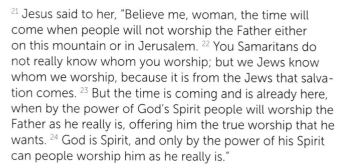

¹⁹ "I see you are a prophet, sir," the woman said.
²⁰ "My Samaritan ancestors worshiped God on this mountain, but you Jews say that Jerusalem is the place where we should worship God."

²¹ Jesus said to her, "Believe me, woman, the time will come when people will not worship the Father either on this mountain or in Jerusalem. ²² You Samaritans do not really know whom you worship; but we Jews know whom we worship, because it is from the Jews that salvation comes. ²³ But the time is coming and is already here, when by the power of God's Spirit people will worship the Father as he really is, offering him the true worship that he wants. ²⁴ God is Spirit, and only by the power of his Spirit can people worship him as he really is."

²⁵ The woman said to him, "I know that the Messiah will come, and when he comes, he will tell us everything."

²⁶ Jesus answered, "I am he, I who am talking with you."

²⁷ At that moment Jesus' disciples returned, and they were greatly surprised to find him talking with a woman. But none of them said to her, "What do you want?" or asked him, "Why are you talking with her?"

²⁸ Then the woman left her water jar, went back to the town, and said to the people there, ²⁹ "Come and see the man who told me everything I have ever done. Could he be the Messiah?" ³⁰ So they left the town and went to Jesus.

³¹ In the meantime the disciples were begging Jesus, "Teacher, have something to eat!"

³² But he answered, "I have food to eat that you know nothing about."

³³ So the disciples started asking among themselves, "Could somebody have brought him food?"

³⁴ "My food," Jesus said to them, "is to obey the will of the one who sent me and to finish the work he gave me to do. ³⁵ You have a saying, 'Four more months and then the

harvest.' But I tell you, take a good look at the fields; the crops are now ripe and ready to be harvested! ³⁶ The one who reaps the harvest is being paid and gathers the crops for eternal life; so the one who plants and the one who reaps will be glad together. ³⁷ For the saying is true, 'Someone plants, someone else reaps.' ³⁸ I have sent you to reap a harvest in a field where you did not work; others worked there, and you profit from their work."

³⁹ Many of the Samaritans in that town believed in Jesus because the woman had said, "He told me everything I have ever done." ⁴⁰ So when the Samaritans came to him, they begged him to stay with them, and Jesus stayed there two days.

⁴¹ Many more believed because of his message, ⁴² and they told the woman, "We believe now, not because of what you said, but because we ourselves have heard him, and we know that he really is the Savior of the world."

Jesus Heals an Official's Son
⁴³ After spending two days there, Jesus left and went to Galilee. ⁴⁴ For he himself had said, "Prophets are not respected in their own country." ⁴⁵ When he arrived in Galilee, the people there welcomed him, because they had gone to the Passover Festival in Jerusalem and had seen everything that he had done during the festival.

⁴⁶ Then Jesus went back to Cana in Galilee, where he had turned the water into wine. A government official was there whose son was sick in Capernaum. ⁴⁷ When he heard that Jesus had come from Judea to Galilee, he went to him and asked him to go to Capernaum and heal his son, who was about to die. ⁴⁸ Jesus said to him, "None of you will ever believe unless you see miracles and wonders."

⁴⁹ "Sir," replied the official, "come with me before my child dies."

⁵⁰ Jesus said to him, "Go; your son will live!"

The man believed Jesus' words and went. ⁵¹ On his way home his servants met him with the news, "Your boy is going to live!"

⁵² He asked them what time it was when his son got better, and they answered, "It was one o'clock yesterday afternoon when the fever left him." ⁵³ Then the father remembered that it was at that very hour when Jesus had told him, "Your son will live." So he and all his family believed.

⁵⁴ This was the second miracle that Jesus performed after coming from Judea to Galilee.

Chapter 5
The Healing at the Pool
¹ After this, Jesus went to Jerusalem for a religious festival. ² Near the Sheep Gate in Jerusalem there is a pool with five porches; in Hebrew it is called Bethzatha. ³ A large crowd of sick people were lying on the porches—the blind, the lame, and the paralyzed. ⁵ A man was there who had been sick for thirty-eight years. ⁶ Jesus saw him lying there, and he knew that the man had been sick for such a long time; so he asked him, "Do you want to get well?"

⁷ The sick man answered, "Sir, I don't have anyone here to put me in the pool when the water is stirred up; while I am trying to get in, somebody else gets there first."

⁸ Jesus said to him, "Get up, pick up your mat, and walk." ⁹ Immediately the man got well; he picked up his mat and started walking.

The day this happened was a Sabbath, ¹⁰ so the Jewish authorities told the man who had been healed, "This is a Sabbath, and it is against our Law for you to carry your mat."

¹¹ He answered, "The man who made me well told me to pick up my mat and walk."

¹² They asked him, "Who is the man who told you to do this?"

¹³ But the man who had been healed did not know who Jesus was, for there was a crowd in that place, and Jesus had slipped away.

¹⁴ Afterward, Jesus found him in the Temple and said, "Listen, you are well now; so stop sinning or something worse may happen to you."

¹⁵ Then the man left and told the Jewish authorities that it was Jesus who had healed him. ¹⁶ So they began to persecute Jesus, because he had done this healing on a Sabbath. ¹⁷ Jesus answered them, "My Father is always working, and I too must work."

¹⁸ This saying made the Jewish authorities all the more determined to kill him; not only had he broken the Sabbath law, but he had said that God was his own Father and in this way had made himself equal with God.

The Authority of the Son

¹⁹ So Jesus answered them, "I tell you the truth: the Son can do nothing on his own; he does only what he sees his Father doing. What the Father does, the Son also does. ²⁰ For the Father loves the Son and shows him all that he himself is doing. He will show him even greater things to do than this, and you will all be amazed. ²¹ Just as the Father raises the dead and gives them life, in the same way the Son gives life to those he wants to. ²² Nor does the Father himself judge anyone. He has given his Son the full right to judge, ²³ so that all will honor the Son in the same way as they honor the Father. Whoever does not honor the Son does not honor the Father who sent him.

²⁴ "I am telling you the truth: those who hear my words and believe in him who sent me have eternal life. They will not be judged, but have already passed from death to life. ²⁵ I am telling you the truth: the time is coming—the time has already come—when the dead will hear the voice of the Son of God, and those who hear it will come to life. ²⁶ Just as the Father is himself the source of life, in the same way he has made his Son to be the source of life.

²⁷ And he has given the Son the right to judge, because he is the Son of Man. ²⁸ Do not be surprised at this; the time is coming when all the dead will hear his voice ²⁹ and come out of their graves: those who have done good will rise and live, and those who have done evil will rise and be condemned.

Witnesses to Jesus

³⁰ "I can do nothing on my own authority; I judge only as God tells me, so my judgment is right, because I am not trying to do what I want, but only what he who sent me wants.

³¹ "If I testify on my own behalf, what I say is not to be accepted as real proof. ³² But there is someone else who testifies on my behalf, and I know that what he says about me is true. ³³ John is the one to whom you sent your messengers, and he spoke on behalf of the truth. ³⁴ It is not that I must have a human witness; I say this only in order that you may be saved. ³⁵ John was like a lamp, burning

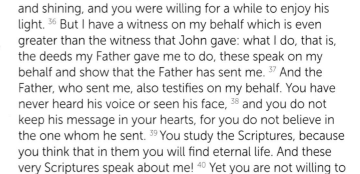

and shining, and you were willing for a while to enjoy his light. ³⁶ But I have a witness on my behalf which is even greater than the witness that John gave: what I do, that is, the deeds my Father gave me to do, these speak on my behalf and show that the Father has sent me. ³⁷ And the Father, who sent me, also testifies on my behalf. You have never heard his voice or seen his face, ³⁸ and you do not keep his message in your hearts, for you do not believe in the one whom he sent. ³⁹ You study the Scriptures, because you think that in them you will find eternal life. And these very Scriptures speak about me! ⁴⁰ Yet you are not willing to come to me in order to have life.

⁴¹ "I am not looking for human praise. ⁴² But I know what kind of people you are, and I know that you have no love for God in your hearts. ⁴³ I have come with my Father's authority, but you have not received me; when, however,

someone comes with his own authority, you will receive him. ⁴⁴ You like to receive praise from one another, but you do not try to win praise from the one who alone is God; how, then, can you believe me? ⁴⁵ Do not think, however, that I am the one who will accuse you to my Father. Moses, in whom you have put your hope, is the very one who will accuse you. ⁴⁶ If you had really believed Moses, you would have believed me, because he wrote about me. ⁴⁷ But since you do not believe what he wrote, how can you believe what I say?"

Chapter 6
Jesus Feeds Five Thousand

¹ After this, Jesus went across Lake Galilee (or, Lake Tiberias, as it is also called). ² A large crowd followed him, because they had seen his miracles of healing the sick. ³ Jesus went up a hill and sat down with his disciples. ⁴ The time for the Passover Festival was near. ⁵ Jesus looked around and saw that a large crowd was coming to him, so he asked Philip, "Where can we buy enough food to feed all these people?" (⁶ He said this to test Philip; actually he already knew what he would do.)

⁷ Philip answered, "For everyone to have even a little, it would take more than two hundred silver coins to buy enough bread."

⁸ Another one of his disciples, Andrew, who was Simon Peter's brother, said, ⁹ "There is a boy here who has five loaves of barley bread and two fish. But they will certainly not be enough for all these people."

¹⁰ "Make the people sit down," Jesus told them. (There was a lot of grass there.) So all the people sat down; there were about five thousand men. ¹¹ Jesus took the bread, gave thanks to God, and distributed it to the people who were sitting there. He did the same with the fish, and they all had as much as they wanted. ¹² When they were all full, he said to his disciples, "Gather the pieces left over; let us not waste a bit." ¹³ So they gathered them all and filled twelve baskets with the pieces left over from the five barley loaves which the people had eaten.

Learn more on page 172.

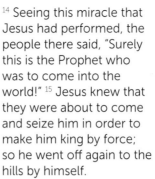
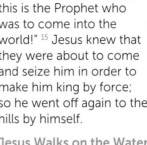

¹⁴ Seeing this miracle that Jesus had performed, the people there said, "Surely this is the Prophet who was to come into the world!" ¹⁵ Jesus knew that they were about to come and seize him in order to make him king by force; so he went off again to the hills by himself.

Jesus Walks on the Water

¹⁶ When evening came, Jesus' disciples went down to the lake, ¹⁷ got into a boat, and went back across the lake toward Capernaum. Night came on, and Jesus still had not come to them. ¹⁸ By then a strong wind was blowing and stirring up the water. ¹⁹ The disciples had rowed about three or four miles when they saw Jesus walking on the water, coming near the boat, and they were terrified. ²⁰ "Don't be afraid," Jesus told them, "it is I!" ²¹ Then they willingly took him into the boat, and immediately the boat reached land at the place they were heading for.

The People Seek Jesus

²² Next day the crowd which had stayed on the other side of the lake realized that there had been only one boat there. They knew that Jesus had not gone in it with his disciples, but that they had left without him. ²³ Other boats, which were from Tiberias, came to shore near the place where the crowd had eaten the bread after the Lord had given thanks. ²⁴ When the crowd saw that Jesus was not there, nor his disciples, they got into those boats and went to Capernaum, looking for him.

Jesus the Bread of Life

²⁵ When the people found Jesus on the other side of the lake, they said to him, "Teacher, when did you get here?"

²⁶ Jesus answered, "I am telling you the truth: you are looking for me because you ate the bread and had all you wanted, not because you understood my miracles. ²⁷ Do

not work for food that spoils; instead, work for the food that lasts for eternal life. This is the food which the Son of Man will give you, because God, the Father, has put his mark of approval on him."

28 So they asked him, "What can we do in order to do what God wants us to do?"

29 Jesus answered, "What God wants you to do is to believe in the one he sent."

30 They replied, "What miracle will you perform so that we may see it and believe you? What will you do? 31 Our ancestors ate manna in the desert, just as the scripture says, 'He gave them bread from heaven to eat.'"

32 "I am telling you the truth," Jesus said. "What Moses gave you was not the bread from heaven; it is my Father who gives you the real bread from heaven. 33 For the bread that God gives is he who comes down from heaven and gives life to the world."

34 "Sir," they asked him, "give us this bread always."

35 "I am the bread of life," Jesus told them. "Those who come to me will never be hungry; those who believe in me will never be thirsty. 36 Now, I told you that you have seen me but will not believe. 37 Everyone whom my Father gives me will come to me. I will never turn away anyone who comes to me, 38 because I have come down from heaven to do not my own will but the will of him who sent me. 39 And it is the will of him who sent me that I should not lose any of all those he has given me, but that I should raise them all to life on the last day. 40 For what my Father wants is that all who see the Son and believe in him should have eternal life. And I will raise them to life on the last day."

41 The people started grumbling about him, because he said, "I am the bread that came down from heaven." 42 So they said, "This man is Jesus son of Joseph, isn't he? We know his father and mother. How, then, does he now say he came down from heaven?"

43 Jesus answered, "Stop grumbling among yourselves.

44 People cannot come to me unless the Father who sent me draws them to me; and I will raise them to life on the last day. 45 The prophets wrote, 'Everyone will be taught by God.' Anyone who hears the Father and learns from him comes to me. 46 This does not mean that anyone has seen the Father; he who is from God is the only one who has seen the Father. 47 I am telling you the truth: he who believes has eternal life. 48 I am the bread of life. 49 Your ancestors ate manna in the desert, but they died. 50 But the bread that comes down from heaven is of such a kind that whoever eats it will not die. 51 I am the living bread that came down from heaven. If you eat this bread, you will live forever. The bread that I will give you is my flesh, which I give so that the world may live."

52 This started an angry argument among them. "How can this man give us his flesh to eat?" they asked.

53 Jesus said to them, "I am telling you the truth: if you do not eat the flesh of the Son of Man and drink his blood, you will not have life in yourselves. 54 Those who eat my flesh and drink my blood have eternal life, and I will raise them to life on the last day. 55 For my flesh is the real food; my blood is the real drink. 56 Those who eat my flesh and drink my blood live in me, and I live in them. 57 The living Father sent me, and because of him I live also. In the same way whoever eats me will live because of me. 58 This, then, is the bread that came down from heaven; it is not like the bread that your ancestors ate, but then later died. Those who eat this bread will live forever."

59 Jesus said this as he taught in the synagogue in Capernaum.

The Words of Eternal Life
60 Many of his followers heard this and said, "This teaching is too hard. Who can listen to it?"

61 Without being told, Jesus knew that they were grumbling about this, so he said to them, "Does this make you want to give up? 62 Suppose, then, that you should see

the Son of Man go back up to the place where he was before? ⁶³ What gives life is God's Spirit; human power is of no use at all. The words I have spoken to you bring God's life-giving Spirit. ⁶⁴ Yet some of you do not believe." (Jesus knew from the very beginning who were the ones that would not believe and which one would betray him.) ⁶⁵ And he added, "This is the very reason I told you that no people can come to me unless the Father makes it possible for them to do so."

⁶⁶ Because of this, many of Jesus' followers turned back and would not go with him any more. ⁶⁷ So he asked the twelve disciples, "And you—would you also like to leave?"

⁶⁸ Simon Peter answered him, "Lord, to whom would we go? You have the words that give eternal life. ⁶⁹ And now we believe and know that you are the Holy One who has come from God."

⁷⁰ Jesus replied, "I chose the twelve of you, didn't I? Yet one of you is a devil!" ⁷¹ He was talking about Judas, the son of Simon Iscariot. For Judas, even though he was one of the twelve disciples, was going to betray him.

Chapter 7
Jesus and His Brothers
¹ After this, Jesus traveled in Galilee; he did not want to travel in Judea, because the Jewish authorities there were wanting to kill him. ² The time for the Festival of Shelters was near, ³ so Jesus' brothers said to him, "Leave this place and go to Judea, so that your followers will see the things that you are doing. ⁴ People don't hide what they are doing if they want to be well known. Since you are doing these things, let the whole world know about you!" (⁵ Not even his brothers believed in him.)

⁶ Jesus said to them, "The right time for me has not yet come. Any time is right for you. ⁷ The world cannot hate you, but it hates me, because I keep telling it that its ways are bad. ⁸ You go on to the festival. I am not going to this festival, because the right time has not come for me." ⁹ He said this and then stayed on in Galilee.

Jesus at the Festival of Shelters
¹⁰ After his brothers had gone to the festival, Jesus also went; however, he did not go openly, but secretly. ¹¹ The Jewish authorities were looking for him at the festival. "Where is he?" they asked.

¹² There was much whispering about him in the crowd. "He is a good man," some people said. "No," others said, "he fools the people." ¹³ But no one talked about him openly, because they were afraid of the Jewish authorities.

¹⁴ The festival was nearly half over when Jesus went to the Temple and began teaching. ¹⁵ The Jewish authorities were greatly surprised and said, "How does this man know so much when he has never been to school?"

¹⁶ Jesus answered, "What I teach is not my own teaching, but it comes from God, who sent me. ¹⁷ Whoever is willing to do what God wants will know whether what I teach comes from God or whether I speak on my own authority. ¹⁸ Those who speak on their own authority are trying to gain glory for themselves. But he who wants glory for the one who sent him is honest, and there is nothing false in him. ¹⁹ Moses gave you the Law, didn't he? But not one of you obeys the Law. Why are you trying to kill me?"

²⁰ "You have a demon in you!" the crowd answered. "Who is trying to kill you?"

²¹ Jesus answered, "I performed one miracle, and you were all surprised. ²² Moses ordered you to circumcise your sons (although it was not Moses but your ancestors who started it), and so you circumcise a boy on the Sabbath. ²³ If a boy is circumcised on the Sabbath so that Moses' Law is not broken, why are you angry with me because I made a man completely well on the Sabbath? ²⁴ Stop judging by external standards, and judge by true standards."

Is He the Messiah?
²⁵ Some of the people of Jerusalem said, "Isn't this the man the authorities are trying to kill? ²⁶ Look! He is talking in public, and they say nothing against him! Can it be that

they really know that he is the Messiah? [27] But when the Messiah comes, no one will know where he is from. And we all know where this man comes from."

[28] As Jesus taught in the Temple, he said in a loud voice, "Do you really know me and know where I am from? I

have not come on my own authority. He who sent me, however, is truthful. You do not know him, [29] but I know him, because I come from him and he sent me."

[30] Then they tried to seize him, but no one laid a hand on him, because his hour had not yet come. [31] But many in the crowd believed in him and said, "When the Messiah comes, will he perform more miracles than this man has?"

Guards Are Sent to Arrest Jesus
[32] The Pharisees heard the crowd whispering these things about Jesus, so they and the chief priests sent some guards to arrest him. [33] Jesus said, "I shall be with you a little while longer, and then I shall go away to him who sent me. [34] You will look for me, but you will not find me, because you cannot go where I will be."

[35] The Jewish authorities said among themselves, "Where is he about to go so that we shall not find him? Will he go to the Greek cities where our people live, and teach the Greeks? [36] He says that we will look for him but will not find him, and that we cannot go where he will be. What does he mean?"

Streams of Life-Giving Water
[37] On the last and most important day of the festival Jesus stood up and said in a loud voice, "Whoever is thirsty should come to me, and [38] whoever believes in me should drink. As the scripture says, 'Streams of life-giving water will pour out from his side.'" [39] Jesus said this about the Spirit,

which those who believed in him were going to receive. At that time the Spirit had not yet been given, because Jesus had not been raised to glory.

Division Among the People
[40] Some of the people in the crowd heard him say this and said, "This man is really the Prophet!"

[41] Others said, "He is the Messiah!"

But others said, "The Messiah will not come from Galilee! [42] The scripture says that the Messiah will be a descendant of King David and will be born in Bethlehem, the town where David lived." [43] So there was a division in the crowd because of Jesus. [44] Some wanted to seize him, but no one laid a hand on him.

The Unbelief of the Jewish Authorities
[45] When the guards went back, the chief priests and Pharisees asked them, "Why did you not bring him?"

[46] The guards answered, "Nobody has ever talked the way this man does!"

[47] "Did he fool you, too?" the Pharisees asked them. [48] "Have you ever known one of the authorities or one Pharisee to believe in him? [49] This crowd does not know the Law of Moses, so they are under God's curse!"

[50] One of the Pharisees there was Nicodemus, the man who had gone to see Jesus before. He said to the others, [51] "According to our Law we cannot condemn people before hearing them and finding out what they have done."

[52] "Well," they answered, "are you also from Galilee? Study the Scriptures and you will learn that no prophet ever comes from Galilee."

Chapter 8
The Woman Caught in Adultery
[1] Then everyone went home, but Jesus went to the Mount of Olives. [2] Early the next morning he went back to the Temple. All the people gathered around him, and he sat down and began to teach them. [3] The teachers of the Law

and the Pharisees brought in a woman who had been caught committing adultery, and they made her stand before them all. ⁴ "Teacher," they said to Jesus, "this woman was caught in the very act of committing adultery. ⁵ In our Law Moses commanded that such a woman must be stoned to death. Now, what do you say?" ⁶ They said this to trap Jesus, so that they could accuse him. But he bent over and wrote on the ground with his finger. ⁷ As they stood there asking him questions, he straightened up and said to them, "Whichever one of you has committed no sin may throw the first stone at her." ⁸ Then he bent over again and wrote on the ground. ⁹ When they heard this, they all left, one by one, the older ones first. Jesus was left alone, with the woman still standing there. ¹⁰ He straightened up and said to her, "Where are they? Is there no one left to condemn you?"

¹¹ "No one, sir," she answered.

"Well, then," Jesus said, "I do not condemn you either. Go, but do not sin again."

Jesus the Light of the World
¹² Jesus spoke to the Pharisees again. "I am the light of the world," he said. "Whoever follows me will have the light of life and will never walk in darkness."

¹³ The Pharisees said to him, "Now you are testifying on your own behalf; what you say proves nothing."

¹⁴ "No," Jesus answered, "even though I do testify on my own behalf, what I say is true, because I know where I came from and where I am going. You do not know where I came from or where I am going. ¹⁵ You make judgments in a purely human way; I pass judgment on no one. ¹⁶ But if I were to do so, my judgment would be true, because I am not alone in this; the Father who sent me is with me. ¹⁷ It is written in your Law that when two witnesses agree, what they say is true. ¹⁸ I testify on my own behalf, and the Father who sent me also testifies on my behalf."

¹⁹ "Where is your father?" they asked him.

"You know neither me nor my Father," Jesus answered. "If you knew me, you would know my Father also."

²⁰ Jesus said all this as he taught in the Temple, in the room where the offering boxes were placed. And no one arrested him, because his hour had not come.

You Cannot Go Where I Am Going
²¹ Again Jesus said to them, "I will go away; you will look for me, but you will die in your sins. You cannot go where I am going."

²² So the Jewish authorities said, "He says that we cannot go where he is going. Does this mean that he will kill himself?"

²³ Jesus answered, "You belong to this world here below, but I come from above. You are from this world, but I am not from this world. ²⁴ That is why I told you that you will die in your sins. And you will die in your sins if you do not believe that 'I Am Who I Am'."

²⁵ "Who are you?" they asked him.

Jesus answered, "What I have told you from the very beginning. ²⁶ I have much to say about you, much to condemn you for. The one who sent me, however, is truthful, and I tell the world only what I have heard from him."

²⁷ They did not understand that Jesus was talking to them about the Father. ²⁸ So he said to them, "When you lift up the Son of Man, you will know that 'I Am Who I Am'; then you will know that I do nothing on my own authority, but I say only what the Father has instructed me to say. ²⁹ And he who sent me is with me; he has not left me

alone, because I always do what pleases him."

30 Many who heard Jesus say these things believed in him.

The Truth Will Set You Free

31 So Jesus said to those who believed in him, "If you obey my teaching, you are really my disciples; 32 you will know the truth, and the truth will set you free."

33 "We are the descendants of Abraham," they answered, "and we have never been anybody's slaves. What do you mean, then, by saying, 'You will be free'?"

34 Jesus said to them, "I am telling you the truth: everyone who sins is a slave of sin. 35 A slave does not belong to a family permanently, but a son belongs there forever. 36 If the Son sets you free, then you will be really free. 37 I know you are Abraham's descendants. Yet you are trying to kill me, because you will not accept my teaching. 38 I talk about what my Father has shown me, but you do what your father has told you."

39 They answered him, "Our father is Abraham."

"If you really were Abraham's children," Jesus replied, "you would do the same things that he did. 40 All I have ever done is to tell you the truth I heard from God, yet you are trying to kill me. Abraham did nothing like this! 41 You are doing what your father did."

"God himself is the only Father we have," they answered, "and we are his true children."

42 Jesus said to them, "If God really were your Father, you would love me, because I came from God and now I am here. I did not come on my own authority, but he sent me. 43 Why do you not understand what I say? It is because you cannot bear to listen to my message. 44 You are the children of your father, the Devil, and you want to follow your father's desires. From the very beginning he was a murderer and has never been on the side of truth, because there is no truth in him. When he tells a lie, he is only doing what is natural to him, because he is a liar and the father of all lies. 45 But I tell the truth, and

that is why you do not believe me. 46 Which one of you can prove that I am guilty of sin? If I tell the truth, then why do you not believe me? 47 He who comes from God listens to God's words. You, however, are not from God, and that is why you will not listen."

Jesus and Abraham

48 They asked Jesus, "Were we not right in saying that you are a Samaritan and have a demon in you?"

49 "I have no demon," Jesus answered. "I honor my Father, but you dishonor me. 50 I am not seeking honor for myself. But there is one who is seeking it and who judges in my favor. 51 I am telling you the truth: whoever obeys my teaching will never die."

52 They said to him, "Now we know for sure that you have a demon! Abraham died, and the prophets died, yet you say that whoever obeys your teaching will never die. 53 Our father Abraham died; you do not claim to be greater than Abraham, do you? And the prophets also died. Who do you think you are?"

54 Jesus answered, "If I were to honor myself, that honor would be worth nothing. The one who honors me is my Father—the very one you say is your God. 55 You have never known him, but I know him. If I were to say that I do not know him, I would be a liar like you. But I do know him, and I obey his word. 56 Your father Abraham rejoiced that he was to see the time of my coming; he saw it and was glad."

57 They said to him, "You are not even fifty years old—and you have seen Abraham?"

58 "I am telling you the truth," Jesus replied. "Before Abraham was born, 'I Am'."

59 Then they picked up stones to throw at him, but Jesus hid himself and left the Temple.

Chapter 9
Jesus Heals a Man Born Blind

1 As Jesus was walking along, he saw a man who had

Learn more on page 179.

been born blind. ² His disciples asked him, "Teacher, whose sin caused him to be born blind? Was it his own or his parents' sin?"

³ Jesus answered, "His blindness has nothing to do with his sins or his parents' sins. He is blind so that God's power might be seen at work in him. ⁴ As long as it is day, we must do the work of him who sent me; night is coming when no one can work. ⁵ While I am in the world, I am the light for the world."

⁶ After he said this, Jesus spat on the ground and made some mud with the spittle; he rubbed the mud on the man's eyes ⁷ and told him, "Go and wash your face in the Pool of Siloam." (This name means "Sent.") So the man went, washed his face, and came back seeing.

⁸ His neighbors, then, and the people who had seen him begging before this, asked, "Isn't this the man who used to sit and beg?"

⁹ Some said, "He is the one," but others said, "No he isn't; he just looks like him."

So the man himself said, "I am the man."

¹⁰ "How is it that you can now see?" they asked him.

¹¹ He answered, "The man called Jesus made some mud, rubbed it on my eyes, and told me to go to Siloam and wash my face. So I went, and as soon as I washed, I could see."

¹² "Where is he?" they asked.

"I don't know," he answered.

The Pharisees Investigate the Healing

¹³ Then they took to the Pharisees the man who had been blind. ¹⁴ The day that Jesus made the mud and cured him of his blindness was a Sabbath. ¹⁵ The Pharisees, then, asked the man again how he had received his sight. He told them, "He put some mud on my eyes; I washed my face, and now I can see."

¹⁶ Some of the Pharisees said, "The man who did this cannot be from God, for he does not obey the Sabbath law."

Others, however, said, "How could a man who is a sinner perform such miracles as these?" And there was a division among them.

¹⁷ So the Pharisees asked the man once more, "You say he cured you of your blindness—well, what do you say about him?"

"He is a prophet," the man answered.

¹⁸ The Jewish authorities, however, were not willing to believe that he had been blind and could now see, until they called his parents ¹⁹ and asked them, "Is this your son? You say that he was born blind; how is it, then, that he can now see?"

²⁰ His parents answered, "We know that he is our son, and we know that he was born blind. ²¹ But we do not know how it is that he is now able to see, nor do we know who cured him of his blindness. Ask him; he is old enough, and he can answer for himself!" ²² His parents said this because they were afraid of the Jewish authorities, who had already agreed that anyone who said he believed that Jesus was the Messiah would be expelled from the synagogue. ²³ That is why his parents said, "He is old enough; ask him!"

²⁴ A second time they called back the man who had been born blind, and said to him, "Promise before God that you will tell the truth! We know that this man who cured you is a sinner."

²⁵ "I do not know if he is a sinner or not," the man replied. "One thing I do know: I was blind, and now I see."

²⁶ "What did he do to you?" they asked. "How did he cure you of your blindness?"

27 "I have already told you," he answered, "and you would not listen. Why do you want to hear it again? Maybe you, too, would like to be his disciples?"

28 They insulted him and said, "You are that fellow's disciple; but we are Moses' disciples. 29 We know that God spoke to Moses; as for that fellow, however, we do not even know where he comes from!"

30 The man answered, "What a strange thing that is! You do not know where he comes from, but he cured me of my blindness! 31 We know that God does not listen to sinners; he does listen to people who respect him and do what he wants them to do. 32 Since the beginning of the world nobody has ever heard of anyone giving sight to a person born blind. 33 Unless this man came from God, he would not be able to do a thing."

34 They answered, "You were born and brought up in sin—and you are trying to teach us?" And they expelled him from the synagogue.

Spiritual Blindness

35 When Jesus heard what had happened, he found the man and asked him, "Do you believe in the Son of Man?"

36 The man answered, "Tell me who he is, sir, so that I can believe in him!"

37 Jesus said to him, "You have already seen him, and he is the one who is talking with you now."

38 "I believe, Lord!" the man said, and knelt down before Jesus.

39 Jesus said, "I came to this world to judge, so that the blind should see and those who see should become blind."

40 Some Pharisees who were there with him heard him say this and asked him, "Surely you don't mean that we are blind, too?"

41 Jesus answered, "If you were blind, then you would not be guilty; but since you claim that you can see, this means that you are still guilty."

Chapter 10
The Parable of the Shepherd

1 Jesus said, "I am telling you the truth: the man who does not enter the sheep pen by the gate, but climbs in some other way, is a thief and a robber. 2 The man who goes in through the gate is the shepherd of the sheep. 3 The gatekeeper opens the gate for him; the sheep hear his voice as he calls his own sheep by name, and he leads them out. 4 When he has brought them out, he goes ahead of them, and the sheep follow him, because they know his voice. 5 They will not follow someone else; instead, they will run away from such a person, because they do not know his voice."

6 Jesus told them this parable, but they did not understand what he meant.

Jesus the Good Shepherd

7 So Jesus said again, "I am telling you the truth: I am the gate for the sheep. 8 All others who came before me are thieves and robbers, but the sheep did not listen to them. 9 I am the gate. Those who come in by me will be saved; they will come in and go out and find pasture. 10 The thief comes only in order to steal, kill, and destroy. I have come in order that you might have life—life in all its fullness.

11 "I am the good shepherd, who is willing to die for the sheep. 12 When the hired man, who is not a shepherd and does not own the sheep, sees a wolf coming, he leaves the sheep and runs away; so the wolf snatches the sheep and scatters them. 13 The hired man runs away because he is only a hired man and does not care about the sheep. 14-15 I am

the good shepherd. As the Father knows me and I know the Father, in the same way I know my sheep and they know me. And I am willing to die for them. [16] There are other sheep which belong to me that are not in this sheep pen. I must bring them, too; they will listen to my voice, and they will become one flock with one shepherd.

[17] "The Father loves me because I am willing to give up my life, in order that I may receive it back again. [18] No one takes my life away from me. I give it up of my own free will. I have the right to give it up, and I have the right to take it back. This is what my Father has commanded me to do."

[19] Again there was a division among the people because of these words. [20] Many of them were saying, "He has a demon! He is crazy! Why do you listen to him?"

[21] But others were saying, "A man with a demon could not talk like this! How could a demon give sight to blind people?"

Jesus Is Rejected

[22] It was winter, and the Festival of the Dedication of the Temple was being celebrated in Jerusalem. [23] Jesus was walking in Solomon's Porch in the Temple, [24] when the people gathered around him and asked, "How long are you going to keep us in suspense? Tell us the plain truth: are you the Messiah?"

[25] Jesus answered, "I have already told you, but you would not believe me. The deeds I do by my Father's authority speak on my behalf; [26] but you will not believe, for you are not my sheep. [27] My sheep listen to my voice; I know them, and they follow me. [28] I give them eternal life, and they shall never die. No one can snatch them away from me. [29] What my Father has given me is greater than everything, and no one can snatch them away from the Father's care. [30] The Father and I are one."

[31] Then the people again picked up stones to throw at him. [32] Jesus said to them, "I have done many good deeds in your presence which the Father gave me to do; for

which one of these do you want to stone me?"

[33] They answered, "We do not want to stone you because of any good deeds, but because of your blasphemy! You are only a man, but you are trying to make yourself God!"

[34] Jesus answered, "It is written in your own Law that God said, 'You are gods.' [35] We know that what the scripture says is true forever; and God called those people gods, the people to whom his message was given. [36] As for me, the Father chose me and sent me into the world. How, then, can you say that I blaspheme because I said that I am the Son of God? [37] Do not believe me, then, if I am not doing the things my Father wants me to do. [38] But if I do them, even though you do not believe me, you should at least believe my deeds, in order that you may know once and for all that the Father is in me and that I am in the Father."

[39] Once more they tried to seize Jesus, but he slipped out of their hands.

[40] Jesus then went back again across the Jordan River to the place where John had been baptizing, and he stayed there. [41] Many people came to him. "John performed no miracles," they said, "but everything he said about this man was true." [42] And many people there believed in him.

Chapter 11

The Death of Lazarus

[1] A man named Lazarus, who lived in Bethany, became sick. Bethany was the town where Mary and her sister Martha lived. ([2] This Mary was the one who poured the perfume on the Lord's feet and wiped them with her hair; it was her brother Lazarus who was sick.) [3] The sisters sent Jesus a message: "Lord, your dear friend is sick."

[4] When Jesus heard it, he said, "The final result of this sickness will not be the death of Lazarus; this has happened in order to bring glory to God, and it will be the means by which the Son of God will receive glory."

[5] Jesus loved Martha and her sister and Lazarus. [6] Yet when he received the news that Lazarus was sick, he

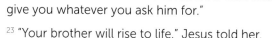

stayed where he was for two more days. 7 Then he said to the disciples, "Let us go back to Judea."

8 "Teacher," the disciples answered, "just a short time ago the people there wanted to stone you; and are you planning to go back?"

9 Jesus said, "A day has twelve hours, doesn't it? So those who walk in broad daylight do not stumble, for they see the light of this world. 10 But if they walk during the night they stumble, because they have no light." 11 Jesus said this and then added, "Our friend Lazarus has fallen asleep, but I will go and wake him up."

12 The disciples answered, "If he is asleep, Lord, he will get well."

13 Jesus meant that Lazarus had died, but they thought he meant natural sleep. 14 So Jesus told them plainly, "Lazarus is dead, 15 but for your sake I am glad that I was not with him, so that you will believe. Let us go to him."

16 Thomas (called the Twin) said to his fellow disciples, "Let us all go along with the Teacher, so that we may die with him!"

Jesus the Resurrection and the Life

17 When Jesus arrived, he found that Lazarus had been buried four days before. 18 Bethany was less than two miles from Jerusalem, 19 and many Judeans had come to see Martha and Mary to comfort them about their brother's death.

20 When Martha heard that Jesus was coming, she went out to meet him, but Mary stayed in the house. 21 Martha said to Jesus, "If you had been here, Lord, my brother would not

Learn more on page 188.

have died! 22 But I know that even now God will give you whatever you ask him for."

23 "Your brother will rise to life," Jesus told her.

24 "I know," she replied, "that he will rise to life on the last day."

25 Jesus said to her, "I am the resurrection and the life. Those who believe in me will live, even though they die; 26 and those who live and believe in me will never die. Do you believe this?"

27 "Yes, Lord!" she answered. "I do believe that you are the Messiah, the Son of God, who was to come into the world."

Jesus Weeps

28 After Martha said this, she went back and called her sister Mary privately. "The Teacher is here," she told her, "and is asking for you." 29 When Mary heard this, she got up and hurried out to meet him. (30 Jesus had not yet arrived in the village, but was still in the place where Martha had met him.) 31 The people who were in the house with Mary comforting her followed her when they saw her get up and hurry out. They thought that she was going to the grave to weep there.

32 Mary arrived where Jesus was, and as soon as she saw him, she fell at his feet. "Lord," she said, "if you had been here, my brother would not have died!"

33 Jesus saw her weeping, and he saw how the people with her were weeping also; his heart was touched, and he was deeply moved. 34 "Where have you buried him?" he asked them.

"Come and see, Lord," they answered.

35 Jesus wept. 36 "See how much he loved him!" the people said.

37 But some of them said, "He gave sight to the blind man, didn't he? Could he not have kept Lazarus from dying?"

Lazarus Is Brought to Life

38 Deeply moved once more, Jesus went to the tomb, which was a cave with a stone placed at the entrance. 39 "Take the stone away!" Jesus ordered.

Martha, the dead man's sister, answered, "There will be a bad smell, Lord. He has been buried four days!"

40 Jesus said to her, "Didn't I tell you that you would see God's glory if you believed?" 41 They took the stone away. Jesus looked up and said, "I thank you, Father, that you listen to me. 42 I know that you always listen to me, but I say this for the sake of the people here, so that they will believe that you sent me." 43 After he had said this, he called out in a loud voice, "Lazarus, come out!" 44 He came out, his hands and feet wrapped in grave cloths, and with a cloth around his face. "Untie him," Jesus told them, "and let him go."

The Plot against Jesus

45 Many of the people who had come to visit Mary saw what Jesus did, and they believed in him. 46 But some of them returned to the Pharisees and told them what Jesus had done. 47 So the Pharisees and the chief priests met with the Council and said, "What shall we do? Look at all the miracles this man is performing! 48 If we let him go on in this way, everyone will believe in him, and the Roman authorities will take action and destroy our Temple and our nation!"

49 One of them, named Caiaphas, who was High Priest that year, said, "What fools you are! 50 Don't you realize that it is better for you to have one man die for the people, instead of having the whole nation destroyed?" 51 Actually, he did not say this of his own accord; rather, as he was High Priest that year, he was prophesying that Jesus was going to die for the Jewish people, 52 and not only for them, but also to bring together into one body all the scattered people of God.

53 From that day on the Jewish authorities made plans to kill Jesus. 54 So Jesus did not travel openly in Judea, but left and went to a place near the desert, to a town named Ephraim, where he stayed with the disciples.

55 The time for the Passover Festival was near, and many people went up from the country to Jerusalem to perform the ritual of purification before the festival. 56 They were looking for Jesus, and as they gathered in the Temple, they asked one another, "What do you think? Surely he will not come to the festival, will he?" 57 The chief priests and the Pharisees had given orders that if anyone knew where Jesus was, he must report it, so that they could arrest him.

Chapter 12

Jesus Is Anointed at Bethany

1 Six days before the Passover, Jesus went to Bethany, the home of Lazarus, the man he had raised from death. 2 They prepared a dinner for him there, which Martha helped serve; Lazarus was one of those who were sitting at the table with Jesus. 3 Then Mary took a whole pint of a very expensive perfume made of pure nard, poured it on Jesus' feet, and wiped them with her hair. The sweet smell of the perfume filled the whole house. 4 One of Jesus' disciples, Judas Iscariot—the one who was going to betray him—said, 5 "Why wasn't this perfume sold for three hundred silver coins and the money given to the poor?" 6 He said this, not because he cared about the poor, but because he was a thief. He carried the money bag and would help himself from it.

7 But Jesus said, "Leave her alone! Let her keep what she has for the day of my burial. 8 You will always have poor people with you, but you will not always have me."

The Plot Against Lazarus

9 A large number of people heard that Jesus was in Bethany, so they went there, not only because of Jesus but also to see Lazarus, whom Jesus had raised from death. 10 So the chief priests made plans to kill Lazarus too, 11 because on his account many Jews were rejecting them and believing in Jesus.

The Triumphant Entry into Jerusalem

¹² The next day the large crowd that had come to the Passover Festival heard that Jesus was coming to Jerusalem. ¹³ So they took branches of palm trees and went out to meet him, shouting, "Praise God! God bless him who comes in the name of the Lord! God bless the King of Israel!"

¹⁴ Jesus found a donkey and rode on it, just as the scripture says,

¹⁵ "Do not be afraid, city of Zion!
    Here comes your king,
    riding on a young donkey."

¹⁶ His disciples did not understand this at the time; but when Jesus had been raised to glory, they remembered that the scripture said this about him and that they had done this for him.

¹⁷ The people who had been with Jesus when he called Lazarus out of the grave and raised him from death had reported what had happened. ¹⁸ That was why the crowd met him—because they heard that he had performed this miracle. ¹⁹ The Pharisees then said to one another, "You see, we are not succeeding at all! Look, the whole world is following him!"

Some Greeks Seek Jesus

²⁰ Some Greeks were among those who had gone to Jerusalem to worship during the festival. ²¹ They went to Philip (he was from Bethsaida in Galilee) and said, "Sir, we want to see Jesus."

²² Philip went and told Andrew, and the two of them went and told Jesus. ²³ Jesus answered them, "The hour has now come for the Son of Man to receive great glory. ²⁴ I am telling you the truth: a grain of wheat remains no more than a single grain unless it is dropped into the ground and dies. If it does die, then it produces many grains. ²⁵ Those who love their own life will lose it; those who hate their own life in this world will keep it for life eternal. ²⁶ Whoever wants to serve me must follow me, so that my servant will be with me where I am. And my Father will honor anyone who serves me.

Jesus Speaks about His Death

²⁷ "Now my heart is troubled—and what shall I say? Shall I say, 'Father, do not let this hour come upon me'? But that is why I came—so that I might go through this hour of suffering. ²⁸ Father, bring glory to your name!"

Then a voice spoke from heaven, "I have brought glory to it, and I will do so again."

²⁹ The crowd standing there heard the voice, and some of them said it was thunder, while others said, "An angel spoke to him!"

³⁰ But Jesus said to them, "It was not for my sake that this voice spoke, but for yours. ³¹ Now is the time for this world to be judged; now the ruler of this world will be overthrown. ³² When I am lifted up from the earth, I will draw everyone to me." (³³ In saying this he indicated the kind of death he was going to suffer.)

³⁴ The crowd answered, "Our Law tells us that the Messiah will live forever. How, then, can you say that the Son of Man must be lifted up? Who is this Son of Man?"

³⁵ Jesus answered, "The light will be among you a little longer. Continue on your way while you have the light, so that the darkness will not come upon you; for the one who walks in the dark does not know where he is going. ³⁶ Believe in the light, then, while you have it, so that you will be the people of the light."

The Unbelief of the People

After Jesus said this, he went off and hid himself from them. ³⁷ Even though he had performed all these miracles

in their presence, they did not believe in him, [38] so that what the prophet Isaiah had said might come true:

"Lord, who believed the message we told?
To whom did the Lord reveal his power?"

[39] And so they were not able to believe, because Isaiah also said,

[40] "God has blinded their eyes
and closed their minds,
so that their eyes would not see,
and their minds would not understand,
and they would not turn to me, says God,
for me to heal them."

[41] Isaiah said this because he saw Jesus' glory and spoke about him.

[42] Even then, many Jewish authorities believed in Jesus; but because of the Pharisees they did not talk about it openly, so as not to be expelled from the synagogue. [43] They loved human approval rather than the approval of God.

Judgment by Jesus' Words

[44] Jesus said in a loud voice, "Whoever believes in me believes not only in me but also in him who sent me. [45] Whoever sees me sees also him who sent me. [46] I have come into the world as light, so that everyone who believes in me should not remain in the darkness. [47] If people hear my message and do not obey it, I will not judge them. I came, not to judge the world, but to save it. [48] Those who reject me and do not accept my message have one who will judge them. The words I have spoken will be their judge on the last day! [49] This is true, because I have not spoken on my own authority, but the Father who sent me has commanded me what I must say and speak. [50] And I know that his command brings eternal life. What I say, then, is what the Father has told me to say."

Chapter 13

Jesus Washes His Disciples' Feet

[1] It was now the day before the Passover Festival. Jesus knew that the hour had come for him to leave this world and go to the Father. He had always loved those in the world who were his own, and he loved them to the very end.

[2] Jesus and his disciples were at supper. The Devil had already put into the heart of Judas, the son of Simon Iscariot, the thought of betraying Jesus. [3] Jesus knew that the Father had given him complete power; he knew that he had come from God and was going to God. [4] So he rose from the table, took off his outer garment, and tied a towel around his waist. [5] Then he poured some water into a washbasin and began to wash the disciples' feet and dry them with the towel around his waist. [6] He came to Simon Peter, who said to him, "Are you going to wash my feet, Lord?"

[7] Jesus answered him, "You do not understand now what I am doing, but you will understand later."

[8] Peter declared, "Never at any time will you wash my feet!"

"If I do not wash your feet," Jesus answered, "you will no longer be my disciple."

[9] Simon Peter answered, "Lord, do not wash only my feet, then! Wash my hands and head, too!"

[10] Jesus said, "Those who have taken a bath are completely clean and do not have to wash themselves, except for their feet. All of you are clean—all except one." ([11] Jesus already knew who was going to betray him; that is why he said, "All of you, except one, are clean.")

[12] After Jesus had washed their feet, he put his outer garment back on and returned to his place at the table. "Do you understand what I have just done to you?" he asked. [13] "You call me Teacher and Lord, and it is right that you do so, because that is what I am. [14] I, your Lord and Teacher, have just washed your feet. You, then, should wash one another's feet. [15] I have set an example for you,

so that you will do just what I have done for you. ¹⁶ I am telling you the truth: no slaves are greater than their master, and no messengers are greater than the one who sent them. ¹⁷ Now that you know this truth, how happy you will be if you put it into practice!

¹⁸ "I am not talking about all of you; I know those I have chosen. But the scripture must come true that says, 'The man who shared my food turned against me.' ¹⁹ I tell you this now before it happens, so that when it does happen, you will believe that 'I Am Who I Am.'

²⁰ I am telling you the truth: whoever receives anyone I send receives me also; and whoever receives me receives him who sent me."

Jesus Predicts His Betrayal

²¹ After Jesus had said this, he was deeply troubled and declared openly, "I am telling you the truth: one of you is going to betray me."

²² The disciples looked at one another, completely puzzled about whom he meant. ²³ One of the disciples, the one whom Jesus loved, was sitting next to Jesus. ²⁴ Simon Peter motioned to him and said, "Ask him whom he is talking about."

²⁵ So that disciple moved closer to Jesus' side and asked, "Who is it, Lord?"

²⁶ Jesus answered, "I will dip some bread in the sauce and give it to him; he is the man." So he took a piece of bread, dipped it, and gave it to Judas, the son of Simon Iscariot. ²⁷ As soon as Judas took the bread, Satan entered into him. Jesus said to him, "Hurry and do what you must!" ²⁸ None of the others at the table understood why Jesus said this to him. ²⁹ Since Judas was in charge of the mon-ey bag, some of the disciples thought that Jesus had told him to go and buy what they needed for the festival, or to give something to the poor.

³⁰ Judas accepted the bread and went out at once. It was night.

The New Commandment

³¹ After Judas had left, Jesus said, "Now the Son of Man's glory is revealed; now God's glory is revealed through him. ³² And if God's glory is revealed through him, then God will reveal the glory of the Son of Man in himself, and he will do so at once. ³³ My children, I shall not be with you very much longer. You will look for me; but I tell you now what I told the Jewish authorities, 'You cannot go where I am going.' ³⁴ And now I give you a new commandment: love one another. As I have loved you, so you must love one another. ³⁵ If you have love for one another, then everyone will know that you are my disciples."

Jesus Predicts Peter's Denial

³⁶ "Where are you going, Lord?" Simon Peter asked him.

"You cannot follow me now where I am going," answered Jesus; "but later you will follow me."

³⁷ "Lord, why can't I follow you now?" asked Peter. "I am ready to die for you!"

³⁸ Jesus answered, "Are you really ready to die for me? I am telling you the truth: before the rooster crows you will say three times that you do not know me.

Chapter 14

Jesus the Way to the Father

¹ "Do not be worried and upset," Jesus told them. "Believe in God and believe also in me. ² There are many rooms in my Father's house, and I am going to prepare a place for you. I would not tell you this if it were not so. ³ And after I go and prepare a place for you, I will come back and take you to myself, so that you will be where I am. ⁴ You know the way that leads to the place where I am going."

5 Thomas said to him, "Lord, we do not know where you are going; so how can we know the way to get there?"

6 Jesus answered him, "I am the way, the truth, and the life; no one goes to the Father except by me. 7 Now that you have known me," he said to them, "you will know my Father also, and from now on you do know him and you have seen him."

8 Philip said to him, "Lord, show us the Father; that is all we need."

9 Jesus answered, "For a long time I have been with you all; yet you do not know me, Philip? Whoever has seen me has seen the Father. Why, then, do you say, 'Show us the Father'? 10 Do you not believe, Philip, that I am in the Father and the Father is in me? The words that I have spoken to you," Jesus said to his disciples, "do not come from me. The Father, who remains in me, does his own work. 11 Believe me when I say that I am in the Father and the Father is in me. If not, believe because of the things I do. 12 I am telling you the truth: those who believe in me will do what I do—yes, they will do even greater things, because I am going to the Father. 13 And I will do whatever you ask for in my name, so that the Father's glory will be shown through the Son. 14 If you ask me for anything in my name, I will do it.

The Promise of the Holy Spirit

15 "If you love me, you will obey my commandments. 16 I will ask the Father, and he will give you another Helper, who will stay with you forever. 17 He is the Spirit, who reveals the truth about God. The world cannot receive him, because it cannot see him or know him. But you know him, because he remains with you and is in you.

18 "When I go, you will not be left all alone; I will come back to you. 19 In a little while the world will see me no more, but you will see me; and because I live, you also will live. 20 When that day comes, you will know that I am in my Father and that you are in me, just as I am in you.

21 "Those who accept my commandments and obey them are the ones who love me. My Father will love those who love me; I too will love them and reveal myself to them."

22 Judas (not Judas Iscariot) said, "Lord, how can it be that you will reveal yourself to us and not to the world?"

23 Jesus answered him, "Those who love me will obey my teaching. My Father will love them, and my Father and I will come to them and live with them. 24 Those who do not love me do not obey my teaching. And the teaching you have heard is not mine, but comes from the Father, who sent me.

25 "I have told you this while I am still with you. 26 The Helper, the Holy Spirit, whom the Father will send in my name, will teach you everything and make you remember all that I have told you.

27 "Peace is what I leave with you; it is my own peace that I give you. I do not give it as the world does. Do not be worried and upset; do not be afraid. 28 You heard me say to you, 'I am leaving, but I will come back to you.' If you loved me, you would be glad that I am going to the Father; for he is greater than I. 29 I have told you this now before it all happens, so that when it does happen, you will believe. 30 I cannot talk with you much longer, because the ruler of this world is coming. He has no power over me, 31 but the world must know that I love the Father; that is why I do everything as he commands me.

"Come, let us go from this place.

Chapter 15
Jesus the Real Vine

1 "I am the real vine, and my Father is the gardener. 2 He breaks off every branch in me that does not bear fruit, and he prunes every branch that does bear fruit, so that it will be clean and bear more fruit. 3 You have been made clean already by the teaching I have given you. 4 Remain united to me, and I will remain united to you. A branch cannot bear fruit by itself; it can do so only if it remains in the vine. In the same way you cannot bear fruit unless you remain in me.

5 "I am the vine, and you are the branches. Those who remain in me, and I in them, will bear much fruit; for you can do nothing without me. 6 Those who do not remain in me are thrown out like a branch and dry up; such branches are gathered up and thrown into the fire, where they are burned. 7 If you remain in me and my words remain in you, then you will ask for anything you wish, and you shall have it. 8 My Father's glory is shown by your bearing much fruit; and in this way you become my disciples. 9 I love you just as the Father loves me; remain in my love. 10 If you obey my commands, you will remain in my love, just as I have obeyed my Father's commands and remain in his love.

11 "I have told you this so that my joy may be in you and that your joy may be complete. 12 My commandment is this: love one another, just as I love you. 13 The greatest love you can have for your friends is to give your life for them. 14 And you are my friends if you do what I command you. 15 I do not call you servants any longer, because servants do not know what their master is doing. Instead, I call you friends, because I have told you everything I heard from my Father. 16 You did not choose me; I chose you and appointed you to go and bear much fruit, the kind of fruit that endures. And so the Father will give you whatever you ask of him in my name. 17 This, then, is what I command you: love one another.

The World's Hatred

18 "If the world hates you, just remember that it has hated me first. 19 If you belonged to the world, then the world would love you as its own. But I chose you from this world, and you do not belong to it; that is why the world hates you. 20 Remember what I told you: 'Slaves are not greater than their master.' If people persecuted me, they will persecute you too; if they obeyed my teaching, they will obey yours too. 21 But they will do all this to you because you are mine; for they do not know the one who sent me. 22 They would not have been guilty of sin if I had not come and spoken to them; as it is, they no longer have any excuse for their sin. 23 Whoever hates me hates my Father also. 24 They would not have been guilty of sin if I had not done among them the things that no one else ever did; as it is, they have seen what I did, and they hate both me and my Father. 25 This, however, was bound to happen so that what is written in their Law may come true: 'They hated me for no reason at all.'

26 "The Helper will come—the Spirit, who reveals the truth about God and who comes from the Father. I will send him to you from the Father, and he will speak about me. 27 And you, too, will speak about me, because you have been with me from the very beginning.

Chapter 16

1 "I have told you this, so that you will not give up your faith. 2 You will be expelled from the synagogues, and the time will come when those who kill you will think that by doing this they are serving God. 3 People will do these things to you because they have not known either the Father or me. 4 But I have told you this, so that when the time comes for them to do these things, you will remember what I told you.

The Work of the Holy Spirit

"I did not tell you these things at the beginning, for I was with you. 5 But now I am going to him who sent me, yet none of you asks me where I am going. 6 And now that I have told you, your hearts are full of sadness. 7 But I am telling you the truth: it is better for you that I go away, because if I do not go, the Helper will not come to you. But if I do go away, then I will send him to you. 8 And when he comes, he will prove to the people of the world that they are wrong about sin and about what is right and about God's judgment. 9 They are wrong about sin, because they do not believe in me; 10 they are wrong about what is right,

because I am going to the Father and you will not see me any more; ¹¹ and they are wrong about judgment, because the ruler of this world has already been judged.

¹² "I have much more to tell you, but now it would be too much for you to bear. ¹³ When, however, the Spirit comes, who reveals the truth about God, he will lead you into all the truth. He will not speak on his own authority, but he will speak of what he hears and will tell you of things to come. ¹⁴ He will give me glory, because he will take what I say and tell it to you. ¹⁵ All that my Father has is mine; that is why I said that the Spirit will take what I give him and tell it to you.

Sadness and Gladness

¹⁶ "In a little while you will not see me any more, and then a little while later you will see me."

¹⁷ Some of his disciples asked among themselves, "What does this mean? He tells us that in a little while we will not see him, and then a little while later we will see him; and he also says, 'It is because I am going to the Father.' ¹⁸ What does this 'a little while' mean? We don't know what he is talking about!"

¹⁹ Jesus knew that they wanted to question him, so he said to them, "I said, 'In a little while you will not see me, and then a little while later you will see me.' Is this what you are asking about among yourselves? ²⁰ I am telling you the truth: you will cry and weep, but the world will be glad; you will be sad, but your sadness will turn into gladness. ²¹ When a woman is about to give birth, she is sad because her hour of suffering has come; but when the baby is born, she forgets her suffering, because she is happy that a baby has been born into the world. ²² That is how it is with you: now you are sad, but I will see you again, and your hearts will be filled with gladness, the kind of gladness that no one can take away from you.

²³ "When that day comes, you will not ask me for anything. I am telling you the truth: the Father will give you whatever you ask of him in my name. ²⁴ Until now you have not asked for anything in my name; ask and you will receive, so that your happiness may be complete.

Victory over the World

²⁵ "I have used figures of speech to tell you these things. But the time will come when I will not use figures of speech, but will speak to you plainly about the Father. ²⁶ When that day comes, you will ask him in my name; and I do not say that I will ask him on your behalf, ²⁷ for the Father himself loves you. He loves you because you love me and have believed that I came from God. ²⁸ I did come from the Father, and I came into the world; and now I am leaving the world and going to the Father."

²⁹ Then his disciples said to him, "Now you are speaking plainly, without using figures of speech. ³⁰ We know now that you know everything; you do not need to have someone ask you questions. This makes us believe that you came from God."

³¹ Jesus answered them, "Do you believe now? ³² The time is coming, and is already here, when all of you will be scattered, each of you to your own home, and I will be left all alone. But I am not really alone, because the Father is with me. ³³ I have told you this so that you will have peace by being united to me. The world will make you suffer. But be brave! I have defeated the world!"

Chapter 17
Jesus Prays for His Disciples

¹ After Jesus finished saying this, he looked up to heaven and said, "Father, the hour has come. Give glory to your Son, so that the Son may give glory to you. ² For you gave him authority over all people, so that he might give eternal life to all those you gave him. ³ And eternal life means to know you, the only true God, and to know Jesus Christ, whom you sent. ⁴ I have shown your glory on earth; I have finished the work you gave me to do. ⁵ Father! Give me glory in your presence now, the same glory I had with you before the world was made.

⁶ "I have made you known to those you gave me out of the world. They belonged to you, and you gave them to

me. They have obeyed your word, ⁷ and now they know that everything you gave me comes from you. ⁸ I gave them the message that you gave me, and they received it; they know that it is true that I came from you, and they believe that you sent me.

⁹ "I pray for them. I do not pray for the world but for those you gave me, for they belong to you. ¹⁰ All I have is yours, and all you have is mine; and my glory is shown through them. ¹¹ And now I am coming to you; I am no longer in the world, but they are in the world. Holy Father! Keep them safe by the power of your name, the name you gave me, so that they may be one just as you and I are one. ¹² While I was with them, I kept them safe by the power of your name, the name you gave me. I protected them, and not one of them was lost, except the man who was bound to be lost—so that the scripture might come true. ¹³ And now I am coming to you, and I say these things in the world so that they might have my joy in their hearts in all its fullness. ¹⁴ I gave them your message, and the world hated them, because they do not belong to the world, just as I do not belong to the world. ¹⁵ I do not ask you to take them out of the world, but I do ask you to keep them safe from the Evil One. ¹⁶ Just as I do not belong to the world, they do not belong to the world. ¹⁷ Dedicate them to yourself by means of the truth; your word is truth. ¹⁸ I sent them into the world, just as you sent me into the world. ¹⁹ And for their sake I dedicate myself to you, in order that they, too, may be truly dedicated to you.

²⁰ "I pray not only for them, but also for those who believe in me because of their message. ²¹ I pray that they may all be one. Father! May they be in us, just as you are in me and I am in you. May they be one, so that the world will believe that you sent me. ²² I gave them the same glory you gave me, so that they may be one, just as you and I are one: ²³ I in them and you in me, so that they may be completely one, in order that the world may know that you sent me and that you love them as you love me.

²⁴ "Father! You have given them to me, and I want them to be with me where I am, so that they may see my glory, the glory you gave me; for you loved me before the world was made. ²⁵ Righteous Father! The world does not know you, but I know you, and these know that you sent me. ²⁶ I made you known to them, and I will continue to do so, in order that the love you have for me may be in them, and so that I also may be in them."

Chapter 18
The Arrest of Jesus

¹ After Jesus had said this prayer, he left with his disciples and went across Kidron Brook. There was a garden in that place, and Jesus and his disciples went in. ² Judas, the traitor, knew where it was, because many times Jesus had met there with his disciples. ³ So Judas went to the garden, taking with him a group of Roman soldiers, and some Temple guards sent by the chief priests and the Pharisees; they were armed and carried lanterns and torches. ⁴ Jesus knew everything that was going to happen to him, so he stepped forward and asked them, "Who is it you are looking for?"

⁵ "Jesus of Nazareth," they answered.

"I am he," he said.

Judas, the traitor, was standing there with them. ⁶ When Jesus said to them, "I am he," they moved back and fell to the ground. ⁷ Again Jesus asked them, "Who is it you are looking for?"

"Jesus of Nazareth," they said.

⁸ "I have already told you that I am he," Jesus said. "If, then, you are looking for me, let these others go." (⁹ He

said this so that what he had said might come true: "Father, I have not lost even one of those you gave me.")

[10] Simon Peter, who had a sword, drew it and struck the High Priest's slave, cutting off his right ear. The name of the slave was Malchus. [11] Jesus said to Peter, "Put your sword back in its place! Do you think that I will not drink the cup of suffering which my Father has given me?"

Jesus Before Annas

[12] Then the Roman soldiers with their commanding officer and the Jewish guards arrested Jesus, tied him up, [13] and took him first to Annas. He was the father-in-law of Caiaphas, who was High Priest that year. [14] It was Caiaphas who had advised the Jewish authorities that it was better that one man should die for all the people.

Peter Denies Jesus

[15] Simon Peter and another disciple followed Jesus. That other disciple was well known to the High Priest, so he went with Jesus into the courtyard of the High Priest's house, [16] while Peter stayed outside by the gate. Then the other disciple went back out, spoke to the girl at the gate, and brought Peter inside. [17] The girl at the gate said to Peter, "Aren't you also one of the disciples of that man?"

"No, I am not," answered Peter.

[18] It was cold, so the servants and guards had built a charcoal fire and were standing around it, warming themselves. So Peter went over and stood with them, warming himself.

The High Priest Questions Jesus

[19] The High Priest questioned Jesus about his disciples and about his teaching. [20] Jesus answered, "I have always spoken publicly to everyone; all my teaching was done in the synagogues and in the Temple, where all the people come together. I have never said anything in secret. [21] Why, then, do you question me? Question the people who heard me. Ask them what I told them—they know what I said."

[22] When Jesus said this, one of the guards there slapped him and said, "How dare you talk like that to the High Priest!"

[23] Jesus answered him, "If I have said anything wrong, tell everyone here what it was. But if I am right in what I have said, why do you hit me?"

[24] Then Annas sent him, still tied up, to Caiaphas the High Priest.

Peter Denies Jesus Again

[25] Peter was still standing there keeping himself warm. So the others said to him, "Aren't you also one of the disciples of that man?"

But Peter denied it. "No, I am not," he said.

[26] One of the High Priest's slaves, a relative of the man whose ear Peter had cut off, spoke up. "Didn't I see you with him in the garden?" he asked.

[27] Again Peter said "No"—and at once a rooster crowed.

Jesus Before Pilate

[28] Early in the morning Jesus was taken from Caiaphas' house to the governor's palace. The Jewish authorities did not go inside the palace, for they wanted to keep themselves ritually clean, in order to be able to eat the Passover meal. [29] So Pilate went outside to them and asked, "What do you accuse this man of?"

[30] Their answer was, "We would not have brought him to you if he had not committed a crime."

[31] Pilate said to them, "Then you yourselves take him and try him according to your own law."

They replied, "We are not allowed to put anyone to death." ([32] This happened in order to make come true what Jesus had said when he indicated the kind of death he would die.)

[33] Pilate went back into the palace and called Jesus. "Are you the king of the Jews?" he asked him.

[34] Jesus answered, "Does this question come from you or have others told you about me?"

[35] Pilate replied, "Do you think I am a Jew? It was your own people and the chief priests who handed you over to me. What have you done?"

[36] Jesus said, "My kingdom does not belong to this world; if my kingdom belonged to this world, my followers would fight to keep me from being handed over to the Jewish authorities. No, my kingdom does not belong here!"

[37] So Pilate asked him, "Are you a king, then?"

Jesus answered, "You say that I am a king. I was born and came into the world for this one purpose, to speak about the truth. Whoever belongs to the truth listens to me."

[38] "And what is truth?" Pilate asked.

Jesus Is Sentenced to Death

Then Pilate went back outside to the people and said to them, "I cannot find any reason to condemn him. [39] But according to the custom you have, I always set free a prisoner for you during the Passover. Do you want me to set free for you the king of the Jews?"

[40] They answered him with a shout, "No, not him! We want Barabbas!" (Barabbas was a bandit.)

Chapter 19

[1] Then Pilate took Jesus and had him whipped. [2] The soldiers made a crown out of thorny branches and put it on his head; then they put a purple robe on him [3] and came to him and said, "Long live the King of the Jews!" And they went up and slapped him.

[4] Pilate went back out once more and said to the crowd, "Look, I will bring him out here to you to let you see that I cannot find any reason to condemn him." [5] So Jesus came out, wearing the crown of thorns and the purple robe. Pilate said to them, "Look! Here is the man!"

[6] When the chief priests and the Temple guards saw him, they shouted, "Crucify him! Crucify him!"

Pilate said to them, "You take him, then, and crucify him. I find no reason to condemn him."

[7] The crowd answered back, "We have a law that says he ought to die, because he claimed to be the Son of God."

[8] When Pilate heard this, he was even more afraid. [9] He went back into the palace and asked Jesus, "Where do you come from?"

But Jesus did not answer. [10] Pilate said to him, "You will not speak to me? Remember, I have the authority to set you free and also to have you crucified."

[11] Jesus answered, "You have authority over me only because it was given to you by God. So the man who handed me over to you is guilty of a worse sin."

[12] When Pilate heard this, he tried to find a way to set Jesus free. But the crowd shouted back, "If you set him free, that means that you are not the Emperor's friend! Anyone who claims to be a king is a rebel against the Emperor!"

[13] When Pilate heard these words, he took Jesus outside and sat down on the judge's seat in the place called "The Stone Pavement." (In Hebrew the name is "Gabbatha.") [14] It was then almost noon of the day before the Passover. Pilate said to the people, "Here is your king!"

[15] They shouted back, "Kill him! Kill him! Crucify him!"

Pilate asked them, "Do you want me to crucify your king?"

The chief priests answered, "The only king we have is the Emperor!"

[16] Then Pilate handed Jesus over to them to be crucified.

Jesus Is Crucified

So they took charge of Jesus. ¹⁷ He went out, carrying his cross, and came to "The Place of the Skull," as it is called. (In Hebrew it is called "Golgotha.") ¹⁸ There they crucified him; and they also crucified two other men, one on each side, with Jesus between them. ¹⁹ Pilate wrote a notice and had it put on the cross. "Jesus of Nazareth, the King of the Jews," is what he wrote. ²⁰ Many people read it, because the place where Jesus was crucified was not far from the city. The notice was written in Hebrew, Latin, and Greek. ²¹ The chief priests said to Pilate, "Do not write 'The King of the Jews,' but rather, 'This man said, I am the King of the Jews.'"

²² Pilate answered, "What I have written stays written."

²³ After the soldiers had crucified Jesus, they took his clothes and divided them into four parts, one part for each soldier. They also took the robe, which was made of one piece of woven cloth without any seams in it. ²⁴ The soldiers said to one another, "Let's not tear it; let's throw dice to see who will get it." This happened in order to make the scripture come true:

"They divided my clothes among themselves and gambled for my robe."

And this is what the soldiers did.

²⁵ Standing close to Jesus' cross were his mother, his mother's sister, Mary the wife of Clopas, and Mary Magdalene. ²⁶ Jesus saw his mother and the disciple he loved standing there; so he said to his mother, "He is your son."

²⁷ Then he said to the disciple, "She is your mother." From that time the disciple took her to live in his home.

The Death of Jesus

²⁸ Jesus knew that by now everything had been completed; and in order to make the scripture come true, he said, "I am thirsty."

²⁹ A bowl was there, full of cheap wine; so a sponge was soaked in the wine, put on a stalk of hyssop, and lifted up to his lips. ³⁰ Jesus drank the wine and said, "It is finished!"

Then he bowed his head and gave up his spirit.

Jesus' Side Is Pierced

³¹ Then the Jewish authorities asked Pilate to allow them to break the legs of the men who had been crucified, and to take the bodies down from the crosses. They requested this because it was Friday, and they did not want the bodies to stay on the crosses on the Sabbath, since the coming Sabbath was especially holy. ³² So the soldiers went and broke the legs of the first man and then of the other man who had been crucified with Jesus. ³³ But when they came to Jesus, they saw that he was already dead, so they did not break his legs. ³⁴ One of the soldiers, however, plunged his spear into Jesus' side, and at once blood and water poured out. (³⁵ The one who saw this happen has spoken of it, so that you also may believe. What he said is true, and he knows that he speaks the truth.) ³⁶ This was done to make the scripture come true: "Not one of his bones will be broken." ³⁷ And there is another scripture that says, "People will look at him whom they pierced."

The Burial of Jesus

³⁸ After this, Joseph, who was from the town of Arimathea, asked Pilate if he could take Jesus' body. (Joseph was a follower of Jesus, but in secret, because he was afraid of the Jewish authorities.) Pilate told him he could have the body, so Joseph went and took it away. ³⁹ Nicodemus, who at first had gone to see Jesus at night, went with Joseph, taking with him about one hundred pounds of spices, a mixture of myrrh and aloes. ⁴⁰ The two men took Jesus' body and wrapped it in linen cloths with the spices according to the Jewish custom of preparing a

body for burial. ⁴¹ There was a garden in the place where Jesus had been put to death, and in it there was a new tomb where no one had ever been buried. ⁴² Since it was the day before the Sabbath and because the tomb was close by, they placed Jesus' body there.

Chapter 20
The Empty Tomb
¹ Early on Sunday morning, while it was still dark, Mary Magdalene went to the tomb and saw that the stone had been taken away from the entrance. ² She went running to Simon Peter and the other disciple, whom Jesus loved, and told them, "They have taken the Lord from the tomb, and we don't know where they have put him!"

Learn more on page 201.

³ Then Peter and the other disciple went to the tomb. ⁴ The two of them were running, but the other disciple ran faster than Peter and reached the tomb first. ⁵ He bent over and saw the linen cloths, but he did not go in. ⁶ Behind him came Simon Peter, and he went straight into the tomb. He saw the linen cloths lying there ⁷ and the cloth which had been around Jesus' head. It was not lying with the linen cloths but was rolled up by itself. ⁸ Then the other disciple, who had reached the tomb first, also went in; he saw and believed. (⁹ They still did not understand the scripture which said that he must rise from death.) ¹⁰ Then the disciples went back home.

Jesus Appears to Mary Magdalene
¹¹ Mary stood crying outside the tomb. While she was still crying, she bent over and looked in the tomb ¹² and saw two angels there dressed in white, sitting where the body of Jesus had been, one at the head and the other at the feet. ¹³ "Woman, why are you crying?" they asked her.

She answered, "They have taken my Lord away, and I do not know where they have put him!"

¹⁴ Then she turned around and saw Jesus standing there; but she did not know that it was Jesus. ¹⁵ "Woman, why are you crying?" Jesus asked her. "Who is it that you are looking for?"

She thought he was the gardener, so she said to him, "If you took him away, sir, tell me where you have put him, and I will go and get him."

¹⁶ Jesus said to her, "Mary!"

She turned toward him and said in Hebrew, "Rabboni!" (This means "Teacher.")

¹⁷ "Do not hold on to me," Jesus told her, "because I have not yet gone back up to the Father. But go to my brothers and tell them that I am returning to him who is my Father and their Father, my God and their God."

¹⁸ So Mary Magdalene went and told the disciples that she had seen the Lord and related to them what he had told her.

Learn more on page 201.

Jesus Appears to His Disciples
¹⁹ It was late that Sunday evening, and the disciples were gathered together behind locked doors, because they were afraid of the Jewish authorities. Then Jesus came and stood among them. "Peace be with you," he said. ²⁰ After saying this, he showed them his hands and his side. The disciples were filled with joy at seeing the Lord. ²¹ Jesus said to them again, "Peace be with you. As the Father sent me, so I send you." ²² Then he breathed on them and said, "Receive the Holy Spirit. ²³ If you forgive people's sins, they are forgiven; if you do not forgive them, they are not forgiven."

Jesus and Thomas
²⁴ One of the twelve disciples, Thomas (called the Twin),

was not with them when Jesus came. ²⁵ So the other disciples told him, "We have seen the Lord!"

Thomas said to them, "Unless I see the scars of the nails in his hands and put my finger on those scars and my hand in his side, I will not believe."

²⁶ A week later the disciples were together again indoors, and Thomas was with them. The doors were locked, but Jesus came and stood among them and said, "Peace be with you." ²⁷ Then he said to Thomas, "Put your finger here, and look at my hands; then reach out your hand and put it in my side. Stop your doubting, and believe!"

Learn more on page 203

²⁸ Thomas answered him, "My Lord and my God!"

²⁹ Jesus said to him, "Do you believe because you see me? How happy are those who believe without seeing me!"

The Purpose of This Book

³⁰ In his disciples' presence Jesus performed many other miracles which are not written down in this book. ³¹ But these have been written in order that you may believe that Jesus is the Messiah, the Son of God, and that through your faith in him you may have life.

Chapter 21

Jesus Appears to Seven Disciples

¹ After this, Jesus appeared once more to his disciples at Lake Tiberias. This is how it happened. ² Simon Peter, Thomas (called the Twin), Nathanael (the one from Cana in Galilee), the sons of Zebedee, and two other disciples of Jesus were all together. ³ Simon Peter said to the others, "I am going fishing."

"We will come with you," they told him. So they went out in a boat, but all that night they did not catch a thing. ⁴ As the sun was rising, Jesus stood at the water's edge, but the disciples did not know that it was Jesus. ⁵ Then he asked them, "Young men, haven't you caught anything?"

"Not a thing," they answered.

⁶ He said to them, "Throw your net out on the right side of the boat, and you will catch some." So they threw the net out and could not pull it back in, because they had caught so many fish.

⁷ The disciple whom Jesus loved said to Peter, "It is the Lord!" When Peter heard that it was the Lord, he wrapped his outer garment around him (for he had taken his clothes off) and jumped into the water. ⁸ The other disciples came to shore in the boat, pulling the net full of fish. They were not very far from land, about a hundred yards away. ⁹ When they stepped ashore, they saw a charcoal fire there with fish on it and some bread. ¹⁰ Then Jesus said to them, "Bring some of the fish you have just caught."

¹¹ Simon Peter went aboard and dragged the net ashore full of big fish, a hundred and fifty-three in all; even though there were so many, still the net did not tear. ¹² Jesus said to them, "Come and eat." None of the disciples dared ask him, "Who are you?" because they knew it was the Lord. ¹³ So Jesus went over, took the bread, and gave it to them; he did the same with the fish.

¹⁴ This, then, was the third time Jesus appeared to the disciples after he was raised from death.

Jesus and Peter

¹⁵ After they had eaten, Jesus said to Simon Peter, "Simon son of John, do you love me more than these others do?"

Learn more on page 204.

"Yes, Lord," he answered, "you know that I love you."

Jesus said to him, "Take care of my lambs." ¹⁶ A second time Jesus said to him, "Simon son of John, do you love me?"

"Yes, Lord," he answered, "you know that I love you."

Jesus said to him, "Take care of my sheep." ¹⁷ A third time Jesus said, "Simon son of John, do you love me?"

Peter became sad because Jesus asked him the third time, "Do you love me?" and so he said to him, "Lord, you know everything; you know that I love you!"

Jesus said to him, "Take care of my sheep. ¹⁸ I am telling you the truth: when you were young, you used to get ready and go anywhere you wanted to; but when you are old, you will stretch out your hands and someone else will tie you up and take you where you don't want to go." ¹⁹ (In saying this, Jesus was indicating the way in which Peter would die and bring glory to God.) Then Jesus said to him, "Follow me!"

Jesus and the Other Disciple

²⁰ Peter turned around and saw behind him that other disciple, whom Jesus loved—the one who had leaned close to Jesus at the meal and had asked, "Lord, who is going to betray you?" ²¹ When Peter saw him, he asked Jesus, "Lord, what about this man?"

²² Jesus answered him, "If I want him to live until I come, what is that to you? Follow me!"

²³ So a report spread among the followers of Jesus that this disciple would not die. But Jesus did not say he would not die; he said, "If I want him to live until I come, what is that to you?"

²⁴ He is the disciple who spoke of these things, the one who also wrote them down; and we know that what he said is true.

Conclusion

²⁵ Now, there are many other things that Jesus did. If they were all written down one by one, I suppose that the whole world could not hold the books that would be written.

151

52 **FEATURED GOSPEL** Stories

On the next 52 pages you will find a selection of **FEATURED GOSPEL** stories. Use the information and reflections on these pages to uncover deeper meaning in some of the most beloved stories of the Gospels.

Look It Up
Use the Bible citations at the top of each page to find the story in the Gospels. Read the whole Scripture passage for yourself.

Quick Summary
Each page provides a quick summary of the story, highlighting the action and message in language that is easy to understand.

Digging Deeper
This section provides meaningful ways in which you can apply the Gospel message in your own life as you live your faith in Christ!

I Pray
Take a moment of prayerful reflection to thank God for speaking to you through the good news of the Gospel.

I'll hear this Gospel story in Mass...
Learn when each of these Gospel stories will be read throughout the 3-Year Liturgical Cycle. Listen for them as you attend Mass.

52 **FEATURED GOSPEL** Stories

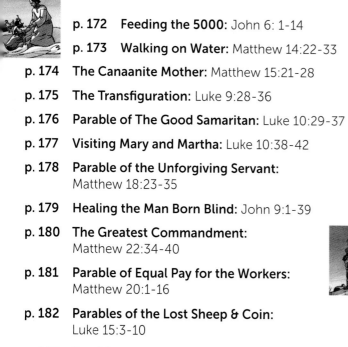

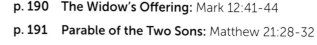

The NATIVITY of JOHN the BAPTIST
Luke 1:5-25, 57-80

News that Left Zechariah Speechless!

Zechariah was a priest who was given the special job of burning incense at the altar of the Lord in the Temple. While he was doing this holy work, the Angel Gabriel appeared to him and told him that he and his wife Elizabeth would have a very special son who would prepare the way for Jesus. But Zechariah could not believe this because he and his wife were very old. So Gabriel told Zechariah that he would not be able to speak until his son was born. Elizabeth soon became pregnant and nine months later, when the baby was born, Zechariah could speak again, and the first words out of his mouth were songs of praise to God for his goodness to him and his family.

At that moment Zechariah was able to speak again, and he started praising God.
Luke 1:64

I Pray

Dear God, open my mouth to proclaim your good news about Jesus. Amen.

Digging Deeper

Zechariah did not believe the good news of Gabriel at first. It is hard for us to believe the good news of God in Jesus Christ sometimes, because it is beyond what we can even imagine. But we have been given the good news that Jesus is coming to save us from our sins so that we can talk about it with everyone we meet. It is a precious gift we have been given to be able to speak and to tell people how much God loves us in Jesus. Use your gift and spread the word!

I'll hear this Gospel story in Mass...

**The Nativity of John the Baptist (June 24)
Liturgical Years A,B,C**

The ANNUNCIATION
Luke 1:26-38, 46-55

> "I am the Lord's servant," said Mary; "may it happen to me as you have said."
> *Luke 1:38*

Nothing Is Impossible with God!

God sent the Angel Gabriel to a young woman named Mary. The angel told Mary that she was blessed and would have a baby boy. His name would be Jesus, and he would be the Son of God. Mary did not understand how this could happen because she was not married yet. Gabriel said, "The Holy Spirit and God's power will make this happen. Nothing is impossible with God." Mary said, "I am the Lord's servant. Let it happen as you said."

Digging Deeper

Mary said "yes" to God even though she felt confused and overwhelmed. When she said "yes," she allowed God's Son to enter the world as a Divine Person with a divine and human nature. We, too, have times when we feel confused and overwhelmed. It happens whenever we are visited by some of the more difficult situations in life. Mary is our model. We, too, can say "yes" to what God asks of us. We can celebrate the times that we have said "yes" to God.

I Pray

Lord, following the example of Mary, help me say "yes" to you. Amen.

I'll hear this Gospel story in Mass...

The 4th Sunday of Advent Liturgical Year B

JOSEPH'S Dream
Matthew 1:18-25

An Angel Speaks to Joseph

When Mary told Joseph she was going to have a baby through the power of the Holy Spirit, Joseph was confused about how this could be. So an angel told Joseph in a dream that what Mary said was true. The angel said, "Marry her and name the baby Jesus. He will save people from their sins." Long ago, God had promised, "A virgin will have a baby boy, who will be called Immanuel (God is with us)." The promise was coming true.

> **She will have a son, and you will name him Jesus—because he will save his people from their sins.**
> *Matthew 1:21*

Digging Deeper

Jesus' name means "God is with us." Someone being with us even though we cannot see them is hard to comprehend. Think about how you can feel someone's presence even if that person is far away. When you are apart from someone, you are still with them in your thoughts. Ponder ways you feel other people's presence when you are at school, church or home.

I Pray

God my Father, you sent your Son, Jesus, to be with me. I thank you for this greatest sign of your love. Amen.

I'll hear this Gospel story in Mass...

**The 4th Sunday of Advent
Liturgical Year A**

The BIRTH of JESUS
Luke 2:1-20

I'll hear this Gospel story in Mass...

The Nativity of Our Lord (Night)
Liturgical Years A,B,C

Digging Deeper

The story of the birth of Jesus shows us in many ways how Jesus came to be our humble King, not wrapped in silk, but in swaddling clothes. He wore no crown and had no proper bed. He came in human form, though he was from God. His humility helps us to realize that Jesus came to us and for us to be like us and dwell with us and ultimately die for us that we might be saved of our sins.

I Pray

Dear Jesus, be born in my heart and life today and dwell with me every moment of my life. Amen.

> **She gave birth to her first son, wrapped him in cloths and laid him in a manger—there was no room for them to stay in the inn.**
> *Luke 2:7*

A Baby Is Born

Mary and Joseph traveled far from their home in Nazareth to the little town of Bethlehem to be counted in the census. But there were no rooms left in the inn for Joseph or Mary, who was about to have a baby. So they found a place to rest for the night in a stable. There the Baby Jesus was born, wrapped in swaddling clothes, and placed in a manger, which is a feeding trough for animals. Shepherds and angels celebrated the birth because, as the angel said, "Unto you is born this day in the city of David, a Savior, which is Christ the Lord."

SIMEON and ANNA
Luke 2:25-38

Jesus Is the Messiah

Joseph and Mary took the infant Jesus to the Temple in Jerusalem to present him to the Lord as the law stated. In Jerusalem, a holy man named Simeon had been promised by the Holy Spirit that he would live to see the Messiah. When Simeon came into the Temple, he took Jesus into his arms and blessed God, saying "Now, Master, you may let your servant go in peace, according to your word, for my eyes have seen your salvation."

> **Simeon took the child in his arms and gave thanks to God.**
> *Luke 2:28*

Digging Deeper

The people of Israel waited centuries for a Savior to come. The people who were poor and marginalized waited for a Savior, too. Simeon, a just and pious man, and Anna, a widow, represented these groups. They recognized their Savior in Jesus, the child who was presented in the Temple that day, forty days after his birth. Filled with hope, Simeon proclaimed him as a light to all nations and the glory of Israel. Anna announced his arrival to many.

I Pray

Jesus, open my heart that I may know you. Help me grow in love for you each day. Amen.

I'll hear this Gospel story in Mass...

**The Holy Family of Jesus, Mary and Joseph
Liturgical Year B**

158

The WISE MEN
Matthew 2:1-12

> **When they saw the child with his mother Mary, they knelt down and worshiped him.**
> *Matthew 2:11*

Guide Us to Jesus

Wise men from the East followed a star to Jerusalem. They asked, "Where is the child who will be king of the Jews?" King Herod told them to go to Bethlehem and let him know when they found the baby. When the wise men found the baby, they gave him special gifts and worshiped him. But they did not go back and tell King Herod where he was.

Digging Deeper

The three kings discovered a rising star. It was the opening act for someone great, so they followed the star in search of that someone—a newborn king. When the star finally rested over Bethlehem, they discovered that the real star was God, revealed in the person of Jesus. God's love is present in the stars and in all of creation. God's love is present in the person of Jesus. God's love is for everyone!

I Pray

O God, let me adore your Son who came into the world for all nations. Amen.

I'll hear this Gospel story in Mass...

**The Epiphany of the Lord
Liturgical Years A,B,C**

BOY JESUS at the TEMPLE
Luke 2:41-52

I'll hear this Gospel story in Mass...

**The Holy Family of Jesus, Mary and Joseph
Liturgical Year C**

Digging Deeper
We often call our parish church the house of God. It is the place where the Word of God is spoken and shared and where people gather to support and encourage one another in their faith. Jesus gives us a good example of what it means to spend time with God. We should be in church as often as we can, listening to what he has to say to us, praying to him and singing his praises.

I Pray
Dear Jesus, help me to enjoy my time in your Father's house. Amen.

Where Is Jesus?
When Jesus was 12 years old, he took a trip with his family to Jerusalem for the festival of Passover, which celebrates the Israelites' escape from Egypt. When the festival was over and Mary and Joseph were heading home, they realized that Jesus was not with them. So they looked high and low for Jesus for three days until they found him in the temple talking to the teachers there. Mary asked why Jesus had done this and he said, "Didn't you know that I had to be in my Father's house?"

On the third day they found him in the Temple, sitting with the Jewish teachers, listening to them and asking questions.
Luke 1:46

JOHN the BAPTIST PREACHES
Matthew 3:1-5; John 1:1-18

> **"Turn away from your sins," [John] said, "because the Kingdom of Heaven is near!"**
> *Matthew 3:2*

Get Ready for the Lord!

John the Baptist was preaching in the desert to everyone who would listen. "Get ready for the Lord! Make a straight path for him." Many people listened to John. They asked forgiveness for their sins and were baptized. Some, however, only pretended to be sorry for their sins. John got very angry with them. He warned them that someone even greater than he was coming to baptize with the Holy Spirit and fire. "Be ready," he said. "Be sorry for your sins."

Digging Deeper

Nothing compares to hearing John the Baptist preach, "Get ready! Repent. Make a straight path for the Lord. He's coming. He's coming!" In today's jargon, John might be preaching, "Stay in the zone." We must let nothing distract us from expressing sorrow for our sins and preparing our hearts and souls to accept Jesus. Emphasize this message in your life.

I Pray

Jesus, prepare my heart to welcome you. Amen.

I'll hear this Gospel story in Mass...

The Nativity of Our Lord (Day)
Liturgical Years A, B, C

The 2nd Sunday of Advent
Liturgical Year A

The BAPTISM of JESUS
John 1:19-34; Matthew 3:13-17

Jesus Is Baptized

People wondered, "Could John be the Messiah?" John said, "No! Someone more powerful than I is coming. He will baptize you with the Holy Spirit and fire." After everyone else had been baptized, Jesus himself was baptized. Afterward, as he prayed, the sky opened up and the Holy Spirit came down upon him in the form of a dove. A voice from heaven said, "You are my own dear Son, and I am pleased with you."

> **God, who sent me to baptize with water, had said to me, "You will see the Spirit come down and stay on a man; he is the one who baptizes with the Holy Spirit."**
> *John 1:33*

Digging Deeper

In this story, we experience all three Persons of the Trinity. We see Jesus being baptized. We hear the voice of the Father. We feel the presence of the Holy Spirit. What a peaceful scene. It gives us hope for the world we live in, which seems anything but peaceful and harmonious. The daily news reports wars and acts of cruelty. Violence comes packaged as entertainment. Hopeless? Not for believers in the power of the Trinity.

I Pray

God my Father, I am blessed to be called your child. May I always be grateful for your love and goodness. Amen.

I'll hear this Gospel story in Mass...

The 2nd Sunday in Ordinary Time
Liturgical Year A

Baptism of Our Lord
Liturgical Year A

JESUS' Temptation
Matthew 4:1-11

Then Jesus answered, "Go away, Satan! The scripture says, 'Worship the Lord your God and serve only him!'"
Matthew 4:10

Jesus Faces Temptation
Jesus went into the desert for forty days, where he was tested by the devil. The devil told Jesus to turn stone into bread. Jesus answered, "No one lives only on food." Then, the devil told Jesus to worship him and he would make him powerful. Jesus answered, "Worship the Lord your God and serve only him!" Finally, the devil dared Jesus to jump from the top of the Temple. Jesus said, "Don't test the Lord, your God."

Digging Deeper
Self-denial helps us develop the discipline and self-ccntrol to live good moral lives. It is always a good time to work on developing more control over our bad habits. In this story, Jesus disciplines himself through fasting and prayer. He knows that if he is to conquer the difficulties and temptations ahead of him, he must have self-control, which does not come from a self-indulgent life.

I Pray
Jesus, help me to remain strong when I feel tempted to break your rules. Help me be more like you. Amen.

I'll hear this Gospel story in Mass...

**The First Sunday of Lent
Liturgical Year A**

163

JESUS Turns WATER into WINE
John 2:1-11

Jesus' First Miracle

Mary, Jesus, and his disciples were all at a wedding. The wine ran out, so Mary told Jesus about it. He said, "Mother, my time has not yet come!" But Mary told the servants, "Do whatever Jesus tells you to do." So Jesus told the servants to fill six stone jars with water, and he turned the water into wine. This was Jesus' first miracle. From then on, his disciples believed in him.

Jesus performed this first miracle in Cana in Galilee; there he revealed his glory, and his disciples believed in him.
John 2:11

Digging Deeper

Most parents believe they have a moral obligation to guide their children, no matter how old they are. We see that kind of parenting in this story. Mary sees a need, knows her son can help, and tells him to do so. Mary also shows faith in her son. This is Jesus' first miracle. Mary's belief in him causes Jesus to do something he's never done before. Her words signal the beginning of Jesus' ministry.

I Pray

Jesus, your miracle of turning water into wine helped the disciples believe. I am your disciple, too, and I believe in you. Amen.

I'll hear this Gospel story in Mass...

**The 2nd Sunday in Ordinary Time
Liturgical Year C**

JESUS Calls PETER, JAMES and JOHN
Luke 5:1-11

> **They pulled the boats up on the beach, left everything, and followed Jesus.**
> *Luke 5:11*

Jesus Helps Simon Believe

When Jesus finished teaching, he told Simon to row his boat into deep water and let down his nets to catch fish. "Master," Simon replied, "we did not catch anything all night. But I will do as you say." They caught so many fish their nets began ripping. When Simon saw this, he said, "Lord, don't come near me! I am a sinner." Jesus said, "From now on you will bring in people instead of fish."

Digging Deeper

Jesus wouldn't let the fishermen quit fishing. Indeed, he gave them an even bigger job of attracting people to God's message. The task Jesus asks of us is to fish until we find the way into others' hearts. We must create a relationship so that we can help people learn about God through our words and actions. We must guide people to choose to live a life of faith.

I Pray

Jesus, you helped Simon know you and believe in you. Help me to know you and believe too. Amen.

I'll hear this Gospel story in Mass...

The 5th Sunday in Ordinary Time Liturgical Year C

The BEATITUDES
Matthew 5:1-12

I'll hear this Gospel story in Mass...

**The 4th Sunday in Ordinary Time
Liturgical Year A**

Digging Deeper

The Gospel shows us attitudes that help us to be rooted and bear fruit during life's adversities. Jesus understood that we need to be rooted to a community and our families. Families offer a sense of belonging, and they help us learn our identity and the values that guide us through life's problems. As members of the family of God, we trust in Jesus' words and give thanks to our Father for his loving care in all circumstances.

I Pray

Lord Jesus, sometimes I am busy wanting things. Instead, help me remember that being loving and kind is the way to be happy. Amen.

Blessed Are You

Jesus said to his disciples: "God will bless you who are poor. You will inherit the kingdom! God will bless you, hungry people. You will have plenty to eat! God will bless you who cry. You will laugh! God will bless you when others hate you and stay away from you, or when people say mean things about you because you follow Jesus. When this happens, be happy, for you will have a great reward in heaven."

Jesus saw the crowds and went up a hill, where he sat down. His disciples gathered around him, and he began to teach them. *Matthew 5:1-2*

BUILD Your HOUSE on the ROCK
Matthew 7:24-27

So then, anyone who hears these words of mine and obeys them is like a wise man who built his house on rock.
Matthew 7:24

Digging Deeper
The solid rock of Jesus on which we build is the Word of God. The promises we find in the Bible remind us that Jesus came to earth to save us by living the perfect life, dying on the Cross and rising on the third day when the rock in front of the tomb was rolled away. Jesus is the only sure thing in a world that will one day crumble and disappear. Grounded in Jesus, we will never be destroyed, but will live in dwelling places prepared for us in Heaven.

I Pray
Jesus, my Rock, keep me firm in my faith always. Amen.

I'll hear this Gospel story in Mass...
The 9th Sunday in Ordinary Time Liturgical Year A

Rock Solid
When people build houses, they should look first at the land they are building on. A house built on sand will not stand. A house built on rock will remain firm. Jesus says that our lives are like houses and that we should build our lives on ground that is solid and firm. Jesus is our firm foundation and the solid rock on which we build. He will never let our lives wash away, but will keep us strong in our faith.

JESUS CALMS the STORM
Mark 4:35-41

Jesus Gives Us Faith

Jesus and the disciples got into a boat and started to cross a lake. Suddenly a windstorm struck. Waves splashed into the boat, and it was about to sink. Jesus was asleep in the boat. His disciples woke him and said, "Teacher, don't you care that we're about to drown?" Jesus ordered the wind and waves to be quiet. Everything became calm. Jesus asked, "Why were you afraid? Don't you have any faith?"

Jesus stood up and commanded the wind, "Be quiet!" and he said to the waves, "Be still!"
Mark 4:39

Digging Deeper

In creation, we have constant reminders of God's goodness. Yet, so often we take the simple gifts around us for granted. We must never forget that all we have is from God. We are also called to look at our personal faith in God. Although Jesus is present in the boat with the Apostles, they are still frightened by the storm and question his concern for them. Jesus calls them, and us, to deeper faith.

I Pray

God my Father, all good things come from you. Help me to be loving and obedient in return. Amen.

I'll hear this Gospel story in Mass...

**The 12th Sunday in Ordinary Time
Liturgical Year B**

PARALYTIC Through the ROOF
Mark 2:1-12

> ### So he said to the paralyzed man, "I tell you, get up, pick up your mat, and go home!"
> *Mark 2:10-11*

I Pray

Dear Jesus, heal me and love me that I may walk with you forever. Amen.

Digging Deeper

When we are in need of help from God, we sometimes get frustrated if nothing seems to happen when we pray or it feels like God is not listening to us. The four friends in this story teach us to never give up. There is always a way to get close to Jesus, and there is always a way for Jesus to help us. Jesus knows that our greatest need is to be healed of our sins and so he forgives us. And Jesus knows that we want to follow him so he gives us a way to walk in his path through our faith in him.

I'll hear this Gospel story in Mass...

The 7th Sunday in Ordinary Time Liturgical Year B

Look Up

A man who was paralyzed had four friends who wanted to help him walk again. When Jesus was in town, they carried their friend to the place where Jesus was. But many other people wanted to hear Jesus and get help from him, and it was so crowded that the men could not get through the front door with their friend. So they got creative and climbed up on the roof, made a hole in the roof and lowered their paralyzed friend down right in front of Jesus. Jesus took notice and first forgave the man's sins and then told the man to get up and walk. So that is what the man did. He took his mat and walked. And the people were amazed.

PARABLE of the SOWER
Matthew 13:1-9, 18-23

Jesus Tells Us to Listen to Him

Jesus told this story: "A farmer went out to sow seed in his field. Some seeds fell along the road and were eaten by birds. Some fell on rocky ground and started growing, but couldn't grow deep roots, so they quickly died. Other seeds fell where thorny bushes grew and choked the plants. But some seeds fell on good ground and produced many, many strong, healthy plants." Then Jesus said, "If you have ears, pay attention!"

> **But some seeds fell in good soil, and the plants bore grain: some had one hundred grains, others sixty, and others thirty.**
> *Matthew 13:8*

Digging Deeper

Jesus' story about the farmer who scattered seeds over several types of soil reminds us to examine the kind of soil we offer for God's Word to grow in us. God's Word grows best in a heart that is ready to accept it—tilled and tender like good soil; a heart that is prepared to keep it growing with watering and weeding. This kind of heart will produce the biggest harvest of Gospel values!

I Pray

Jesus, plant the seeds of faith in me. Help me to grow closer to you. Amen.

I'll hear this Gospel story in Mass...

**The 15th Sunday in Ordinary Time
Liturgical Year A**

Raising JAIRUS' DAUGHTER
Mark 5:21-24, 35-43

I'll hear this Gospel story in Mass...

The 13th Sunday in Ordinary Time Liturgical Year B

Digging Deeper

Jesus listens to the man whose daughter is dying and goes with him to help. Even when people tell the man that his daughter is dead, Jesus tells him not to worry. Jesus lives up to his promises and helps the man's daughter by bringing her to life again. We must trust that Jesus will help us, no matter how bad things look. He has the power to make all things good again.

I Pray

Lord Jesus, help me to have faith that you will do what you say. Amen.

> **[Jesus] took her by the hand and said to her, "Talitha, koum," which means, "Little girl, I tell you to get up!"**
> *Mark 5:41*

Jesus Gives New Life

Jairus, a Jewish leader, approached Jesus and said, "My daughter is dying! Please touch her, so she will live." Some men met them on the way to Jairus' house and said, "She has died!" Jesus said to Jairus, "Don't worry. Have faith!"

Then Jesus took the girl's father and mother and three disciples to where the girl was. He held her hand and said, "Little girl, get up!" She got up and started walking around.

FEEDING the 5000
John 6:1-14

Jesus Feeds a Large Crowd

Jesus and the disciples went up on a mountain. When Jesus saw a crowd coming, he asked Philip how they would feed all the people. Philip answered that it would take almost a year's wages to feed the crowd. A boy shared his five small loaves of barley bread and two fish. Jesus took the bread in his hands and gave thanks to God. Then he passed the bread to the people. He did the same with the fish. The people ate all they wanted. The leftovers filled twelve large baskets.

> **Jesus took the bread, gave thanks to God, and distributed it to the people who were sitting there. He did the same with the fish, and they all had as much as they wanted.**
> *John 6:11*

Digging Deeper

A person who works with the poor told a story of a family that was given some food. Instead of hoarding the food, however, they shared it with another hungry family. They understood that they could not let their neighbors starve while they had the security of eating for two or three days. Like the boy in the story, they shared the little they had. Their generosity multiplied a small gift into a great gift.

I Pray

Merciful Jesus, teach me to share all the gifts I have with others. Help me to have a generous heart. Amen.

I'll hear this Gospel story in Mass...

**The 17th Sunday in Ordinary Time
Liturgical Year B**

WALKING on WATER
Matthew 14:22-33

Jesus spoke to them at once. "Courage!" he said. "It is I. Don't be afraid!"
Matthew 14:27

We Have Faith in Jesus

One stormy night, Jesus told the disciples to take the boat out and leave him on shore. Later they saw Jesus walking toward them on the water! They couldn't believe it! Peter said, "Lord, if it is really you, tell me to come to you." "Come on!" Jesus said. Peter started walking on the water, but then got scared and started to sink. "Save me," he cried. Jesus saved him and said, "Why do you doubt, Peter?"

Digging Deeper

Who but Jesus could be so reassuring when the waters are churning? Life is full of stormy waters that shake our faith just as the stormy waters distracted Peter's focus from Jesus. It can be easy to be distracted by our weaknesses. And it's easy to be distracted by our busy schedules. Don't be afraid to keep your focus on Jesus. And don't be afraid to call for his help!

I Pray

Jesus, give me strength and courage to believe in you always. Amen.

I'll hear this Gospel story in Mass...

The 19th Sunday in Ordinary Time Liturgical Year A

173

The CANAANITE Mother
Matthew 15:21-28

Jesus Can Heal Us

A Canaanite woman was begging Jesus to heal her daughter. "Have pity!" she cried. Jesus said, "I was sent only to the Israelites! It isn't right to take food from children and feed it to dogs." The woman answered, "That's true, but even dogs get the crumbs that fall from the table." Jesus said, "Dear woman, you have a lot of faith, and you will get what you want." At that moment, her daughter was healed.

> "That's true, sir," she answered, "but even the dogs eat the leftovers that fall from their masters' table."
> *Matthew 15:27*

Digging Deeper

In this story, Jesus was reluctant to respond to the Canaanite woman. After all, his mission, or ministry, involved the Israelites, not the Canaanites. The woman persisted and Jesus relented. Not only did he cure her daughter, but he praised her faith. Ministry is a way to show God's love. Jesus did not limit his love to any particular group. He showed that God's love includes all people. Does yours?

I Pray

Jesus, you healed many people.
May you heal me from my hurts,
fears, and sadness. Amen.

I'll hear this Gospel story in Mass...

**The 20th Sunday in Ordinary Time
Liturgical Year A**

The TRANSFIGURATION
Luke 9:28-36

I'll hear this Gospel story in Mass...

**The Second Sunday of Lent
Liturgical Year C**

Digging Deeper

In this story, Jesus takes Peter, James, and John to the top of the mountain to pray. While they are there, they experience the majesty and wonder that is God. It is good for us to strengthen our relationship with God through prayer.
The Church provides opportunities to pray through retreats, services, and Mass. Sometimes, like the Apostles, we need something different to help us experience God in a new way.

I Pray

Loving Father, help me to know and follow your Son, Jesus. Amen.

> **While he was praying, his face changed its appearance, and his clothes became dazzling white.**
> *Luke 9:29*

Jesus Is God's Chosen One

Jesus took Peter, John, and James up on a mountain to pray. The three disciples fell asleep. When they woke, they saw that Jesus was changed. They also saw Moses and Elijah speaking with him. When Moses and Elijah were about to leave, Peter said, "Let us make three shelters—one for each of you." Then a cloud's shadow covered them and a voice said, "This is my chosen Son. Listen to what he says!"

Parable of the GOOD SAMARITAN
Luke 10:29-37

Caring for Others

Jesus told this story: A man was traveling from Jerusalem to Jericho when robbers beat him and took everything he had. They left him half dead. Two people passed by without helping. Then a Samaritan passed by. When he saw the man, he treated his wounds with olive oil and bandaged them. He put the man on his own donkey and took him to an inn. The Samaritan was a real neighbor. We are to do as he did.

> **But a Samaritan who was traveling that way came upon the man, and when he saw him, his heart was filled with pity.**
> *Luke 10:33*

Digging Deeper

The Good Samaritan story is familiar. All people are our neighbors. Now, God does not expect us to put ourselves or our loved ones in harm's way to help others. But if we see an obvious need, and we feel that we are not personally in danger, we are obliged as Christians to help. The point Jesus was making was that it should not matter who needs help. Every person is our neighbor.

I Pray

Lord Jesus, when I find it difficult to act with kindness, help me remember your words and your example. Make me a person who acts with love. Amen.

I'll hear this Gospel story in Mass...

**The 15th Sunday in Ordinary Time
Liturgical Year C**

Visiting MARY and MARTHA
Luke 10:38-42

> **The Lord answered her, "Martha, Martha! You are worried and troubled over so many things, but just one is needed."**
> *Luke 10:41-42*

Digging Deeper
This story often leaves us with the impression that some people's gifts and talents are more desirable than other people's. Not so! Like Mary and Martha, each of us has a unique combination of gifts and talents. We also have our unique weaknesses. In families, problems can arise if we value certain gifts and talents more than others. While it may be easy to appreciate and relate to certain gifts in one person, it is important that another person not feel undervalued.

I Pray
Jesus, help me know what is most important in your kingdom. Help me to always put you first in my life. Amen.

I'll hear this Gospel story in Mass...

The 16th Sunday in Ordinary Time Liturgical Year C

Jesus Visits Martha and Mary
The Lord and his disciples traveled to a village where a woman named Martha welcomed him into her home. Martha had a sister named Mary, who sat in front of the Lord and listened to what he said. Martha was worried about all that needed to be done. She went to Jesus and said, "Lord, tell her to come help me!" The Lord answered, "Mary has chosen what is best, and it will not be taken away from her."

Parable of the UNFORGIVING Servant
Matthew 18:23-35

God Wants Us to Show Mercy

A man owed the king money. The king could have thrown the man and his family out on the street, but the man begged for mercy. The king felt sorry for him and forgave his debt. This man then met someone who owed him money and he got very angry at this person. He even had that man thrown into prison! The king was very angry at this, so he made the first man pay back everything he owed.

> **The king felt sorry for him, so he forgave him the debt and let him go.**
> *Matthew 18:27*

Digging Deeper

You know what it means to say, "I'm sorry. I was wrong." When caught doing something upsetting to someone, lots of people will sometimes utter these words quickly to avoid punishment. Everybody needs to say, "I'm sorry," when a stressful situation occurs. Being able to apologize to another person teaches us that we all need forgiveness. Family life becomes better when all members give forgiveness to one another.

I Pray

Lord, help me to forgive others as I would like others to forgive me. May I always remember that you are kind and merciful. Amen.

I'll hear this Gospel story in Mass...

**The 24th Sunday in Ordinary Time
Liturgical Year A**

HEALING the Man BORN BLIND
John 9:1-39

> "Go and wash your face in the Pool of Siloam." (This name means "Sent.") So the man went, washed his face, and came back seeing.
> *John 9:7*

Jesus Cures the Man Who Was Blind

Jesus cured a man who had been blind from birth. People were amazed! The Pharisees tried to make the man take back his story about how Jesus cured him, but he wouldn't. Jesus asked the man if he believed in the Son of Man. The man said he would if he knew who the Son of Man was. Jesus said, "You are talking to him." The man said, "Lord, I put my faith in you."

Digging Deeper

God sees things differently than we do. Sometimes we think we have the right perspective on a situation, and then God shows us a whole different way of seeing it. We may be blind and not even know it. This is a good thing to talk about within your family. Think about different types of events and ponder different people's points of view. Practice looking at people and events from all sides of a situation.

I Pray

Lord Jesus, may I put my faith in you every day. Amen.

I'll hear this Gospel story in Mass...

The Fourth Sunday of Lent Liturgical Year A

The GREATEST Commandment
Matthew 22:34-40

I'll hear this Gospel story in Mass...
**The 30th Sunday in Ordinary Time
Liturgical Year A**

Digging Deeper
This story reminds us that love of God and love of neighbor go hand in hand. This caring about God and others is what Jesus commands his Church to do. We are the Church Jesus founded, and what happens in our lives should reflect what we believe in faith. Love is at the center of our lives. It extends to forgiveness, compassion, respectfulness, and all those other virtues that form a holy person.

I Pray
Lord, help me grow in love for you. Teach me to treat others with love every day. Amen.

Love the Lord your God with all your heart, with all your soul, and with all your mind.
Matthew 22:37

Jesus Teaches About Love
The Pharisees again tried to trick Jesus. One of them asked him, "What is the most important commandment?" Jesus answered, "Love the Lord your God with all your heart, soul, and mind. This is the first and most important commandment. And the second most important is: 'Love others as much as you love yourself.' All the Law of Moses and the Prophets are based on these two commandments."

Parable of EQUAL PAY for the WORKERS
Matthew 20:1-16

> **Call the workers and pay them their wages, starting with those who were hired last and ending with those who were hired first.**
> *Matthew 20:8*

God's Ways Are Not Our Ways

Jesus told the story of a man who hired some workers very early one morning. They agreed on their pay for the day's work. Throughout the day, the man hired more workers at different times. When he paid the workers at the end of the day, those who worked the longest expected more pay. But the man said, "I paid you what we agreed. If I want to be generous, I can be." Jesus added, "The last shall be first."

Digging Deeper

What does it mean to be fair? Both Isaiah the prophet and Jesus tell us that God is much more fair to us than we can imagine. Sometimes you may think someone is being unfair. We all have many hard decisions to make, and people learn what is best when they are included as much as possible in the decision-making. When we work together, fairness on all levels will be easier.

I Pray

Lord, remind me to be generous to all people. Let me never forget your generosity to me. Amen.

I'll hear this Gospel story in Mass...

The 25th Sunday in Ordinary Time Liturgical Year A

Parables of the LOST SHEEP & COIN
Luke 15:3-10

The Lost Is Found

Jesus told two parables about things that were lost. He first told about a shepherd who had a hundred sheep, but lost one. Most shepherds would probably let that sheep go. But not this shepherd. This shepherd looked all over the pasture for the lost sheep until he found it and put it on his shoulders and brought that sheep back into the fold. Jesus also talked about a woman who lost a coin. Again, other people might just let that little coin go. But not this woman. She swept and searched until she found that lost coin, celebrating with her friends and neighbors when she did.

> **Then you call your friends and neighbors together and say to them, "I am so happy I found my lost sheep. Let us celebrate!"**
> *Luke 15:6*

Digging Deeper

These parables remind us that Jesus never leaves us behind when we get lost in sin and trouble. He takes the time to go out and get us so that we can enjoy being in his presence with his people. There is no length to which Jesus will not go to save the lost. He died on the Cross for our sins and opened the way for us to live together with all believers in Heaven. In him our joy is found.

I Pray

Thank you, O Jesus, for searching for me when I am lost and finding me that I might celebrate the love you have for us all. Amen.

I'll hear this Gospel story in Mass...

**The 24th Sunday in Ordinary Time
Liturgical Year C**

Parable of the PRODIGAL SON
Luke 15:11-32

He was still a long way from home when his father saw him; his heart was filled with pity, and he ran, threw his arms around his son, and kissed him.
Luke 15:20

The Forgiving Father

A father had two sons. The younger son was foolish and greedy. The older son was loyal and hard working. The younger son left home. After he wasted all his money, he returned home. The father was overjoyed to see him and threw him a big party. This made the older son angry. He had worked hard, but his father never gave him a party. "That's not fair!" he said. The father said to him, "Son, all that I have is yours, but your brother was lost and now is found. Because of this, we celebrate!"

Digging Deeper

Family members often experience a need to apologize to one another—to be forgiven and to forgive. In this story, we hear again about God's capacity for "loving us anyway" when we have done wrong. This is a good time to look within our own relationships and examine how willing we are to forgive others, and how willing we are to ask others for forgiveness.

I Pray

God, my Father, you are always loving and ready to forgive. Help me always to count on your love. Amen.

I'll hear this Gospel story in Mass...

The 24th Sunday in Ordinary Time Liturgical Year C

Parable of the RICH MAN and LAZARUS
Luke 16:19-31

I'll hear this Gospel story in Mass...
The 26th Sunday in Ordinary Time
Liturgical Year C

Digging Deeper
Sometimes we may find it difficult to give to others, but we need to remember how blessed we really are. Most of us live in ways considered luxurious in many parts of the world. Reflect on things we take for granted—everyday things like clean running water, milk in the refrigerator, and a bed to sleep in every night. Remember that we are among the few people in the world who have so much.

I Pray
Jesus, sometimes I forget to care for others. Help me to treat others just as I want to be treated. Amen.

The Rich Man and Lazarus
Once there was a poor man named Lazarus. He wore rags and ate food thrown away by a rich man, who was not kind to Lazarus. When the two men died, Lazarus went to heaven, where he was very happy. But because the rich man had been selfish and mean, he faced eternal suffering. The rich man begged to be freed from his eternal suffering, but because he had not listened when he was told to follow God, he had to endure it forever.

But Abraham said, "If they will not listen to Moses and the prophets, they will not be convinced even if someone were to rise from death."
Luke 16:31

Healing the TEN LEPERS
Luke 17:11-19

**When one of them saw
that he was healed,
he came back, praising God
in a loud voice.**
Luke 17:15

Remember to Thank God
One day, ten men, all covered in sores, begged Jesus to cure them. They had a terrible disease called leprosy. Jesus told them to go see the priests, who could decide if the men were no longer sick. On their way, the men saw that their sores were gone. Jesus had healed them! One man went back to thank Jesus. "Weren't ten men healed? Why did only one come back to thank me?" Jesus asked.

Digging Deeper
It's so easy to take things for granted. We wake each day and expect that we will get clean water from our faucets, eat fresh food from our local grocery, even have our favorite TV show to watch. This story about the ten lepers reminds us of the need to feel grateful. Gratitude is a deeper sense of appreciation for all that we have and a realization that our blessings are not ours by right, but by the goodness of God.

I Pray
Lord Jesus, you give me so
many blessings each day.
Help me to be thankful. Amen.

I'll hear this Gospel story in Mass...

**The 28th Sunday in Ordinary Time
Liturgical Year C**

185

JESUS and the CHILDREN
Mark 10:13-16

Jesus Welcomes the Children

Some people brought their children to Jesus to be blessed. The disciples told the people to leave Jesus alone. When Jesus saw what the disciples did, he said, "Let the little children come to me! People who are like children belong to the kingdom of God. Unless you accept it the way a child does, you cannot get into God's kingdom." Then gathering the children in his arms, Jesus blessed them.

> **Whoever does not receive the Kingdom of God like a child will never enter it.**
> *Mark 10:15*

Digging Deeper

In this story, Jesus reminds us that unless we become open to love, we will not understand the Kingdom of God. Little children learn from example, and the friendships they see influence their future friendships. We should all model loyalty and love in our relationships with one another. Friendship is important because we all need somebody with whom we can share ourselves.

I Pray

Jesus, your love for me is wonderful. You welcome me as a friend. Thank you for your love and friendship. Amen.

I'll hear this Gospel story in Mass...

**The 27th Sunday in Ordinary Time
Liturgical Year B**

ZACCHAEUS
Luke 19:1-10

> **So [Zacchaeus] ran ahead of the crowd and climbed a sycamore tree to see Jesus, who was going to pass that way.**
> *Luke 19:4*

Zacchaeus Promises to Change

A great crowd gathered to see Jesus. Among them was Zacchaeus, a man who got rich by cheating people. Because he was short, Zacchaeus climbed a tree so he could see Jesus. "Zacchaeus, come down. I want to visit your house," Jesus shouted. Zacchaeus was thrilled but others were angry and jealous. Zacchaeus told Jesus, "I am sorry for cheating people and will pay everyone back." Jesus said, "I came to save people like you who were on the wrong path."

Digging Deeper

God's mercy is sometimes hard for us to understand and accept. This story tells us about Jesus and his encounter with Zacchaeus, the tax collector. Jesus shocks everyone by accepting Zacchaeus as he is, while challenging him to be better. Zacchaeus feels free to be himself but, because of Jesus' love, he decides to be better.

I Pray

Lord Jesus, Zacchaeus climbed a tree to see you. He promised to change and be good. I want to seek you when I do something wrong, and to do my best to do better. Amen.

I'll hear this Gospel story in Mass...

The 31st Sunday in Ordinary Time Liturgical Year C

Raising of LAZARUS
John 11:1-44

Jesus Gives Lazarus New Life

When Lazarus was sick, Mary and Martha sent for Jesus. By the time he arrived, however, their brother was dead and buried. Everyone was crying. Jesus cried too. Martha said to Jesus, "If you had been here, he would not have died." Jesus said, "I am the one who raises the dead to life. Everyone who believes in me will live forever." Then Jesus called Lazarus out of his grave and returned him to life.

After [Jesus] had said this, he called out in a loud voice, "Lazarus, come out!"
John 11:43

Digging Deeper

Learning to recognize, admit, and deal with feelings is a lifelong task. We are often eager to share what is going on in our lives. But sometimes we tend to hide what we feel because we aren't quite sure what feelings will be acceptable to others. We should find safe places to share the daily adventures of our lives. We can also bring our feelings to Jesus, who listens to us and loves us always.

I Pray

Jesus, I believe in you. I pray that I will one day live with you forever in Heaven. Amen.

I'll hear this Gospel story in Mass...

**The Fifth Sunday of Lent
Liturgical Year A**

ENTRY into JERUSALEM
Luke 19:28-40

I'll hear this Gospel story in Mass...

**The Palm Sunday Processional
Liturgical Years C**

Digging Deeper

Jesus gives us opportunities for caring and loving one another. We are called by Christ to make sacrifices for one another. Sometimes we take the people with whom we live for granted. Sometimes we selfishly think everything will work out for us when it may not always happen that way. Sometimes we fail to see the uniqueness in each other. We may not always notice the people who need our help. Jesus calls us to accept his great gift of love as shown in his life, Death, and Resurrection. Only through Christ's love are we able to live selflessly.

I Pray

Jesus, I welcome you into my life and my heart. Amen.

"God bless the king who comes in the name of the Lord! Peace in heaven and glory to God!"
Luke 19:38

The People Welcome Jesus

Jesus and his disciples were close to Jerusalem when Jesus said, "Go into the next village. You will find a donkey and her colt. Bring them to me." When they got back, Jesus sat on the donkey and rode toward the city. People all along the way greeted him with joyful shouts of "Hosanna!" and made a path for him out of palm branches. Everyone was excited because the prophet from Nazareth had come.

The WIDOW'S Offering
Mark 12:41-44

The Poor Widow Gives All She Has

Jesus was sitting in the Temple near the offering box. He noticed that many rich people gave a lot of money. Finally, a poor widow came up and put in two coins that were worth only a few pennies. Jesus told his disciples, "This poor widow has put in more than all the others. Everyone else gave what they didn't need. But she is very poor and gave everything she had."

> **A poor widow came along and dropped in two little copper coins, worth about a penny.**
> *Mark 12:42*

Digging Deeper

Sacrifice. When we are little, we may have no idea what this word means. Then when we are older, we may not think of sacrifice as a good thing. But as we grow older, we understand what sacrifice means. After all, most of us make sacrifices every day for the benefit of someone else. With help from God, we can understand that sacrifice is its own reward, as we are shown the fruit of our labors and our losses. Best of all, sacrifice is a way of expressing our love for God.

I Pray

Jesus, I want to be generous with what I have, but sometimes it is hard. Help me to share with a generous heart. Amen.

I'll hear this Gospel story in Mass...

**The 32nd Sunday in Ordinary Time
Liturgical Year B**

Parable of the TWO SONS
Matthew 21:28-32

Which one of the two did what his father wanted?"
Matthew 21:31

Walk in the Lord's Ways

Jesus told the chief priests and leaders a story about a father who asked his older son to work in the vineyard. The son said, "No," but later he did it anyway. The father asked his younger son to work in the vineyard. He said, "Yes," but he didn't do the work. When Jesus asked which son obeyed the father, the people said the older son. Jesus then said, "Cheating tax collectors and other sinners who believed John the Baptist and changed their ways will get into Heaven before you."

Digging Deeper

In this story, Jesus addresses honesty and obedience. He calls us to mean what we say and say what we mean. He calls us to believe what John the Baptist preached and change anything that could lead us astray. Strong families help one another in our journey to the Kingdom of God. Being a good disciple means that we will be honest and follow through on our promises.

I Pray

Lord, help me to change my ways. Show me the path to Heaven. Amen.

I'll hear this Gospel story in Mass...

The 26th Sunday in Ordinary Time Liturgical Year A

Parable of the WEDDING FEAST
Matthew 22:1-14

I'll hear this Gospel story in Mass...

**The 28th Sunday in Ordinary Time
Liturgical Year A**

Digging Deeper

Parties are events that most people don't want to miss. Parties bring us together. God calls us to be family. God calls us to spend quality time encouraging one another. If it takes a party to call people together, then by all means find a reason to have one. The more time we can gather around our family banquet table, the better prepared we will be to celebrate the great party God invites us to.

I Pray

Lord, help me to recognize your voice in my life. May I always be ready to listen to you. Amen.

Come to the Lord's Banquet

Jesus told a story about a king who gave a wedding banquet for his son. None of the invited guests came. The king sent his servants to remind the guests that the banquet was ready, but they still refused to come. The king was so angry that he told his servants to go out on the streets and invite everyone they met, good and bad alike. And they did. And the banquet hall was filled with guests.

Now go to the main streets and invite to the feast as many people as you find.
Matthew 22:9

Parable of the TEN YOUNG WOMEN
Matthew 25:1-13

> **The five who were ready went in with him to the wedding feast, and the door was closed.**
> *Matthew 25:10*

Jesus Says Be Ready for Him

Jesus told this story: Ten girls went to a wedding to greet the groom. Five were wise and took extra oil for their lamps and five did not. When the groom was almost there, the lamps all ran out of oil. The five girls with no extra oil had to leave to buy more. While they were gone, the groom came, and the five wise girls went into the wedding and the doors were closed.

Digging Deeper

In this story, we meet the ten girls waiting with their oil lamps. Five are prepared with extra oil in tow. Five are not. The lesson of the story is clear: Be prepared for the unexpected. We learn this by becoming involved in the preparations for special events such as parties or holidays. Preparing your own meal prayers for your family and nighttime prayers to say with your mom or dad is one way for you to have spiritual responsibility.

I Pray

Lord, may I be prepared to meet you when you come again. May my life be pleasing to you. Amen.

I'll hear this Gospel story in Mass...

The 32nd Sunday in Ordinary Time Liturgical Year A

193

Parable of the THREE SERVANTS
Matthew 25:14-30

God Wants Us to Do Our Best

Jesus told this story about the Kingdom of God: A man went away and put three servants in charge of his money. He gave the first servant 5,000 coins, the second got 2,000 coins, and the third got 1,000. When the man came back, he asked them all what they had done with his money. The one left with 5,000 coins had earned 5,000 more. "Wonderful," the man said, "you are a good and faithful servant."

"Well done, you good and faithful servant!" said his master. "You have been faithful in managing small amounts, so I will put you in charge of large amounts. Come on in and share my happiness!"
Matthew 25:23

Digging Deeper

This story calls us to look at the gifts and talents God has given us and how we use them. The old saying, "You can't pick your family," is true. But you do have something to say about what part you play in your family. You can take stock of each member of your family, identify specific gifts, and work toward helping your fellow family members grow those gifts for the sake of the world. Each of us can use our gifts in a unique way.

I Pray

Lord, you have given me unique talents and gifts. May I always do good deeds with them. Amen.

I'll hear this Gospel story in Mass...
**The 33rd Sunday in Ordinary Time
Liturgical Year A**

The FINAL JUDGMENT
Matthew 25:31-46

> "I tell you, whenever you did this for one of the least important of these followers of mine, you did it for me!"
> *Matthew 25:40*

You Have Done It unto Me

Jesus told this story about a shepherd who separates the sheep from the goats. After he has separated them, he says to the sheep, "Welcome to my kingdom. You helped me out when I was hungry and thirsty and naked and sick!" The sheep say, "When did we do this all to you?" And the shepherd says, "When you did it to the lowliest among you, you did it to me." Then the shepherd says to the goats, "Get away from me. You are not welcome here because you did not help me when I was hungry and thirsty and naked and sick!" The goats say, "When did we not do this to you?" Jesus says, "When you didn't do this to the lowliest among you, you did not do to me."

Digging Deeper

This parable shows us that we are to be like Christ in how we treat one another. We should help out those who are in need around us, no matter who they are. We should not look away from or discard the people who are poor or helpless or strangers to us. Jesus came for all. He ate with tax collectors and sinners and other people society did not like. And we should too. We serve Jesus out of love for him when we serve every person we see.

I Pray

Help me, Lord, to serve those around me as you have served me so faithfully. Amen.

I'll hear this Gospel story in Mass...

**Christ the King Sunday
Liturgical Year A**

195

The LORD'S SUPPER
Matthew 26:17-19, 26-30

Jesus Gives Us the Eucharist

Jesus and the disciples were eating the Passover meal in the Upper Room. Jesus took some bread, blessed it, and broke it. Then he gave it to his disciples to eat and said, "This is my body." Jesus picked up a cup of wine and gave thanks to God. He gave it to his disciples to drink and said, "This is my blood, which is poured out for many people."

I tell you, I will never again drink this wine until the day I drink the new wine with you in my Father's Kingdom.
Matthew 26:29

Digging Deeper

Our experience at Mass should be a life-changing experience. We must be open to letting God touch our lives in the Word, in one another, and, of course, in the Eucharist. If we do this, people will sense something different in the way we treat them and deal with whatever challenges we face. God wants to be an active presence in our lives. That is why he gave us the gift of the Eucharist.

I Pray

Lord Jesus, help me to know you.
Open my heart to welcome you. Amen.

I'll hear this Gospel story in Mass...

**Palm Sunday of the Passion of Our Lord
Liturgical Year A**

JESUS in the GARDEN
Luke 22:39-45

I'll hear this Gospel story in Mass...

**Palm Sunday of the Passion of Our Lord
Liturgical Year C**

Digging Deeper

The scene in the Garden of Gethsemane reveals to us that Jesus was just as human as we are. He was nervous and scared and did not want to go through with what God had planned for him. But because that was what God had in mind for him, Jesus did what his Father asked. Sometimes it is hard for us to do what God asks us to do. But God gives us strength and power and faith from him to move forward in the tasks God sets before us. We should not be like the disciples who fell asleep. We should be awake and ready to follow God's will.

I Pray

O Son of God, give me vision
to see your plan for me and
follow through. Amen.

Then he went off from them about the distance of a stone's throw and knelt down and prayed.
Luke 22:41

Thy Will Be Done

After Jesus and his disciples ate the Eucharist meal, they left the Upper Room and went to the Garden of Gethsemane to pray. Jesus went off away from the disciples to pray more privately to the heavenly Father. He prayed that this cup of suffering he was about to experience on the cross would be taken away. But he obediently said, "Not my will, but yours be done." He prayed so hard that his sweat became like great drops of blood. When he was done praying, he came back to find his disciples sleeping.

Peter's DENIAL
Luke 22:31-34, 54-62

The Rooster Crow

On the night that Jesus was arrested, Peter told Jesus he would never deny him, but Jesus said that before the rooster crowed, Peter would deny him three times. When Jesus was being tried in court hours later, Peter stood in the courtyard outside warming himself by the fire. Then a young girl said Peter was with Jesus. Peter said he did not know the man. Then a man said Peter was one of Jesus' disciples. Peter said no. Then another person said that Peter's accent connected him to Jesus. But Peter swore that was not true. Right then, the rooster crowed, Jesus looked straight at Peter and Peter went out and wept bitterly.

> **"I tell you, Peter,"** Jesus said, **"the rooster will not crow tonight until you have said three times that you do not know me."**
> *Luke 22:34*

Digging Deeper

Like Peter, we so often think that we would never deny Jesus. But we do it all the time when people make fun of Jesus and we don't say anything. We do it when we are afraid to pray in a restaurant because we worry what people will think. We do it when we hide our Bible when we are in public because we don't want people to know we are Christian. But we have a Savior who loves us and he forgives us every time we deny him, just like Jesus forgave Peter on the beach after Jesus rose from the dead.

I Pray

Help me, O Jesus, to proclaim that I belong to you wherever I go. Amen.

I'll hear this Gospel story in Mass...

Palm Sunday of the Passion of Our Lord Liturgical Year C

The CRUCIFIXION
Matthew 27:33—28:5; John 18:28-19:16

> **They crucified him and then divided his clothes among them by throwing dice.**
> *Matthew 27:35*

Jesus Dies on the Cross

Even though Pilate found Jesus innocent, he handed Jesus over to the soldiers to be hung on a cross between two criminals. On the cross, Jesus said, "Forgive them, Father, for they don't know what they're doing!" The soldiers said to Jesus, "If you are the king of the Jews, save yourself!" The sky turned dark and stayed that way until mid-afternoon. Jesus cried out, "Father, into your hands I put my spirit!" Then he died.

Digging Deeper

Depending on where we are in our lives and faith, we may approach the crucifixion of Jesus differently. For instance, we may not want to remember Jesus' pain and suffering, or we might draw comfort from the fact that our Savior really knows life's pain and suffering. No matter our attitude, the Cross always reminds us of what it means to be a follower of Jesus.

I Pray

Lord Jesus, I want to always be among those who know you and believe in you. Give me faith and courage. Amen.

I'll hear this Gospel story in Mass...

Good Friday of the Passion of Our Lord Liturgical Years A,B,C

Palm Sunday of the Passion of Our Lord Liturgical Year A

The RESURRECTION
John 20:1-10

Listen for this Gospel story on:

**The Resurrection of Our Lord
Liturgical Years A,B,C**

Digging Deeper

Our faith and our Church are built on the story of the Resurrection. We believe the tomb was empty because Jesus rose from the dead. He is the Risen Lord who continues to be with us as we celebrate the sacraments, especially the Eucharist. His words and actions continue to guide us as a faith community.

I Pray

Jesus, through your Death and Resurrection you bring me new life. I praise you for your great love for us. Amen.

Jesus Is Risen!

On Sunday morning, Mary Magdalene went to the tomb, where she saw that the stone covering the entrance had been rolled away. She ran to Simon Peter and the disciple Jesus loved and said, "They have taken the Lord!" The men ran to the tomb. The other disciple got there first and saw the strips of linen cloth lying inside. Then Simon Peter went into the tomb and saw the strips of cloth.

Then the other disciple, who had reached the tomb first, also went in; he saw and believed.
John 20:8

The RESURRECTION
John 20:11-18; Mark 16:1-9

> **Jesus said to her, "Mary!" She turned toward him and said in Hebrew, "Rabboni!" (This means "Teacher.")**
> *John 20:16*

I Pray
Dear Jesus, keep teaching me new things about you. Amen.

Digging Deeper
Mary learned many things from Jesus. That is why she called him Teacher. She had listened to his preaching. She had witnessed his miracles. Yet she still had more to learn from him. Jesus revealed to her that he was going back to Heaven. Mary must have marveled at what she encountered at the tomb. Everything was so surprising—a stone rolled away, angels appearing and Jesus standing next to her alive. As students of our Savior, we, too, are just as surprised and excited about what Mary learned that first Easter. Jesus has overcome death, Heaven rejoices, and Christ's Resurrection changes our lives forever.

Rabboni!
Mary Magdalene was crying outside of the empty tomb of Jesus. She did not know what to think now that there was no body in the grave. Then two angels appeared to her right where Jesus' body had been. They asked her why she was crying. She answered by saying she didn't know where Jesus was. Then she heard another voice behind her asking why she was crying. She thought it was the gardner, so she asked him if he knew where Jesus was. But then, when the man said, "Mary," she realized it was Jesus. She exclaimed, "Rabboni!" (which means teacher). This term of endearment shows how close Mary and Jesus were. Jesus told Mary to tell the disciples that he was returning to the Father, so she ran and told them what she saw and what Jesus said.

Listen for this Gospel story on:

The Resurrection of Our Lord
Liturgical Years A,B,C

The ROAD to EMMAUS
Luke 24:13-35

Jesus Appears to the Disciples

Two disciples were walking along when a man joined them. The two disciples were sad and gloomy because Jesus, their Messiah, had died. The man, using the Scriptures, explained many things to them about Jesus. When they stopped to eat, the man blessed and broke the bread. That was when the two disciples knew that the man was Jesus. The disciples returned to Jerusalem to tell others, and they learned that others had also seen Jesus alive.

> And Jesus explained to them what was said about himself in all the Scriptures, beginning with the books of Moses and the writings of all the prophets.
> *Luke 24:27*

Digging Deeper

It is a good thing to create good memories for others. It is important for us to find ways and opportunities to discover the joys of life. This might require going an extra step outside of the daily routine—asking to have a picnic lunch, planning a game night for your family, or helping to set up a tent in the backyard to sleep under the stars. Just like Jesus made his disciples' journey memorable in this story, we can make our time with loved ones special.

I Pray

Jesus, help me to always know that you are with me in the Eucharist. Amen.

I'll hear this Gospel story in Mass...

**The 3rd Sunday of Easter
Liturgical Year A**

Doubting THOMAS
John 20:19-29

Thomas said to them, "Unless I see the scars of the nails in his hands and put my finger on those scars and my hand in his side, I will not believe."
John 20:25

Jesus Helps Thomas Believe
The Apostle Thomas was not with the others when Jesus appeared to them. They told him, "We have seen the Lord!" Thomas said, "I won't believe until I touch the wounds in his hands and side!" A week later, when the Apostles were gathered, Jesus appeared before them. He said to Thomas, "Put your finger on my hand; put your hand in my side. Stop doubting and have faith!" Thomas answered, "My Lord and my God!"

Digging Deeper
When Thomas returned to the room where the other disciples had seen Jesus, he found some ecstatic friends. Although he probably wanted to believe what they said, he found it unbelievable. Jesus returned and gave Thomas proof. We have all heard about how someone turned their life around or was successful because of someone else's faith in them. We understand what a gift it is to that person. Faith is a gift. Our faith in God is one of our greatest gifts.

I Pray
Lord, like the Apostle Thomas, sometimes my faith is weak. Help me to be strong in my beliefs. Amen.

I'll hear this Gospel story in Mass...

**The 2nd Sunday of Easter
Liturgical Years A,B,C**

BREAKFAST on the SEASHORE
John 21:1-19

Jesus Appears to the Disciples

Some of the disciples went fishing one evening. The next morning, Jesus stood on the shore, but the disciples did not realize who he was. Jesus shouted, "Have you caught anything?" When they said no, Jesus said, "Let your net down on the right side of the boat." They did, and the net filled with 153 fish. Then Jesus' favorite disciple said to Peter, "It's the Lord!" When the disciples got out of the boat, Jesus said, "Come and eat!"

He said to them, "Throw your net out on the right side of the boat, and you will catch some."
John 21:6

Digging Deeper

The events of Jesus' Passion, Crucifixion, and Resurrection probably caused powerful emotions within the Apostles. In such extraordinary situations, people often fall back on familiar routines. Because the Apostles were fishermen, they went fishing. Then Jesus appeared again at the seashore and prepared breakfast for them. He extended the invitation to "Come and eat." Jesus extends this same invitation to us each time we attend Mass.

I Pray

Jesus, sometimes you are present in my life but I do not recognize you. Open my eyes and help me to know you. Amen.

I'll hear this Gospel story in Mass...

**The 3rd Sunday of Easter
Liturgical Year C**

The ASCENSION / Great COMMISSION
Matthew 28:16-20

I'll hear this Gospel story in Mass...

**The Ascension of the Lord
(The 7th Sunday of Easter)
Liturgical Year A**

Digging Deeper
Jesus is going home to his beloved Father. For many people, returning to their childhood homes brings a sense of excitement and anticipation. Sacred memories surface. Our thoughts turn to the people who love us in ways no others do. We are creating sacred memories for each other. As you enter your home every day, feel the warmth, love, and safety radiating from it through Jesus.

I Pray
May I follow you to Heaven, O Lord. While on earth, help me to teach others about you. Amen.

Jesus drew near and said to them, "I have been given all authority in heaven and on earth."
Matthew 28:18

Jesus Ascends to Heaven
Jesus told his disciples, "Go and preach the Good News to everyone in the world. Whoever believes in me and is baptized will be saved." Then the Lord Jesus was taken back up to Heaven, where he sat down at the right side of God.

Gospel Reading Plan: **ADVENT**

First Sunday of Advent: Luke 21:25-28, 34-36
Monday: Matthew 8:5-11
Tuesday: Matthew 4:18-22
Wednesday: Matthew 15:29-37
Thursday: Matthew 7:21, 24-27
Friday: Matthew 9:27-31
Saturday: Matthew 9:35—10:1, 5a, 6-8

Second Sunday of Advent: Luke 3:1-6
Monday: Luke 5:17-26
Tuesday: Matthew 18:12-14
Wednesday: Matthew 11:28-30
Thursday: Matthew 11:11-15
Friday: Matthew 11:16-19
Saturday: Matthew 17:9a, 10-13

Third Sunday of Advent: Luke 3:10-18
Monday: Matthew 21:23-27
Tuesday: Matthew 21:28-32
Wednesday: Luke 7:18b-23
Thursday: Luke 7:24-30
Friday: Matthew 1:1-17
Saturday: Matthew 1:18-25

Fourth Sunday of Advent: Luke 1:39-45
Monday: Luke 1:26-38
Tuesday: Luke 1:46-56
Wednesday: Luke 1:57-66
Thursday: Luke 1:67-79
Friday: Luke 2:1-20
Saturday: John 1:1-18

Build anticipation for the Nativity of Our Lord through Gospel reading during the Advent Season.

Gospel Reading Plan: **LENT**

Observe the prayerful practice of Gospel reading throughout the season of Lent.

Ash Wednesday: Matthew 6:1-6, 16-18
Thursday: Luke 9:22-25
Friday: Matthew 9:14-15
Saturday: Luke 5:27-32

First Sunday of Lent: Luke 4:1-13
Monday: Matthew 25:31-46
Tuesday: Matthew 6:7-15
Wednesday: Luke 11:29-32
Thursday: Matthew 7:7-12
Friday: Matthew 5:20-26
Saturday: Matthew 5:43-48

Second Sunday: Luke 9:28b-36
Monday: Luke 6:36-38
Tuesday: Matthew 23:1-12
Wednesday: Matthew 20:17-28
Thursday: Luke 16:19-31
Friday: Matthew 21:33-43, 45-46
Saturday: Luke 15:1-3, 11-32

Third Sunday: John 4:5-42
Monday: Luke 4:24-30
Tuesday: Matthew 18:21-35
Wednesday: Matthew 5:17-19
Thursday: Luke 11:14-23
Friday: Mark 12:28-34
Saturday: Luke 18:9-14

Fourth Sunday: John 9:1-41
Monday: John 4:43-54
Tuesday: John 5:1-16
Wednesday: John 5:17-30
Thursday: John 5:31-47
Friday: John 7:1-2, 10, 25-30
Saturday: John 7:40-53

Fifth Sunday of Lent: John 8:1-11
Monday: John 11:1-45
Tuesday: John 8:21-30
Wednesday: John 8:31-42
Thursday: John 8:51-59
Friday: John 10:31-42
Saturday: John 11:45-56

Palm/Passion Sunday: Luke 19:28-40
Monday: John 12:1-11
Tuesday: John 13:21-33, 36-38
Wednesday: Matthew 26:14-25
Holy Thursday: John 13:1-15
Good Friday: John 18:1—19:42
Holy Saturday: Luke 24:1-12

Gospel Reading Plan: **EASTER**

Easter Sunday: John 20:1-9
Monday: Matthew 28:8-15
Tuesday: John 20:11-18
Wednesday: Luke 24:13-35
Thursday: Luke 24:35-48
Friday: John 21:1-14
Saturday: Mark 16:9-15

Second Sunday: John 20:19-31
Monday: Mark 16:15-20
Tuesday: John 3:7-15
Wednesday: John 3:16-21
Thursday: John 3:31-36
Friday: John 6:1-15
Saturday: John 6:16-21

Third Sunday: John 21:1-19
Monday: John 6:22-29
Tuesday: John 14:6-14
Wednesday: John 6:35-40
Thursday: John 6:44-51
Friday: John 6:52-59
Saturday: John 6:60-69

Fourth Sunday: John 10:27-30
Monday: John 10:1-10
Tuesday: John 10:22-30
Wednesday: John 12:44-50
Thursday: John 13:16-20
Friday: John 14:1-6
Saturday: John 15:9-17

Fifth Sunday: John 13:31-35
Monday: John 14:21-26
Tuesday: John 14:27-31a
Wednesday: John 15:1-8
Thursday: John 15:9-11
Friday: John 15:12-17
Saturday: John 15:18-21

Sixth Sunday: John 14:23-29
Monday: John 15:26—16:4a
Tuesday: John 16:5-11
Wednesday: John 16:12-15
Thursday: John 16:16-20
Friday: John 16:20-23
Saturday: John 16:23b-28

Seventh Sunday: Luke 24:46-53
Monday: John 16:29-33
Tuesday: John 17:1-11a
Wednesday: John 17:11b-19
Thursday: John 17:20-26
Friday: John 21:15-19
Saturday: John 21:20-25

Celebrate our Lord's Resurrection through Gospel reading throughout the Easter Season.

Read all four Gospels over a 40-day period, any time of the year!

Day 1: Matthew 1-3
Day 2: Matthew 4-6
Day 3: Matthew 7-9
Day 4: Matthew 10-12
Day 5: Matthew 13-14
Day 6: Matthew 15-16
Day 7: Matthew 17-18

Day 8: Matthew 19-20
Day 9: Matthew 21-22
Day 10: Matthew 23-24
Day 11: Matthew 25-26
Day 12: Matthew 27-28
Day 13: Mark 1-3
Day 14: Mark 4-6

Day 15: Mark 7-9
Day 16: Mark 10-12
Day 17: Mark 13-14
Day 18: Mark 15-16
Day 19: Luke 1-3
Day 20: Luke 4-6
Day 21: Luke 7-9

Day 22: Luke 10-12
Day 23: Luke 13-14
Day 24: Luke 15-16
Day 25: Luke 17-18
Day 26: Luke 19-20
Day 27: Luke 21-22
Day 28: Luke 23-24

Day 29: John 1-2
Day 30: John 3-4
Day 31: John 5-6
Day 32: John 7-8
Day 33: John 9-10
Day 34: John 11-12
Day 35: John 13-14
Day 36: John 15-16
Day 37: John 17-18
Day 38: John 19
Day 39: John 20
Day 40: John 21

LECTIO DIVINA

Lectio Divina is a traditional practice of Scripture reading, meditation and prayer that was first performed by monks. Each stage of the **Lectio Divina** (LEX-ee-oh dee-VEE-nah) is meant to draw us deeper into communion with Christ by either meditating on his Word or the fruits of his Word found in the Catechism.

The outline of **Lectio Divina** (Latin for "Divine Reading") is as follows:

LECTIO (LEX-ee-oh) **(reading)**

Select a specific passage of Scripture or teaching in the Catechism that you would like to meditate on.

MEDITATIO (med-ee-TAH-tee-oh) **(meditation)**

Once you've selected the specific passage, start meditating on the text. What words or phrases stand out to you? What strikes your heart?

ORATIO (oh-RAH-tee-oh) **(prayer)**

After careful meditation, the next step is to call upon the Holy Spirit for guidance in praying on the passage chosen. This involves an intentional act of prayer. Recite the passage vocally or quietly in an act of prayer and devotion.

CONTEMPLATIO (cone-tem-PLAH-tee-oh) **(contemplation)**

In this final step, respond to God's call about how to live out your faith and discover what God is asking of you.

LECTIO DIVINA

VISUALIZATION

As you meditate, close your eyes and imagine you were actually present within the Scripture passage you read. You can either act as an outside observer or imagine being one of the people in the passage. Think about your senses: What would you see, smell, hear, touch, or taste? Think about how you would feel if you were there.

STORIES

What personal stories does reading this passage bring to your mind? Ponder those stories and make personal connections in your mind to bring you closer to Jesus.

SPONTANEOUS PRAYER

Say or write a spontaneous prayer to God after reading and meditating on the passage. What do you want to say to God? What kind of prayer would be most appropriate: blessing and adoration, petition, intercession, thanksgiving, or praise?

CONVERSATION WITH CHRIST

A common Lectio Divina practice is to have people imagine they are sitting next to Jesus and having a conversation with him. What would you say to Jesus or ask him about this passage? What would he say in response? Write down your reflections on a sheet of paper or in a journal.

SILENCE

Take some time to sit in prayerful silence and think about what you've read and prayed. Give the Lord a chance to speak to you or instill in you a desire for change during these moments of silence.

MASS and the GOSPELS

The Mass has two main parts.

I. The Liturgy of the Word
- We listen to the **Word of God** from Scripture (the Bible).

- We say the **Creed** together. Remember, the Creed is the statement of what the Church believes and teaches.

II. The Liturgy of the Eucharist
- We offer **bread and wine.** The bread is made from wheat and the wine is made from grapes.

- We thank God for all of his blessings, especially the gift of Jesus, his Son.

- The priest **consecrates** the bread and wine. With the blessing of the Holy Spirit, the priest says the words of Jesus at **the Last Supper**. "For this is my Body, which will be given up for you." "For this is the chalice of my Blood, the Blood of the new and eternal covenant, which will be poured out for you and for many." The bread and wine truly become **the Body and Blood of Christ.**

- We receive Jesus in **Holy Communion.** We welcome Jesus into our body and soul. Jesus is so close to us. Jesus is so happy to be with us.

Readings from Scripture are part of every Mass.

At least two readings, **one always from the Gospels,** (three on Sundays and solemnities) make up the **Liturgy of the Word.** In addition, a psalm or canticle is sung. These readings are typically read from a Lectionary, not a Bible, though the Lectionary is taken from the Bible.

A **Lectionary** is composed of the readings and the responsorial psalm assigned for each Mass of the year (Sundays, weekdays and special occasions). The readings are divided by the day or the theme (baptism, marriage, vocations, etc.) rather than according to the books of the Bible. Introductions and conclusions have been added to each reading. Not all of the Bible is included in the Lectionary.

Individual readings in the Lectionary are called **pericopes**, from a Greek word meaning a "section" or "cutting." Because the Mass readings are only portions of a book or chapter, introductory phrases, called **incipits,** are often added to begin the Lectionary reading, for example, "In those days," "Jesus said to his disciples," etc.

MASS and the GOSPELS

The Lectionary is arranged in two cycles, one for Sundays and one for weekdays.

The **Sunday cycle** is divided into **three years, labeled A, B, and C.** For example, 2020 was Year A; 2021, Year B; 2022, Year C; etc. In **Year A**, we read mostly from the Gospel of Matthew. In **Year B**, we read the Gospel of Mark and chapter 6 of the Gospel of John. In **Year C**, we read the Gospel of Luke. The Gospel of John is read during the Easter season in all three years. The first reading, usually from the Old Testament, reflects important themes from the Gospel reading. The second reading is usually from one of the epistles, a letter written to an early Church community. These letters are read semi-continuously. Each Sunday, we pick up close to where we left off the Sunday before, though some passages are never read.

The **weekday cycle** is divided into two years, Year I and Year II. **Year I** is read in odd-numbered years (2021, 2023, etc.) and **Year II** is used in even-numbered years (2020, 2022, etc.) The Gospels for both years are the same. During the year, the Gospels are read semi-continuously, beginning with Mark, then moving on to Matthew and Luke. The Gospel of John is read during the Easter season. For Advent, Christmas, and Lent, readings are chosen that are appropriate to the season. The first reading on weekdays may be taken from the Old Testament or the New Testament. Typically, a single book is read semi-continuously (i.e., some passages are not read) until it is finished and then a new book is started.

The year of the cycle does not change on January 1, but on the **First Sunday of Advent** (usually late November) which is the beginning of the **Liturgical Year**.

In addition to the Sunday and weekday cycles, the Lectionary provides readings for feasts of the saints, common celebrations such as Marian feasts, ritual Masses (weddings, funerals, etc.), votive Masses and other various needs. These readings have been selected to reflect the themes of each particular celebration.

The prayers and actions of the Mass make up one great prayer, one awesome act of worship.

Praying the **ROSARY**

How To Pray the Rosary

1. Make the **Sign of the Cross**. Pray the **"Apostles' Creed"** as you hold the cross.
2. Pray the **"Our Father"** on the first large bead of the Rosary.
3. Pray three **"Hail Marys"** for Faith, Hope, and Charity on the three smaller beads.
4. Pray the **"Glory Be"** to praise God the Father, God the Son, and God the Holy Spirit.
5. Announce the **First Mystery** and then pray the **"Our Father"**.
6. Pray **"Hail Marys"** on the next ten beads while meditating on the Mystery.
7. Pray the **"Glory Be"** in the space between the beads. (Optional: Say the "O My Jesus" prayer requested by the Blessed Mother, Mary, at Fatima.)
8. Announce the Next **Mystery**; then pray the **"Our Father"** and repeat these steps (6 through 8) as you continue through the remaining Mysteries.
9. At the end of the Rosary we pray the **"Hail Holy Queen"**.

Prayers

Sign of the Cross: In the name of the Father, and of the Son, and of the Holy Spirit. Amen.

Apostles' Creed: I believe in God, the Father almighty, creator of heaven and earth, and in Jesus Christ, his only Son, our Lord, who was conceived by the Holy Spirit, born of the Virgin Mary, suffered under Pontius Pilate, was crucified, died, and was buried; he descended into hell; on the third day he rose again from the dead; he ascended into heaven, and is seated at the right hand of God, the Father almighty; from there he will come to judge the living and the dead. I believe in the Holy Spirit, the holy catholic Church, the communion of saints, the forgiveness of sins, the resurrection of the body, and life everlasting. Amen.

Our Father: Our Father, who art in heaven, hallowed be thy name; thy kingdom come, thy will be done on earth as it is in heaven. Give us this day our daily bread, and forgive us our trespasses, as we forgive those who trespass against us, and lead us not into temptation, but deliver us from evil. Amen.

Praying the **ROSARY**

Hail Mary: Hail Mary, full of grace, the Lord is with thee! Blessed art thou among women, and blessed is the fruit of thy womb, Jesus. Holy Mary, Mother of God, pray for us sinners, now and at the hour of our death. Amen.

Glory Be: Glory be to the Father, and to the Son, and to the Holy Spirit. As it was in the beginning, is now, and ever shall be, world without end. Amen.

O My Jesus: O my Jesus, forgive us our sins, save us from the fires of hell, and lead all souls to heaven, especially those in most need of thy mercy.

Hail Holy Queen: Hail, holy Queen, mother of Mercy. Hail, our life, our sweetness and our hope. To thee do we cry, poor banished children of Eve; to thee do we send up our sighs, mourning and weeping, in this vale of tears. Turn then, most gracious advocate, thine eyes of mercy toward us; and after this our exile, show unto us the blessed fruit of thy womb, Jesus. O clement, O loving, O sweet virgin Mary.

The Mysteries of the Rosary

Joyful Mysteries:
The Annunciation,
The Visitation, The Nativity,
The Presentation in the Temple,
The Finding in the Temple

Sorrowful Mysteries:
The Agony in the Garden,
The Scourging at the Pillar,
The Crowning with Thorns,
The Carrying of the Cross, The Crucifixion

Glorious Mysteries:
The Resurrection, The Ascension,
The Descent of the Holy Spirit,
The Assumption of the Blessed Virgin Mary,
The Coronation of the Blessed Virgin Mary

Luminous Mysteries:
The Baptism of Jesus, The Wedding at Cana,
The Proclamation of the Kingdom of God and the
Call to Conversion, The Transfiguration,
The Institution of the Eucharist

Catholic Practices: THE SACRAMENTS

Sacraments are rituals through which we receive God's grace. Grace is a gift of God's love and strength, given freely to us to help us live good and just lives. Sacraments always involve signs appealing to our senses that point to God's saving presence in our lives.

Baptism

In the sacrament of Holy Baptism, we are made children of God by water and the Word. Water is poured over us in the name of the Father and of the Son and of the Holy Spirit. Through Baptism, we are cleansed of Original Sin and born into new life in Christ.

Confirmation

In Confirmation, we affirm our belief in God, Father, Son, and Holy Spirit, first given to us in Baptism. Moved by the Holy Spirit, we declare our faith before the Church and embrace our role as a member of the Body of Christ, ready to serve him and those around us through prayer, devotion and acts of love.

Eucharist

The Eucharist is receiving the Body and Blood of Jesus Christ, under the appearance of bread and wine, given and shed for us for the forgiveness of our sins. Each time we eat and drink his Body and Blood, we proclaim Christ's Death until he comes, and we give thanks to him in remembrance of the gift of himself for us.

Penance and Reconciliation

In this sacrament, you confess (or admit) your sins to a priest. You do penance by committing to do something good to show that you want to make up for the wrong you have done. The priest forgives your sins in the name of Jesus Christ. This is called reconciliation or the reconnection to God.

Anointing of the Sick

In this sacrament, blessed oil is placed upon a sick person by a priest to aid in physical and spiritual healing. This sacrament renews faith in God and strengthens against discouragement and despair at the thought of death, and it prevents from losing Christian hope in God's justice, truth and salvation.

Marriage

In the Sacrament of Marriage, God's love is joined with the love of a man and a woman who are committing themselves to a lifelong partnership with each other as husband and wife.

Holy Orders

Holy Orders is the sacrament of ordaining bishops, priests, and deacons into ministry in the Church.

Works of Mercy are the acts of compassion we perform to those around us. When we welcome people and treat them with kindness, love and respect, we remember what Jesus says in the Bible: "Whatever you did for one of these least brothers of mine, you did for me." So, you can tell Jesus you love him in your prayers, but you can show your love with action! When you do good things for Jesus' "least brothers," you're doing exactly what he asks.

Corporal Works of Mercy

The Corporal Works of Mercy are these kind actions we can perform to extend God's compassion to those in physical need. Since God is merciful to us, we should be loving to others struggling bodily.

- **Feed the Hungry**
- **Visit the Imprisoned**
- **Give Drink to the Thirsty**
- **Bury the Dead**
- **Shelter the Homeless**
- **Give Alms to the Poor**
- **Visit the Sick**

Spiritual Works of Mercy

The Spiritual Works of Mercy are acts of compassion toward those who are spiritually and emotionally in need. Since God is caring of our souls, we should also care for the health of each other's souls.

- **Counsel the Doubtful**
- **Forgive Injuries**
- **Instruct the Ignorant**
- **Bear Wrongs Patiently**
- **Admonish the Sinner**
- **Pray for the Living and the Dead**
- **Comfort the Sorrowful**

The King will reply, "I tell you, whenever you did this for one of the least important of these followers of mine, you did it for me!"
Matthew 25:40

Catholic **PRAYERS**

The Sign of the Cross
In the name of the Father, and of the Son, and of the Holy Spirit. Amen.

Our Father
Our Father, who art in heaven, hallowed be thy name; thy kingdom come, thy will be done on earth as it is in heaven. Give us this day our daily bread, and forgive us our trespasses, as we forgive those who trespass against us, and lead us not into temptation, but deliver us from evil. Amen.

Hail Mary
Hail Mary, full of grace, the Lord is with thee! Blessed art thou among women, and blessed is the fruit of thy womb, Jesus. Holy Mary, Mother of God, pray for us sinners, now and at the hour of our death. Amen.

Glory Be
Glory be to the Father, and to the Son, and to the Holy Spirit. As it was in the beginning, is now, and ever shall be, world without end. Amen.

Guardian Angel Prayer
Angel of God, my guardian dear, to whom God's love commits me here, ever this day, be at my side, to light and guard, rule and guide. Amen.

Short Prayer of Love
Jesus, I love you with my whole heart. Amen.

Act of Contrition
My God, I am sorry for my sins with all my heart. In choosing to do wrong and failing to do good, I have sinned against you whom I should love above all things. I firmly intend, with your help, to do penance, to sin no more, and to avoid whatever leads me to sin. Our Savior Jesus Christ suffered and died for us. In His name, My God, have mercy. Amen.

Prayer of Sorrow
Jesus, I am sorry for the wrong things I do. Amen.

Catholic **PRAYERS**

The Memorare

Remember, O most gracious Virgin Mary, that never was it known that anyone who fled to thy protection, implored thy help, or sought thine intercession was left unaided. Inspired by this confidence, I fly unto thee, O Virgin of virgins, my mother; to thee do I come, before thee I stand, sinful and sorrowful. O Mother of the Word Incarnate, despise not my petitions, but in thy mercy hear and answer me. Amen.

Salve Regina (Hail, Holy Queen)

Hail, holy Queen, mother of Mercy. Hail, our life, our sweetness and our hope. To thee do we cry, poor banished children of Eve; to thee do we send up our sighs, mourning and weeping, in this vale of tears. Turn then, most gracious advocate, thine eyes of mercy toward us; and after this our exile, show unto us the blessed fruit of thy womb, Jesus. O clement, O loving, O sweet virgin Mary. Amen.

Prayer of Saint Francis of Assisi

Lord, make me an instrument of your peace. Where there is hatred, let me sow love. Where there is injury, pardon. Where there is doubt, faith. Where there is despair, hope. Where there is darkness, light. Where there is sadness, joy. O Divine Master, grant that I may not so much seek to be consoled, as to console; to be understood, as to understand; to be loved, as to love. For it is in giving that we receive. It is in pardoning that we are pardoned, and it is in dying that we are born to Eternal Life. Amen.

Blessing Before Meals

Bless us, O Lord, and these thy gifts, which we are about to receive from thy bounty, through Christ, our Lord. Amen.

Grace After Meals

We give you thanks, O Lord, for these thy gifts, which we have received from thy goodness, through Christ, our Lord. Amen.

Morning Prayer

I give to you, my God, this day all I do, and think, and say. Amen.

Night Prayer

Now I lay me down to sleep. I pray you, Lord, your child to keep. Your love be with me through the night, and wake me with the morning light. Amen.

The **HOLY LAND** in the **GOSPELS**

The Holy Land

Keep track of Jesus' location as you read about his ministry and miracles in the Gospels. Note that the distance from **Nazareth** to **Bethlehem** is about 65 miles or 147 km.

When Jesus entered **Jerusalem**, the whole city was thrown into an uproar. "Who is he?" the people asked. "This is the prophet Jesus, from **Nazareth** in **Galilee**," the crowds answered. *Matthew 21:10-11*

Many people from the province of **Judea** and the city of **Jerusalem** went out to hear John. They confessed their sins, and he baptized them in the **Jordan River**. *Mark 1:5*

Joseph went from the town of **Nazareth** in **Galilee** to the town of **Bethlehem** in **Judea**, the birthplace of King David. *Luke 2:4*

A man named Lazarus, who lived in **Bethany**, became sick. **Bethany** was the town where Mary and her sister Martha lived. *John 11:1*

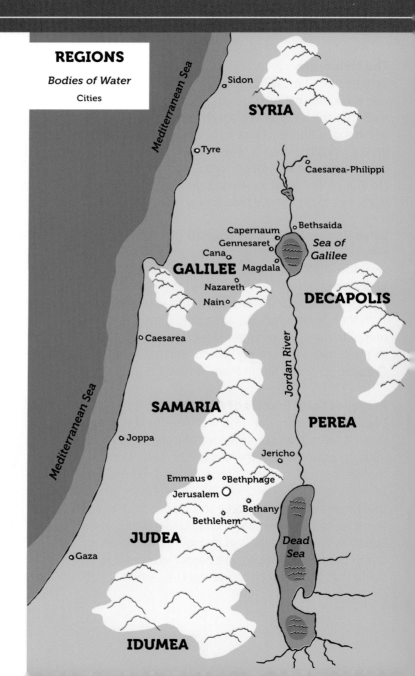

REGIONS

Bodies of Water

Cities

Mediterranean Sea

Sidon

SYRIA

Tyre

Caesarea-Philippi

Capernaum
Bethsaida
Gennesaret
Sea of Galilee
Cana
GALILEE Magdala
Nazareth
Nain
DECAPOLIS

Caesarea

Jordan River

SAMARIA

PEREA

Joppa

Jericho

Emmaus Bethphage
Jerusalem
Bethany
Bethlehem

Mediterranean Sea

JUDEA

Dead Sea

Gaza

IDUMEA

JERUSALEM in the GOSPELS

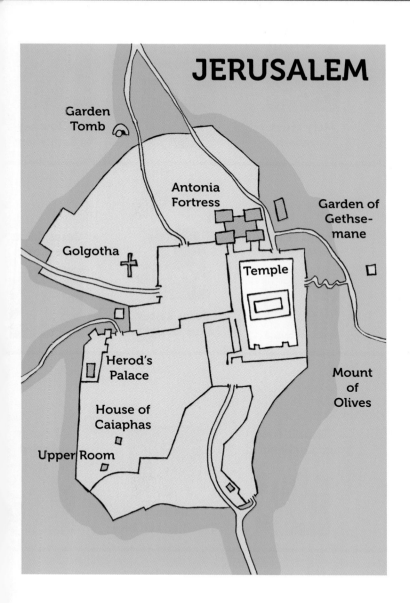

Jerusalem

Throughout the Gospels, we read of Jesus traveling from his home in Nazareth up to the hilly city of Jerusalem. From his entry in Jerusalem on Palm Sunday to his appearance to Mary at the **Garden Tomb**, all the action of Holy Week takes place in and around the city and its **Temple**.

Those who had arrested Jesus took him to the **house of Caiaphas**, the High Priest, where the teachers of the Law and the elders had gathered together.
Matthew 26:57

As they approached Jerusalem, near the towns of Bethphage and Bethany, they came to the **Mount of Olives**. Jesus sent two of his disciples on ahead.
Mark 11:1

One day Zechariah was doing his work as a priest in the **Temple**, taking his turn in the daily service.   *Luke 1:8*

Early on Sunday morning, while it was still dark, Mary Magdalene went to the **tomb** and saw that the stone had been taken away from the entrance.
John 20:1

The Gospels **TIME LINE**

Gabriel Appears to Zechariah

Gabriel Appears to Mary

Joseph Has a Dream

Mary Visits Elizabeth

The Birth of John the Baptist

The Journey to Bethlehem

Jesus Raises Lazarus

Jesus is Transfigured

Jesus Feeds the Multitude

Jesus Raises Jairus' Daughter

Jesus Calms the Storm

Jesus Enters Jerusalem

The Last Supper

Jesus Prays in the Garden

Jesus is Tried and Condemned

Jesus is Crucified and Dies

Jesus is Buried

A Savior is Coming   Jesus' Early Life   Jesus' Ministry

The Gospels TIME LINE

The Birth of Jesus

Presentation in the Temple

The Visit of the Magi

The Flight to Egypt

Boy Jesus at the Temple

The Sermon on the Mount

Jesus' First Miracle in Cana

Jesus Calls the First Disciples

Tempted in the Wilderness

The Baptism of Jesus

The Lord is Risen

The Road to Emmaus

Jesus Appears to Thomas

Breakfast on the Seashore

Jesus Ascends into Heaven

Holy Week   Easter and Beyond

PARABLES of JESUS

PARABLES of JESUS

MIRACLES of JESUS

Parable of the Sower
Matthew 13:1-23

Parable of the Weeds
Matthew 13:24-30

Parable of the Yeast
Matthew 13:33

Parable of the Hidden Treasure
Matthew 13:44

Parable of the Pearl
Matthew 13:45-46

Parable of the Net
Matthew 13:47-50

Parable of the Lost Sheep
Matthew 18:10-14

The Final Judgment
Matthew 25:31-46

A Lamp Under a Bowl
Mark 4:21-25

The Growing Seed
Mark 4:26-29

The Mustard Seed
Mark 4:30-34

Tenants in the Vineyard
Mark 12:1-12

The Good Samaritan
Luke 10:25-37

The Rich Fool
Luke 12:13-21

Humility & Hospitality
Luke 14:7-14

Wedding in Cana
John 2:1-11

Healing an Official's Son
John 4:43-54

The Disciples' Great Catch
Luke 5:1-11

Simon's Mother-in-Law
Mark 1:30-31

Healing an Officer's Servant
Matthew 8:5-13

Raising a Widow's Son
Luke 7:11-17

Jesus Calms a Storm
Matthew 8:23-27

Two Men with Demons
Matthew 8:28-34

Healing A Paralyzed Man
Mark 2:1-12

Jairus' Daughter
Luke 8:40-56

Healing Two Blind Men
Matthew 9:27-31

A Man Who Could Not Speak
Matthew 9:32-33

The Transfiguration
Luke 9:28-36

The Healing at the Pool
John 5:1-9

A Paralyzed Hand
Matthew 12:9-14

Feeding Five Thousand
Matthew 14:13-21

The Parable of the Lost Sheep
Luke 15:1-7

The Parable of the Lost Coin
Luke 15:8-10

The Parable of the Lost Son
Luke 15:11-32

The Widow and the Judge
Luke 18:1-8

The Pharisee and the Tax Collector
Luke 18:9-14

The Parable of the Rich Man and Lazarus
Luke 16:19-31

The Unforgiving Servant
Matthew 18:21-35

Workers in the Vineyard
Matthew 20:1-16

The Two Sons
Matthew 21:28-32

The Wedding Feast
Matthew 22:1-14

The Fig Tree
Matthew 24:32-35

The Faithful Servant
Matthew 24:45-51

Ten Young Women
Matthew 25:1-13

The Three Servants
Matthew 25:14-30

MIRACLES of JESUS

WOMEN of the GOSPELS

GOSPEL FRIENDS

Jesus Heals Ten Men
Luke 17:11-19

Lazarus is Brought to Life
John 11:1-46

Jesus Heals Two Blind Men
Matthew 20:30-34

Jesus Curses the Fig Tree
Matthew 21:18-22

Jesus Heals a Servant's Ear
Luke 22:50-51

The Resurrection
Luke 24:1-12

Jesus Appears to Seven Disciples
John 21:1-14

Elizabeth
Luke 1:39-44, 56-66

Mary, the Mother of Jesus
Luke 1:26-38

Anna the Prophet
Luke 2:36-37

Jairus' Daughter
Mark 5:21-43

Woman who Touched Jesus' Cloak
Matthew 9:20-22

The Canaanite Mother
Matthew 15:21-28

Mary of Bethany
Luke 10:38-42

Martha of Bethany
John 11:17-27

Joseph, Husband of Mary
Matthew 1:18-25

Simeon
Luke 2:25-35

John the Baptist
Luke 3:1-20

Simon Peter
Matthew 16:13-20

James & John
Mark 1:19-20

Nicodemus
John 3:1-21

A Man Born Blind
John 9:1-39

Zacchaeus
Luke 19:1-10

GOSPEL FRIENDS

WOMEN of the GOSPELS

MIRACLES of JESUS

Boy with Fish and Bread
John 6:1-13

Lazarus
John 12:1-9

Bartimaeus
Mark 10:46-52

Simon of Cyrene
Luke 23:26

The Criminal on the Cross
Luke 23:39-43

The Centurion
Matthew 27:45-54

Joseph of Arimathea
Mark 15:42-47

Thomas
John 20:19-29

Samaritan Woman at the Well
John 4:1-42

Lost Coin
Luke 15:8-10

"Cast the First Stone"
John 8:3-11

The Widow's Offering
Mark 12:41-44

The Ten Young Women
Matthew 25:1-13

Mary and John
John 19:25-27

Women at the Tomb
Luke 24:1-10

Mary Magdalene
John 20:11-18

Jesus Walks on the Water
Matthew 14:22-33

A Woman's Faith
Matthew 15:21-28

Jesus Heals a Deaf-Mute
Mark 7:31-37

A Blind Man at Bethsaida
Mark 8:22-26

A Boy with a Demon
Matthew 17:14-21

A Man Born Blind
John 9:1-41

Jesus Heals on the Sabbath
Luke 13:10-17

Jesus Heals a Sick Man
Luke 14:1-4